Saigon, U.S.A.

Books by Alfred Hassler

DIARY OF A SELF-MADE CONVICT

SAIGON, U.S.A.

☆ ☆ ☆ ☆ ☆ ☆ ☆ ☆ ☆ ☆ ☆ ☆ ☆ ☆ ☆

Saigon, U.S.A.

☆ ☆ ☆ ☆ ☆ ☆ ☆ ☆ ☆ ☆ ☆ ☆ ☆ ☆ ☆

Alfred Hassler

WITH AN INTRODUCTION BY
Senator George McGovern

ϒ

RICHARD W. BARON

NEW YORK 1970

TO

Phuong, Phuong Anh, Bao,

Ai, Tai,

and all their brave and

dedicated associates.

Contents

Introduction

As the 1960's come to an end, the President of the United States has said that our concern is not how we got into Vietnam, but how we can bring the war there to an honorable conclusion. I think a nation such as ours, with its high moral traditions and commitments, has a further responsibility to know how we became drawn into this conflict, and to learn what lessons it has to teach us for the future. Otherwise, how can we hope to redeem the all too great sacrifice of the young men on both sides who have fallen in this interminable war?

I would hope that with that knowledge we can structure the foreign policy, not of a nation that seeks to play policeman for the world, but of a nation that sees itself as an important part of the community of man and a nation that understands that the physician who would heal the patient must first heal himself.

Alfred Hassler offers additional insight into the forces which have trapped American men and resources in the jungles of Southeast Asia for the past decade. In *Saigon, U.S.A.*, he writes of the Third Force in Vietnam and of the struggle of the independent Vietnamese caught between the National Liberation Front and the military régime of Thieu and Ky. His analysis of the Buddhist

movement and the important part it has played in modern Vietnamese history suggests a constructive alternative to the warring
extremes in Vietnam.

Hassler's portrait of the Vietnamese people who, by the thousands, risk death and torture to raise their own cry of "Give peace
a chance" underscores the lesson that we ought to learn above
all else. We do not have the right and we do not have the capacity
to save a political régime abroad that does not have the respect
of its own people. That has been at the bottom of our dilemma
and our frustration these many years in Southeast Asia.

I think we can learn further from our experience that there are
problems in this world we cannot reach with massive technology
and that we cannot reach with a B-52, even one carrying napalm
and the worst instruments of destruction ever devised by man.
Such efforts only underscore the self-defeating nature of a foreign
policy built on the illusion that national strength is measured by
military power, without reference to the fundamental forces moving around the globe. This is our urgent need in the 1970's—to
learn what lessons the experience of Vietnam has for us, and to
apply that wisdom to produce a new policy more calculated
toward peace and less likely to involve us in hopeless ventures of
this kind that destroy others in the name of freedom while poisoning the wellsprings of our own national life.

And above all, our need is for a leadership which rejects the
counsels of war and moves to end the killing, turning our energies
back to the great unfinished business of America. Perhaps the
greatest cost of our military operations in Vietnam is not what we
have done to Vietnam but what we have done to ourselves. While
we have fought the Vietcong, we have neglected the enemies
within our own society—the blight of our cities, the ugly scars of
racism, the pollutions of air, water and land, the joblessness, the
bad housing, the ill health, the dull schools, and the hunger of the
poor. We have waged war abroad while surrendering to the enemies seizing our own land.

All the while, the Vietnam war has been taking more than a million lives. We have squandered our young men in a war we cannot win beside an ally we cannot save. The Saigon régime is not worth the 44,000 young Americans who have died. It is not worth the 9,000 who have died in 1969. It is not worth the scores who will die this week. It is not worth one additional young life.

Nor is any continuation of that bloody struggle worth the cost we inflict on ourselves as a people with the commission of horrible atrocites against the civilian population of Vietnam. The massacre at Mylai is not, in any moral sense, an aberrant episode of civilian extermination. Together with the massive bombardment of Vietnam from the air and the calculated destruction of "free fire" artillery zones on the ground, it is dreadful evidence that this war is eroding our sensitivity to violence both at home and abroad. Surely no policy which encourages that awful product is in the national interest.

There is no way to end it except to remove our troops, returning our youth from the bloodshed in Asia to join in the redemption of our troubled land.

GEORGE MCGOVERN

Washington, D.C.
December, 1969

The Sights of
SAIGON, U. S. A.

Independence Palace, from which South Vietnam is governed by two of its most unpopular citizens, President Nguyen Van Thieu and Vice President Nguyen Cao Ky. In a controlled and fraudulent election, complete with censorship, intimidation, and exclusion from the ballot of the two most likely candidates, they could still get only one-third of the vote.

Chi Hoa Prison, where the man who came in second in the presidential election is serving a five-year sentence for daring to campaign for peace and neutralism.

Tu Nghiem Pagoda, where Phan Thi Mai, a young Vietnamese student-nun, burned herself to death to draw American attention to pleas that the war be ended. Thousands of Vietnamese turned her funeral procession into a peace demonstration so long that it took five hours to pass a single point.

An Quang Pagoda. headquarters of the "militant" Buddhists and their leader, Thich Tri Quang. Despite its twenty-four-hour police guard, it is thronged repeatedly by thousands of Vietnamese demonstrating for a representative government that would make peace.

Saigon University, where faculties and student bodies have denounced the war and their government, and have been sent to prison as a consequence. It includes the *Medical School,* from one of those third-floor windows a student with hands tied behind him was hurled to his death; the police called it suicide.

Tong Nha, headquarters of the National Police, which, with dozens of other secret police and intelligence agencies, has imprisoned, often without trial, close to 200,000 Vietnamese who have opposed their government or pleaded for peace.

Mat Vu, Interrogation Center No. 8, where political prisoners are tortured in the search for information and in an effort to intimidate into silence all neutralists and peace forces.

Third Force Headquarters, address unknown, which, in the face of imprisonment, exile, and torture, goes on with demonstrations, petitions, strikes, and pleas for a representative government and peace. Still it remains the best choice for ending the war.

The United States Embassy, representing the country that fights the Vietnamese civil war, finances its army, police, and prisons, keeps Generals Thieu and Ky in power, and helps them to suppress the Third Force.

Saigon, U.S.A.

1

The Secret War in Vietnam

June, 1969, was an important month in the history of Vietnam. Some of its events were well reported in the West, where their significance was obvious. But much of what happened was widely known only in Vietnam and was almost totally ignored in the West. June, 1969, was the fifty-second month of war in Vietnam since American planes began extensive bombing of North Vietnam and the thirteenth month of talks in Paris intended to end that war. It was a month during which Richard M. Nixon met Nguyen Van Thieu on Midway Island and announced the withdrawal of 25,000 American troops, and a month when various unidentified American generals in Saigon expressed restrained horror at the notion that the United States would begin to "chicken out" just when the enemy was "hurting" and victory was—again—in sight. It was the month in which the National Liberation Front of South Vietnam announced in Paris its transformation into the Provisional Revolutionary Government of South Vietnam and repeated its adamant refusal to participate in arrangements with the puppet Thieu-Ky Government to end the war. It was the month in which *Life* magazine devoted twelve pages to printing the photographs and names of 242 young Americans who had died in a single week in the Vietnam war.

But in Vietnam it was also a month bracketed on May 30 by the action of a young Buddhist priest who, before a congregation of three thousand, held his finger in a flame for an hour and fifty minutes, until it was completely burned, to demonstrate for peace, and on July 1 by the self-immolation of Vo Van Be, a 40-year-old South Vietnamese marine and the first soldier to take such an action for peace.

It was a month during which the rector and faculty of Saigon University received a farewell letter from eleven of the top student leaders of that institution who were on their way to "an tri"—detention without trial—for their peace activities; [1] a month during which the runner-up in South Vietnam's 1967 presidential election was moved from the notorious prison on Con Son Island—the country's "Devil's Island"—to a Saigon jail.

It was the month, moreover, during which an ad hoc committee of American religious leaders of all faiths sent out the United States Study Team on Religious and Political Freedom in Vietnam, a development that had several immediate consequences and from which others are still flowing. The team's arrival in Saigon undoubtedly prompted the transfer of Truong Dinh Dzu, the defeated presidential candidate, to the Chi Hoa jail, and its presence as clearly contributed to the ability of twenty-three of South Vietnam's leading intellectuals and political figures to announce the formation of the Progressive National Force to call for a "total cease-fire" and a "government of reconciliation." For the team clearly exposed a situation that it summed up in a telegram to President Nixon: "There must be no illusion that this climate of political and religious suppression [in South Vietnam] is compatible with either a representative or a stable government."

[1] See Appendix 12.

The team's visit was in part the culmination of a relationship that had begun four years before with the visit of another, similar group of American and European religious leaders. I had organized and led that earlier team, and so began to know and understand a substantial, unreported, largely underground movement for peace and neutralism that permeates South Vietnam and is of critical importance in any prospect of ending the war.

The Fellowship of Reconciliation, of which I am executive director, is a peace organization with more than a half-century's experience of trying to stop wars and preparations for wars. It was inevitable that we would become deeply involved in the war in Vietnam as it mushroomed from a disquieting localized conflict half a world away into a major American war. The beginning of extensive bombing of North Vietnam in the winter of 1965 sounded the alarm; I was asked to cut short a trip in order to draft a statement and a program. People from this country's religious community, with whom the Fellowship has always worked closely, especially were asking for some specific action.

The statement, approved by the Fellowship's executive committee, was circulated to some 30,000 clergymen for their approval, and then was published in *The New York Times* on April 4, 1965. Signed by 2,700 ministers, priests, and rabbis, it was one of the first, if not the first, of the full-page advertisement-statements on the war in Vietnam that were to manifest the deep disquiet of a growing segment of the American people, and it was one of the most famous. Its headline read: *"MR. PRESIDENT, In the Name of God STOP IT!"* [2]

That we had touched a sensitive nerve was immediately apparent in the flood of mail that came in response. A few letters were virulently hostile—one reader, wielding a rubber stamp, printed the word "Death" all over the ad and returned it—others were critical, but most were openly grateful that

[2] See Appendix 1.

someone at last had spoken out. Hundreds of the clergy of all faiths asked us to add their names to the newly formed Clergymen's Emergency Committee for Vietnam. A few days after the ad appeared President Johnson made his famous speech at Johns Hopkins University, variously interpreted as offering hope for peace and as laying the groundwork for an escalated war. The morning after the speech, a State Department official telephoned me to ask what the Clergymen's Emergency Committee had thought of it and to imply, ever so delicately, that the committee's statement had caused the President to modify his remarks—said modifications remaining undisclosed.

Whatever the President's intent, the facts were observably in the direction of escalation. By June, 1965, the United States had committed its 23,000 "advisers" in South Vietnam to combat and begun the process that was to see 160,000 more American troops in that country by the end of the year. Thoroughly alarmed, the Fellowship decided to mobilize its clergymen's committee to send a team of religious leaders to South Vietnam to see for themselves what was going on and to make contact with their opposite numbers to determine if they could find ways for cooperative efforts for peace.

The team made its visit in the oppressive heat of July. It comprised twelve Americans and two Europeans, one of whom was the famous Pastor Martin Niemoeller, "Hitler's prisoner" during World War II and a Fellowship member himself. Among the Americans were such distinguished names as Dr. Edwin T. Dahlberg, who as president of the National Council of Churches had coined the expression "massive reconciliation" to set against the "massive retaliation" of John Foster Dulles, then Secretary of State; Episcopal Bishop William Crittenden; the Methodist Harold Bosley and Dana McLean Greeley, president of the Unitarian-Universalist Association; the Right Rev. Edward Murray, consultor to the Roman Catholic Archdiocese of Boston; and Rabbi Jacob Weinstein, president of the

Central Conference of American Rabbis.[3] While we were in Saigon we received a cablegram from the Rev. Dr. Martin Luther King, Jr., commending us on our "all-important mission to Vietnam" and calling, as we were, for an immediate end to the war.

The trip was valuable in many ways. Splitting up into subgroups, as our study team four years later was also to do, we were able to meet and talk not only with religious leaders of all faiths, but also with scores of others—students, soldiers, news correspondents, young volunteer workers, labor union leaders, teachers, officials of both governments, defectors from the NLF, neutralists, and supporters of the NLF and North Vietnam. These experiences, translated into reports and unnumbered speeches, articles and television and radio appearances at home, were to move official and unofficial church groups into far more vigorous action on the war than had characterized them before. Yet perhaps the most important accomplishment was the contact we made with leaders of the Unified Buddhist Church, and the discovery of how little we really knew of the war, of the people in whose land it was being fought, and particularly of the priests and *bonzes* (clerical figures)—"militants" [4] the press called them—who had emerged from their monasteries to lead their people's struggle for peace.

[3] Other members of the team were the Rev. James Lawson, minister of Centenary Methodist Church, Memphis, Tenn.; Miss Elmira Kendrick, president of the National Student Christian Federation; Dr. Howard Schomer, president of Chicago Theological Seminary; Mrs. Elsie Schomer and the Rev. Annalee Stewart, both of the Women's International League for Peace and Freedom; the Rev. André Trocmè of the Church of St. Gervais, Geneva; and myself.

[4] The word "militant" was first applied to Vietnamese Buddhists as a consequence of their participation in the actions in 1963 that led to the unseating of President Ngo Dinh Diem, and its similarity to the word "military" has led some Americans to assume that the word in this case may be synonymous with "violence." As the study team noted in its report, the Buddhists are deeply committed to nonviolence, and "militant" in this case carries its French meaning of "an active supporter or worker."

Our ignorance was especially brought home to us at two
meetings. The first was in a tin-roofed building at the headquarters of the Buddhists' Vien Hoa Dao, or secular affairs division.
Facing us were three monks and their interpreter, a young professor from the University of Hue. We caught their names—
at the left, next to the interpreter, the Venerable Thich Tam
Chau, chairman of the Vien Hoa Dao; in the middle, a portly
monk, Thich Phap Tri, who said nothing throughout the conversation; at the right, a powerful looking young monk with intense eyes, Thich Tri Quang. Someone muttered that these were
the men who had brought down President Ngo Dinh Diem two
years before; someone else remarked that Tri Quang could
"bring 50,000 people out on the streets in fifteen minutes."

Politely we expressed our gratitude for the opportunity to
meet them; politely they told of their appreciation for our visit
and its intentions. Then we began to ask questions, our conversation periodically interrupted by spasms of monsoon rain beating on the tin roof. Soon Tri Quang tapped Tam Chau on the
arm and they changed places; from then on Tri Quang was the
spokesman, his powerful, passionate concerns probing and
thrusting. We were moved, but uncomfortable. We asked questions, knowing as we did so that they were somehow not the
right ones.

What were Buddhist monks, who were understood to be con-
templatives, doing on the firing line in the war? What were they
doing, anyway? Whose side were they on? They answered, and
we did not always understand the answers. We had read a great
deal about the war in Vietnam and its antecedents, but they had
been written from a Western perspective, and we were conscious of it that day. We were not prepared to probe Tri Quang
as he was prepared to probe us; consequently we were not able
to respond as we could have wished.

The second meeting took place a day later at Van Hanh University, with one of Tri Quang's closest friends and associates,
the Venerable Thich Nhat Hanh. His voice was so quiet, his

manner so serene, that we almost missed the rare quality of the man—poet, educator, editor, organizer, theoretician par excellence for the peace movement in Vietnam. He talked with an almost painful earnestness of the sufferings of his people, and especially of the peasants, with whom he spent much of his time, and their longing for peace. He spoke of the alignment of forces in Vietnam in ways that sometimes confirmed our presuppositions and sometimes did not. He was kind to the United States and gave it the benefit of every doubt as he spoke of its stated reasons for intervening, but he was firm and unambiguous in condemning that intervention. He spoke somewhat mysteriously of a "third solution," and we were intrigued but unconvinced.

We had sense enough to realize that more Americans needed to meet and hear some of these men, and we left open-end invitations with Tri Quang, Tam Chau, and Nhat Hanh to visit us. A year later Nhat Hanh did.

His coming was a deliberate risk on his part. "Militant" Buddhists could not easily get permission to leave the country, especially with the new struggle between them and the government of Premier Nguyen Cao Ky drawing to a climax. Through the help of the Interuniversity Committee for Debate on Foreign Policy, Nhat Hanh was invited to lecture on contemporary Buddhism at Cornell University, and the Government permitted him a limited leave for that purpose.

But Nhat Hanh had much more in mind than lecturing on contemporary Buddhism. He was, and is, an exemplar of the new "engaged Buddhism," about which he had already published three books. Engaged Buddhism had emerged out of the agony of the South Vietnamese and the slow realization by leading monks that every other organized voice of the people had been destroyed in their country. It sought no political power for itself or its spokesmen; it was caught simply and inextricably in the suffering of its people and the necessity to become actively involved in the attempt to relieve that suffering, much as Christian and Jewish clergymen in the United States at about the same time were similarly recognizing their need to become involved in the struggle for racial equality.

"There is a pagoda and a priest in every village," Nhat Hanh would tell his audiences. "They are the center of the village, for counselling as well as for meditation. At services the priest preaches sermons, as clergymen do at services in the West. How can he preach as though the war were not going on? How can he refrain from speaking his mind about it? Who would listen to him if he did? And how can he speak against the war and not involve himself in the struggle for peace?"

It was a question that Nhat Hanh had answered for himself in 1963 when, after the fall of President Ngo Dinh Diem, his friend Tri Quang had summoned him home from his studies and lecturing at Columbia University. He had plunged immediately into Buddhism's engagement with life. Recognizing his country's twin need for peace and for cadres of trained young people prepared to deal with its new economic and social problems, he had written passionate peace poetry while helping to organize Van Hanh University, creating the School of Youth for Social Service, editing the Buddhist weekly *Thien My,* and turning out one book after another. A combined publishing house-activist center called *La Boi* (Leaf of the Boi Tree) came into existence; significantly, Nhat Hanh and the other young monks who constituted it set up a "coffeehouse group" with a number of progressive young Catholic priests and laymen who had created *Song Dao* (Live Religion), itself both a movement and a newspaper. The process of merging the peace forces of the two religious groups, once so hostile to each other, had begun.

By 1966 they had concluded that they must seek allies and help outside Vietnam. Americans especially, they thought, surely must not understand how the Vietnamese were suffering, or they would not allow the war to continue. Someone who could speak with authority and credibility must go. Nhat Hanh, youthful although twenty-five years a monk, articulate, passionate, and with experience in the United States, was clearly the choice, and the Cornell invitation provided the opportunity.

His subsequent travels, back and forth across the United States, then through Western Europe and to Australia, New Zealand, the Philippines, Japan, and once again through the United States were under the auspices of the International Committee of Conscience on Vietnam, created by the Fellowship of Reconciliation in the early winter of 1966 out of much the same need for united international effort as had moved the Buddhist monks. The committee's statement, "They Are Our Brothers Whom We Kill!", had won the signatures of 10,000 religious leaders of all faiths from more than forty countries when it appeared as a two-page advertisement in *The New York Times* on January 23, 1966. One of those signatures, identified in the ad as simply "A Vietnamese Buddhist Monk," was that of Thich Nhat Hanh; the anonymity had been our decision, not his. The statement, appropriately for so international a sponsorship, laid the heaviest responsibility for the war on the United States and called on it to stop, but the statement reminded all the other parties to the conflict of their responsibilities for peace also, pleading the cause of the suffering human beings caught between the two fires, insisting that no matter what the justification, "they are our brothers whom we kill." [5]

In the United States, the slight, fervent monk was greeted with a warmth and hospitality that surprised him and led him to feel even more strongly that the Americans would surely stop the war if they knew how terrible were the sufferings of his people. At first his speeches were confined to that subject. His audiences were moved to tears as he spoke for the "voiceless peasants" and their longing for an end to the war that had torn their lives apart, and told of the young girls who sold their bodies to American soldiers in order to buy the rice that would

[5] See Appendix 2.

keep their families alive. "A prostitute in Danang," Nhat Hanh
would say in a voice barely audible, "can earn enough to support four people; a laborer cannot earn enough to keep himself
alive." He recounted stories of the corruption that robbed even
the helpless refugees in their camps of the pitiful seven piastres
a day (about five cents) allotted them for food, and pleaded
with the Americans to stop the war.

But the audiences, moved though they were, wanted other
answers to their questions, political answers. How could the
war be stopped? What would happen if it stopped under these
conditions, or those? Inevitably, of course, if the United States
were to withdraw militarily, would not the Communists take
over, would there not be a "blood bath"?

Nhat Hanh tried to steer a delicate path in his answers. First,
he would say with gentle firmness, that "what happens to the
Vietnamese when they are dealing with one another is not your
business."

"I am not a Communist; I am a monk," he would say. "I
know that if communism dominates in my country there will be
difficult times for me, but if a Vietnamese Communist and I
stood side by side on this platform, our answer would have to
be the same: It is not your affair."

But of course that was not enough for most audiences, and
he would go on to explain that the Vietnamese were a cultured
people who have been sickened by all the killing and were not
likely to engage in more slaughter when the fighting ended, or
support any who did. There might be some, he acknowledged,
but Americans should consider the blood bath they were already inflicting on his countrymen and ask themselves whether
anything they feared as a sequel to the war could be as bad.

Elaborating, he told of the resistance to the war that had
gone on since 1963, almost entirely nonviolent, by thousands of
Vietnamese living in the cities and exposed to the reprisals of
the police-state regime the United States had imposed on them.
He told of the thousands of political prisoners—students,

monks, labor leaders, intellectuals, peasants—not Communists or members of the Vietcong, but South Vietnamese longing for peace and a society in which social justice would be combined with personal freedom. He outlined the "third solution" by which these groups hoped the war might be ended, extricating the United States from its entanglement without excessive loss of face while giving the Vietnamese a genuine chance at what both sides in the war professed to champion—their right to decide their own destiny.

The Fellowship arranged Nhat Hanh's itinerary and engagements, with the help of the national Committees of Conscience that had sprung up in nineteen countries, and I traveled with him through much of the United States and Western Europe. Alone or with me he met with many dignitaries. In Washington, members of the Senate and the House, singly or in groups, talked with him, and Secretary of Defense Robert S. McNamara doubled the time he had allotted to question the Vietnamese monk closely. Senator Eugene J. McCarthy, the day before he announced his candidacy for the presidency, closed the door of his private office against the hubbub of his staff and listened attentively and courteously to Nhat Hanh's presentation, asked thoughtful and informed questions, and when presented with a small collection of Nhat Hanh's poetry, in turn gave a book of contemporary Greek poetry to the monk. Later, in New Hampshire, the Minnesota Senator was to quote from the Vietnamese poet's works.

In London, Nhat Hanh met with forty members of the House of Commons; in Stockholm with members of the Swedish Parliament and the Foreign Minister; in Rome with Pope Paul VI, to whom, when asked how His Holiness could help the cause of peace, he suggested a visit to Vietnam, "first to Hanoi, because then the Americans would stop bombing Hanoi, but also to Saigon, to urge your children there not to hate the Buddhists but to work with them for a common peace." He added diffidently that he did not mean to be presumptuous but had only thought

that it was what Jesus Christ might have done. (Shortly there-
after a papal mission headed by Monsignor Sergio Pignedoli, a
personal friend of the Pope, did go to Saigon to plead for joint
Catholic-Buddhist efforts for peace, precipitated, according to
the Rome correspondent of *The National Catholic Reporter,* by
Nhat Hanh's visit.)

It was a rewarding, provocative experience for me. I was
also interested in the politics of extrication. The antiwar movement had moral outrage in plentiful quantity, but there was no
sign that it would be able to compel the Johnson Administration to pull out unilaterally in the foreseeable future unless outrage could be combined with some plausible proposal for withdrawing without humiliation. I had no interest in saving face
for either Mr. Johnson or his Government per se—indeed, I
shared the feeling that the United States might well profit from
experiencing humiliation—but I did want the war stopped.
The blood-bath argument did not impress me; past experience
suggested that the most likely victims of such reprisals would
be well out of the way in time, enjoying the comforts of the
French Riviera on fortunes amassed in Swiss banks during the
war, but I sympathized also with the Vietnamese who longed
for a chance to build their own form of society, free from dicta-
tion either by American puppets or Communist ideologues.
The political proposals articulated by Nhat Hanh seemed to
offer a hope for both.

But more than a political proposal was emerging. As he answered questions from widely varied audiences, and as we
talked privately between meetings, there began to appear the
vague outlines of an approach that was more than political, of a
perspective rooted deep in the compassionate teachings of
Buddhism that could be of vital importance to a West caught in
the depersonalizing grip of a technology guided by materialism
and greed. There was an underground peace movement that
spread through the five universities of South Vietnam, complete
with its own newspaper, recruiting students and professors

alike; there were simple people who would march by the thousands for peace in the face of the police of a government whose laws made acts for peace punishable by imprisonment, exile, or death; there were intellectuals casting up the form of a future society that would seek to combine the best contributions of the technology of the West with the deep humaneness of the Buddhist East; there were, again and again, glimpses of the thousands upon thousands of men, women, and children, peasants and intellectuals, laborers and students, sitting in the prisons of South Vietnam because of their stand for peace.

In the spring of 1966, Nhat Hanh wrote a book intended for the American people.[6] It had a fairly good distribution in this country, but it was published as well in eight other languages and nine other countries. Interestingly, its most spectacular success was in South Vietnam itself, where a smuggled-in version was printed illegally and sold more than 100,000 copies (this in a country where a 3,000 sale constitutes a best-seller).

Early in 1967 I made my second and third trips to South Vietnam, each a week long and separated by a week in Hong Kong in order to avoid the necessity of getting a visa. I went at Nhat Hanh's request, armed with introductions from him that were to be indispensable in the tensely suspicious atmosphere of Saigon, to meet the peace forces of South Vietnam and discuss ideas and actions for ending the war.

The relationship and the cooperation have continued. They produced in 1969 not only the report of the United States Study Team on Religious and Political Freedom in South Vietnam, but also a new, interreligious committee of Eastern Buddhists and Western Christians, Jews, and humanists, committed to peace both in Vietnam and in a world threatened with extinction unless it manages to achieve peace.

The events of June, 1969, at Midway and Paris were the predictable steps in the minuet of conflict between combatants

[6] *Vietnam: Lotus in a Sea of Fire,* Foreword by Thomas Merton (New York: Hill and Wang, 1967).

willing to end the war only on a basis of maximum advantage to their own side. The sacrifices of the monk and the marine, the formation of the Progressive National Force, the jailing of the students—and the continued imprisonment of perhaps 200,000 other political and religious dissenters—were surface indications of another struggle in Vietnam that has been so unmarked in the West as to justify describing it as a "secret" war.

It is not surprising that it has gone largely unmarked and unreported. People like the rights and wrongs of their conflicts to be clear and uncomplicated, with good and evil as distinguishable as black and white, and the choice for belief and support correspondingly simple. For millions of Americans the issue in Vietnam is one of repelling aggressive communism and defending the freedom of a small people to determine their own destiny. Even for many who doubt the wisdom of our having intervened in a struggle in so small a country so far away, there is no doubt about the validity of that description of the reason for our intervention. If they hear of an occasional newspaper closed, a dissenter jailed, they see it as the regrettable but understandable excesses of a government only gradually moving toward democratic procedures while beset by war.

Other millions in this country and elsewhere find it just as easy to describe the conflict as an example of "American imperialism." The United States is seen as having intervened solely in the interest of spreading and reinforcing its power in the world, with the Vietnamese people unitedly—with a handful of contemptible exceptions—engaged in resisting it through the agency of the National Liberation Front (Vietcong) and its allies, the North Vietnamese.

For both sets of partisans it is unsettling to hear that there is a third position and that multitudes of South Vietnamese, perhaps the majority, support it. That there should be such a position, and that it has been the focus of a struggle that has gone on persistently though nonviolently for the last six years, is too complicated a thought to be seriously entertained. Even the press, which has missed what may be one of the seminal movements toward world community in modern history, is too busy reporting the obvious currents and cross-currents of political and military developments to explore the significance of crowded prisons, massive demonstrations, and stories of extended torture.

There is more than just the human longing for simple situations, of course. "Truth is the first casualty of war," wrote Samuel Johnson, and it remains so. The dynamics of war do not permit qualified assertions of righteousness; each party, believing itself to be fighting for its very existence, tolerates no compromise in its claim to being absolutely justified and the enemy absolutely wrong. The propaganda apparatus of each side in any war is very nearly as important as the military, and sometimes perhaps even more so. As the war continues, the pressure to be partisan mounts; those who do not commit themselves to one side or the other are poltroons or traitors. Until the war begins, and even in its early stages, qualification of the absolute claim is permissible, but not as the tempo of the conflict mounts and the casualties increase.

It is so in all wars. Both sides lie with fluency and conviction as they see it necessary to bolster their respective causes. The "credibility gap" attributed to Lyndon Johnson was not unique; what distinguished it was the willingness of millions of Americans to acknowledge that their own government was lying to its own people.

There is always a secret history of every war, and an element of it is made up of the people in the combatant countries who occupy some middle ground, who have not been swept up into total partisanship for one side or the other. Such groups are usually small and ineffective, isolated and alienated from their fellows, as were the pacifist minorities on both sides during the Second World War. The difference in Vietnam is that this middle group makes up probably the largest part of the population, and certainly of the politically involved population, and its activities have been decisive in the past and may be again. It is the story of this group and what has happened to it that makes up this book.

As I write it, I am at one with all those Americans who are caught in a situation that shames and outrages them, wanting desperately to end the war and to extricate our country from the infamous role that it is playing, but seeking also to avoid the simple answer that sees opposition to one combatant as automatic support for the other. I have tried to understand, and to interpret here, the feelings of the Vietnamese themselves, to see them as fellow humans should see one another and not as distant strangers longing only to resume their separate ways. The Vietnamese and we have indelibly stamped each other with our marks. We have destroyed beyond hope of remaking parts of their ancient culture; they have destroyed our innocence and belief in our own goodness. Neither of us can avoid the consequences of our collision, but each can gain from our future relationships if we will. It is a sign of the impact of the Vietnamese on me that I think the West in general and Americans in particular will be the greater gainers in the exchange.

2

The Man Who Went
to Jail for Almost
Becoming President

In a swiftly moving world it is dangerous to venture predictions that will be published months later, yet I have little hesitation about saying that until the United States clearly abandons its support of the Thieu-Ky Government in South Vietnam, nothing of substance will happen at the Paris talks. There is a simple sequence of reasons why this is so.

First, the National Liberation Front and its ally, North Vietnam, are committed to an independent Vietnam free of a Western military presence. The issues of whether that Vietnam is to be governed by Communists or coalition, whether it is to be neutral or absorbed into the Communist bloc, whether it is to be unified or—for the time being—divided are negotiable, but independence is not. North Vietnam and the NLF have fought too long and suffered too greatly to be willing to sustain the defeat that a continued American military presence would represent.

Second, no settlement of the war which enables the present
South Vietnamese Government to continue to exercise power can
lead to independence, because that government can remain in
power only so long as overwhelming American military force
remains to prop it up.

The Thieu-Ky Government is not only the enemy of the
Vietcong; it is also the enemy of its own people, and they see it
as such. They have made several attempts to overthrow it, the
most serious having been the "struggle movement" in 1966,
and were prevented only by the Americans; if the Americans
were to withdraw, or even to make unequivocal their intention
to withdraw, little time would elapse before Thieu and Ky
would be replaced.

The negotiators and the government of the NLF—now the
Provisional Revolutionary Government—and the North Vietnamese, know this; most Americans, including the President,
seem not to. All Vietnamese know that their ablest and most
respected leaders outside the Provisional Revolutionary Government are behind bars or in exile and that they will continue
to be there so long as the Thieu-Ky regime remains in power.
The case of Truong Dinh Dzu, who went to jail for almost becoming President, is dramatic evidence.

Before the fall of 1967 it was unlikely that any citizen of
South Vietnam thought of Truong Dinh Dzu as a potential
President, with the possible exception of Mr. Dzu himself.[1] A
prosperous Saigon lawyer with several American corporations
among his clients, he had no standing as a national political

---

[1] In Vietnamese, as in Chinese, the first name is the surname, the third is
the given name. Therefore, it is proper to refer to Truong Dinh Dzu as
Mr. Truong. However, there are so few family names in Vietnam that such
a practice would lead to total confusion. President Thieu, Vice President
Ky and thousands of others have the same family name, Nguyen, from
a family that played a dynastic role in Vietnamese history. References
throughout, therefore, will be to the third, or given, name: President Thieu,
Vice President Ky, Mr. Dzu. The only exception is in the case of the Buddhist *bonzes* (clerical figures), where the full name has religious significance.

leader, nor was he widely known outside Saigon. Those familiar
with him regarded him with suspicion. Don Luce, the young
American director of the International Voluntary Service in
Vietnam who resigned in protest against the war, referred to
Dzu as "somewhat disreputable." [2] ; Richard Dudman of *The
St. Louis Post-Dispatch* wrote bluntly (July 8, 1969) that Dzu
is "generally regarded as a crook," and cited his "eight house-
maids, three chauffeurs, three automobiles, and two concu-
bines" as evidence of an income somewhat larger than Vietnamese lawyers ordinarily earn. He is rumored to have gotten
most of his wealth through special influence with the hated
Diem regime, and had been disbarred by the Lawyers' Council
of Vietnam because of his generally unsavory reputation. Even
the South Vietnamese Government, in defending its imprisonment of Mr. Dzu, pointed to the fact that he had given his
daughter a French name—Monique—as proof that he was
not closely related to his people.

Yet Truong Dinh Dzu not only ran for the presidency in
the elections of September, 1967, but came in second in a
field of eleven, with 18 per cent of the vote. Generals Thieu
and Ky, who won, received only 34.8 per cent. When one of
President Johnson's "observers" suggested that so small a mar-
gin argued against the use of fraud, Dzu was reported to have
said wryly that without fraud they would have gotten only 10
per cent.

Dzu's success, while illustrating the South Vietnamese people's passionate desire for peace, proved a personal disaster for
him. He was promptly arrested, sentenced to five years at hard
labor, and sent to the notorious "Devil's Island" prison on Con
Son, 80 miles off the Vietnamese coast. It is as though Senator
McCarthy, having successfully raised a stormy debate about the
war and then failed to win the Democratic nomination, had
been sentenced to a Federal penitentiary for having discomfited

[2] Don Luce and John Sommer, *Vietnam, the Unheard Voices* (Ithaca:
Cornell University Press, 1969), p. 61.

Lyndon Johnson. Truong Dinh Dzu rocketed from obscurity to runner-up and then went on to become his country's best-known convict for the same reason: He had challenged his government's policy on the war and demanded an end to it.

Dzu launched his peace campaign two weeks before the September 3 elections. In that brief time, with very limited access to the electorate, he made a slashing attack on the Ky Government as unrepresentative and corrupt, demanded an immediate cease-fire, and called for negotiations with the National Liberation Front, looking toward a coalition government. The unexpected assault unsettled the Ky regime, which had gone to great pains to avoid just such a development. Even though Dzu's earlier reputation denied him the support he sought from the Buddhists and other peace forces in the country, his candidacy gave an unexpected opportunity for the expression of the deep popular aversion to the Ky Government and the war. Just how deep that aversion ran was emphasized by so large a vote for a candidate so personally unattractive.

It was characteristic of the ruling junta, which reversed leadership roles after the election but otherwise changed very little, that when General Thieu had been safely installed as President, one of his first acts was to have Dzu dragged from a hospital bed and placed under arrest. At the same time another potential rival and peace advocate, Au Truong Thanh, a highly respected economist and cabinet member in three governments, was also arrested, even though the junta had succeeded in keeping him off the ballot entirely. Thanh, whose reputation was as impressive as Dzu's was not, was kept under house arrest until Thieu, under pressure from a number of indignant United States Senators and a reluctant American embassy, finally permitted him to go with his family into exile in France. Dzu was treated more cavalierly. The Con Dao Polo Condor prison on Con Son has a reputation of being one of the most brutal in the world, and Dzu was kept there until the imminent arrival of the study team from the United States in June, 1969, prompted the

Government to bring him back to slightly better facilities in Saigon. Before that happened, from the tiny shack in which he was confined he wrote to his son in America that "there are terrible moments when I feel I am cracking." A delegation from the National Assembly had visited the island, he wrote, and though he had promised the director that he would not try to see them, "my guardian had clamped with lumber every door and window of the little shack for two days and there wasn't any food coming in. After the delegation had left, then I was let out." The letter was quoted by James Wechsler in *The New York Post* March 13, 1969.

Other residents of Con Son, unknown to the public, which maintained some interest in Mr. Dzu, were less fortunate. Officially there are 7,021 men held in Con Dao Prison; only 1,021 of those are held for "formal crimes," the governor of the prison admitted to the study team; [3] the rest were political prisoners, draft resisters, and deserters.

Pham Tam, a noted Vietnamese journalist and authority on prisons who spent four years as a political prisoner, insists that both the total and the proportions are much higher. There are more than 15,000 prisoners on Con Son, he says, and most of them are political.[4] Their treatment ranges from the inhuman to the indescribably brutal. In an article in *Commonweal* by Tom Fox, one veteran of the "struggle movement" of 1966, a Hue University student who spent fourteen months on Con Son, told of the special torture sections and related how he was "chained to a cement slab by all fours, then beaten. I couldn't utter a sound and they threw excrement and urine on me from above, making the smell unbearable." [5]

Another student told Fox of his torture as he, with others, was put naked into one of the notorious "tiger cages": "The

[3] See Appendix 14, report of the United States Study Team on Religious and Political Freedom in Vietnam. See also Chapter III.

[4] *Imprisonment and Torture in South Vietnam,* Published by the Fellowship of Reconciliation, July, 1969. 50¢

[5] "Devil's Island Off Vietnam," *Commonweal,* July 11, 1969.

cage was without a toilet; occasionally guards would beat us with sticks. A mixture of water, blood, excrement, and white rice vomited by the prisoners after beating is more disgusting than one can imagine."

The tiger cages are literally cages—thirty of them in each of two long concrete buildings. The cages are too short for even the small Vietnamese to lie full-length in them, and the ceilings are so low that the inmates can barely stand. A catwalk on the bars that form the top of the cage is used by guards to keep watch over the prisoners and, at intervals, to pour water on them. Occasionally they vary this routine by urinating on a prisoner or dropping excrement on him. Pham Tam relates that a supervisor at the prison told him that his first view of the liquid swilling around on the floors of the cages, a mixture of water, urine, excrement, and vomit, had made it impossible for him to eat for three days. From time to time prisoners charged with "ordinary crimes" are brought to the tiger cages to beat the political prisoners. Although many prisoners are kept in the cages for fairly brief periods designed to terrorize them into submission and "good behavior," others stay in them for months. Less than a third of those survive.

Sixty punishment cells, however brutal, does not sound like a large number for a prison of 15,000 inmates, or even 7,000. The tiger cages actually are not the only punishment cells in Con Dao Prison, but even if they were, the psychological effect of knowing they exist is enough to terrify even brave men.

Why should men inflict such suffering on their fellows? It is easy, but false, to take refuge in the thought that a few sadists have accidentally come to power and that a government preoccupied with fighting for its life has not had time to correct the situation. Some Americans have even sought to resurrect the old canard that Orientals have a lower regard for human life than do we more compassionate Westerners. Leaving aside the consideration that we compassionate Westerners have been engaged in an indiscriminate slaughter in Vietnam that has horrified much of the world, the fact is that the brutalities of Con Dao and other prisons in South Vietnam are visited almost entirely on political prisoners and are the deliberate expression of the determination of a detested government to stay in power by suppressing all dissent. The 1967 elections, effectually misrepresented to the American public as an example of constitutional democracy in action, have been the most dramatic example to date of how deep that disaffection runs, and Truong Dinh Dzu has been the almost accidental means of dramatizing it. To understand how this is so, it is necessary to look at the elections and the events preceding them.

The collapse of the hated regime of President Ngo Dinh Diem in 1963 was greeted with great joy throughout South Vietnam. People called happily to each other in the streets; spontaneous celebrations and dancing burst out almost everywhere. The public looked for a new government that would achieve its dearest wish—peace. Instead, the next eighteen months saw a succession of short-lived governments-by-coup, culminating in the spring of 1965 in the accession to power —again by coup—of the glamorous young Air Force marshal, Nguyen Cao Ky. With Ky as the all-powerful Premier backed by a junta of generals, most of them North Vietnamese, who had earlier fought on the side of the French, the chances of peace had obviously gone glimmering. Like Diem a decade before, Ky was the darling of the Americans, recipient of their help, and in return committed to continuing and even expanding the war.

Within a year popular desperation manifested itself in revolt, largely nonviolent, in the central Vietnam cities of Hue and Danang, led by the Buddhists and called *phong trao tranh dau* (the struggle movement). It was crushed when Ky's paratroopers and tanks were flown into Hue by American planes, but it came very close to unseating Ky and confirmed the deep and widespread antagonism to his regime. Ky, pressed by a worried United States Government, had already moved to set up the machinery by which a constitution would be written and provision made for the "democratic election" of a government to replace his.

The first step in this process was the election of a Constituent Assembly to write the Constitution and make arrangements for national elections. The Hue uprising had occurred in May and June, 1966; elections for the Constituent Assembly were scheduled for September 11, 1966. By early July the Unified Buddhist Church had announced its intention not to cooperate with the elections, and on July 9 its stand was supported by unanimous vote of the All-Religion Citizens and Political Parties Bloc, including, in addition to the Unified Buddhist Church, representatives of a Catholic group headed by the Rev. Hoang Quynh, the Cao Dai and Hoa Hao sects, a small Protestant group, the General Association of Buddhists, the National Revolutionary Council, the Vietnam Kuomintang, the Representative Council of the Saigon Students Conference, and the National Union Front.

In Saigon and through their overseas office in Paris, the Buddhists, whose candidates had won overwhelming victories in the municipal and provincial elections a year before, explained why they were boycotting an election that their own pressure had brought about. Recognizing that observers abroad might be impressed by the Ky Government's apparent willingness to submit itself to the democratic will, the Buddhists carefully explained why they were convinced that the proposed elections would be a "mockery of democracy."

They recalled the words of General Nguyen Van Thieu at his inauguration as Chief of State the previous year. Thieu had categorically rejected any possibility of holding national elections for at least the ten years that he described as necessary to defeat the Communists, pacify the country, and "root out" every Communist and neutralist. Even then, he said, it would take the Administration several years more to "educate" the people in the theories and practices of democracy before elections could be safely held.

In May, 1966, Premier Ky had held a press conference in Saigon at which he declared that, although the decree providing for the election had been signed, no government that tried to settle the Vietnam war peacefully would be permitted to stay in office, but would be overthrown by his air force.

Then, the Buddhists pointed out, following the suppression of the struggle movement at Hue, Ky had arrested most of the Buddhist and student leaders, and in all but two of the forty-four provinces had replaced the elected officials with military officers who would, of course, supervise the elections.

Finally, all "unreliable" citizens were charged with being Communists and denied registration; and the voting cards distributed to the remainder were identified as ration cards, valid to obtain food only if they were stamped at the polling booths. In the weeks just before the election, thousands of government cadres went into the provinces to stage a "Go to the polls" drive, warning that nonvoters would automatically be considered Communists and supporters of the National Liberation Front, with no right to government-held stocks of rice, fish sauce, sugar, and milk, staples of the Vietnamese diet and all in short supply because of the war.

On election day, government trucks and cars transported voters to the polling places, troops set up road blocks to bar any who could not show their stamped voting cards, and soldiers and government employees were shuttled to the voting places in large numbers.

The Government reported triumphantly that 81 per cent of the registered voters had actually voted. The National Liberation Front released its estimate that 27 per cent of the voting population had been "forced to go to the polls"; the reliable Paris newspaper *Le Monde* put the figure at "less than 50 per cent of the voting population," and the Buddhists estimated that of that half of the population that had been registered, probably 60 per cent had voted.[6]

[6] *Tin Tuong* (Witness), Sept. 1 and Sept. 30, 1966. The Buddhist estimate (30 per cent) corresponds closely to that of the NLF (27 per cent).

The Constituent Assembly thus elected was predictably sympathetic to the junta's ideas of the way in which governments and elections should be run, though it occasionally showed flashes of independence and included a handful of men who displayed possibilities of becoming dangerous to the junta. Most prominent of these was a delegate named Tran Van Van; within two months of his installation he was assassinated on a Saigon street. The alleged assassin, a youth, was seized and rushed out of public view by the Government, which subsequently identified him as a Vietcong agent. A month later *The Guardian,* Saigon's leading English-language newspaper, was closed for having reported the widespread suspicion that the assassin had in fact been working for the Government.

The Assembly labored and in due time produced a Constitution. It was not a bad Constitution: indeed, its safeguards of the civil liberties of persons accused of crimes were subsequently described by the study team as "among the most generous and progressive of any democracy in the world." Yet the Assembly also, with only two dissenting votes, excluded from the Constitution any provision for land reform and laid the groundwork for the persecution of political dissent by prohibiting, in Article 4, "every activity designed to publicize or carry out Communism in any form," a prohibition that has been used to describe advocates of peace, neutrality, a coalition government, or negotiations as guilty of publicizing or practicing communism.

The Assembly's most urgent task was to establish the basis for elections and to write the rules under which they would be held. The decisions as to who would win the elections were largely made in that process, and particularly in the decision that the President and Vice President needed only a plurality to win, rather than a majority. Since the absence of established political parties meant that the decision to run would be largely an individual one, a considerable slate of candidates would make it possible for a President to be elected with perhaps 20 per cent of the vote, or even less. Most countries that have a large number of candidates for a post, as in France, provide for a run-off election between the two top winners.

The Constitution made other provisions. Candidates desiring to be on the ballot must make themselves known and be approved by the Assembly. Any candidate holding political or military office must resign in order to campaign. Political campaigning could not begin until August 1, with the election scheduled for September 3.

Even with the provision for victory by a plurality vote, the outlook was grave for the generals. Marshal Ky and his Chief of State, Thieu, ambitious, power-hungry men, both announced themselves as candidates for the presidency. Two of the most popular leaders in South Vietnam, General Duong Van Minh and Au Truong Thanh, also announced that they would run. "Big Minh," hero of the coup that overthrew President Diem, was living in exile in Thailand, where he had been banished after his Government in turn had been overthrown by General Nguyen Khanh. Au Truong Thanh, formerly Minister of Finance under Marshal Ky, announced that he would campaign on a straight peace platform, with a crossed-out bomb as his symbol and "Cease-fire" as his slogan. A committee of the Assembly, noting that neither Ky nor Thieu had resigned his post as required, summoned them to give an explanation and, when they refused to appear, recommended that they be excluded from the ballot.

It was time for the junta to take a hand. True, both Ky and Thieu had made it plain that they would not allow a civilian government, or one committed to making peace, to take power, but that would not go well with the Americans, who were watching uneasily. The junta, whose most powerful member was Thieu, insisted that the generals must not divide the already shaky vote they could count on. Ky obediently announced that he would accept the nomination for Vice President on the same ticket with Thieu.

The Assembly, meanwhile, had had a "first reading" of the

ballot and approved for inclusion on it, among others, the
names of Minh and Thanh. They had hardly done so when
Marshal Ky announced that Minh would not be permitted to
return from exile, and that his police had discovered that
Thanh was a Communist. The Assembly met for its second
reading in an atmosphere of tension heightened by the discovery that the head of the National Police, the notorious General
Nguyen Ngoc Loan, and two of his lieutenants, armed with automatic rifles, were leaning over the balcony rail above them observing loudly that those who did not heed their words would
hear their guns. The Assembly meekly reversed its own committee and placed Thieu and Ky on the ballot. Then it completed its surrender by declaring "Big Minh" and Au Truong
Thanh ineligible for the ballot.

The stage was set for a sure thing, but the generals were taking no chances. It is a truism that free elections are not possible
in the absence of a free press, and General Ky set about assur-
ing that there would be no free press. Censorship, prohibited in
the Constitution, became so blatant as to embarrass even the
American embassy, which was said to have brought heavy pressure on Ky to eliminate at least its most obvious
manifestations—large white spaces appearing regularly on the
pages of Vietnamese newspapers where the censor had removed
entire articles judged offensive to the Government. Other newspapers were suspended, and Marshal Ky warned that any criticism of his Administration would be regarded as support for
the enemy. Shortly before the elections, the Government announced once more that there would be no more censorship;
then, on the day before the voting, General Thieu announced
the suspension "for an indefinite period" of *Than Chung,* one
of Saigon's most widely circulated newspapers, and a smaller
paper, *Song*. "Even in a democracy," Thieu explained, "one
has a right to suspend newspapers that support totalitarians"
—a charge that both publishers vigorously denied.

Newspaper publishers had already taken their lives in their

hands, not only when they published anything critical of the Government but even when they permitted their papers to appear with the censor's white spaces unfilled. In addition to being in danger of the sudden charge of "publicizing communism," they were constantly under the threat of having their allocation of newsprint, determined by the Government, cut off and their businesses destroyed. Thus very little appeared in the press about the positions or even the identity of the opposition candidates, or about what had happened to the excluded Minh and Thanh, while the papers were regularly filled with the statements and activities of Thieu and Ky.

The "rules" provided that campaigning could not begin until August 1, one month before the election. General Ky, insisting that other candidates adhere rigorously to this regulation, began campaigning in June. Posters advocating Thieu and Ky's candidacy bloomed throughout the country; the names and faces of the other candidates remained a mystery to most voters. Ky did most of the campaigning for himself and Thieu, while requiring that the ten other sets of candidates appear jointly on a single platform, an arrangement that gave each of them about five minutes to speak. Often they did not get even that as government-provided planes mysteriously failed to show up and, in one case, landed at an American air base instead of the city where a large crowd was waiting. On that occasion, as some of the candidates complained bitterly but vainly, the only transportation available was an American army garbage truck, in which the crestfallen candidates were obliged to ride.

The obedient Assembly had produced a ballot with eleven sets of candidates. Ten were civilian; one—Thieu and Ky —military. Two civilian candidates, Phan Khac Suu and Tran Van Huong, were former Premiers and fairly well known, though neither was a dynamic or popular leader. The rest, except for the virtually unknown Dzu, were political figures in their own localities and regions, with no national standing.

With both the press and the candidates cared for, the Saigon

Government turned its attention to the registration of voters. Excluded immediately were all those living in "insecure" areas, which meant areas controlled all or part of the time—usually at night—by the forces of the National Liberation Front. Excluded also were all voters considered "unreliable," which in South Vietnam means people believed to be supporters of or sympathetic to the NLF, or to stand for peace or neutralism, which are considered to be synonymous with communism. Professor Michael Novak of St. Mary College in Xavier, Kansas, reporting for *The National Catholic Reporter,* wrote that in a random sampling of Saigon students he found that three out of eight families had been disqualified from voting. Thus the enormous "peace vote" that emerged was all the more significant, since the Government had already tried to exclude all those likely to vote in this way.

By the time the elections, and the twenty-two American observers, arrived, everything possible had been done to secure the victory for the generals. Most experts assumed that Thieu and Ky would get a comfortable vote of nearly 50 per cent, with Huong expected to run second and Suu a possible close third. Thieu himself had predicted that he would poll between 40 and 50 per cent of the vote and observed that it would be impossible to govern with less than 40 per cent.

Except for an obscure candidate named Pham Huy Co, who received only 106,000 of the 4,700,000 votes reported, all of the candidates campaigned on peace platforms. (Co called for an invasion of North Vietnam.) Even though their programs were, until Dzu threw his peace bombshell in mid-August, bland and unspecific, the popular longing for peace was so evident that Thieu himself, as the campaign drew to an end, felt compelled to say that if he were elected he would initiate a bombing pause and seek negotiations with the NLF.

With this by way of prelude, South Vietnam on September 3 went to the polls. Voting cards again had been identified with ration cards, and multiple cards had been given to army units, which were driven to the polls in trucks. By the United States Government's own figures, *The New York Times* reported on September 8, 1967, 70 per cent of South Vietnam's electorate had registered, and of these 83 per cent were reported to have voted. Thus 56 per cent of the population of voting age went to the polls, even if the balloting could be considered strictly honest. Of this, the Thieu-Ky ticket got 34.8 per cent; the opposing candidates totaled 65 per cent. Dzu, Huong, and Suu, the top three opposition entries, together polled more than the Thieu-Ky ticket. Consequently, even if the voting could be considered honest, Generals Thieu and Ky received just slightly more than one-third of the votes cast, with those opposing them, in spite of the handicaps put in their way, getting two-thirds.

But who could consider that the voting has been honest? "You could send 10,000 observers," an election official told Professor Novak, "and they would never know how I cheat. . . . In the villages soldiers will fire their guns in the air one kilometer away. They will say VC attack. People will not come to vote. The official, he will count their vote anyway. He will count 1-2-3-4-41-42-43-56 . . ." He went on to explain that the count of the balloting would be written up in the evening by the senior election official—a military officer appointed by Ky—and the ballots then destroyed.

In the villages, under such circumstances, the Thieu-Ky ticket rolled up big majorities, sometimes seven and eight to one against the combined totals of their opponents. In the cities, like Saigon, Hue, and Danang, where fraud and terror were not so easily managed, the military ticket lost in every case.

"In small towns and in the countryside," wrote Vo Van Ai, secretary-general of the Overseas Vietnamese Buddhist Association, in *Tin Tuong* (September 15, 1967), "people come to vote under the watch of the police and secret police. It is safer for the peasants to vote for those who organize the elections. Just the same as under the regime of Ngo Dinh Diem. We went to vote twice under the Diem regime and know perfectly how

the peasants feel. So only the voting in the cities can prove
something. . . . To be defeated in the cities is to be defeated
throughout the country."

So the Constitution was fulfilled, the elections completed,
government by a junta of North Vietnamese military men confirmed, and South Vietnam, in the words of American Government spokesmen, "took a significant step toward democratic
self-government." In fact, fraud and intimidation on a massive
scale, supported fully by the United States in order to legitimize
an illegitimate government, failed to accomplish its task when
subjected even to the slightest critical scrutiny. Even Ambassador Ellsworth Bunker, when the returns were in, admitted
wryly that "It represents the desire of the country, of everyone,
for peace."

Most Americans are hung up on the relationship between democracy and elections. Not exactly that elections *are* democracy, but that they *prove* it. Granted that political parties and
politicians are frequently corrupt, that "deals" and graft are
equally common, that appeals to the electorate for votes are
usually on a level that is a parody of a genuine political
debate—still the appeals *are* to the electorate, and when
election day comes the voters can at least "turn the rascals
out" in favor of a new set.

Elections are a contest, a debate, and the opportunity to
make a choice. They are a restraint on the power of the office-
holder, a veto on any attempt to perpetuate a person or a group
in power. And the essence of an election is that it must be free
and secret—open to all to express their own choices in secret, free from observation and the fear of reprisals. Never
mind that we have denied the freedom of election to 20 million
of our own black citizens. The myth is still there; it is the easi-
est test by which to determine the validity of any government's
claims to be democratic. Sophisticated students of government
may have their reservations about whether two-party parlia-
mentary democracy is the best possible arrangement for emerging countries; the people know that an election in a Communist

society in which only one party is represented on the ballot and the winner receives 98.9 per cent of the vote is a travesty of democracy, a proof of the totalitarianism of the government in question.

The 1967 Vietnamese elections were such a travesty, a theatrical performance written to appeal to the election-conscious audience in the United States and directed and stage-managed with consummate skill.

Americans had begun to become restive about Vietnam. The official explanation of their country's involvement in a war in an obscure country halfway around the world was that the "free" country of South Vietnam had been invaded by the Communists from North Vietnam, supported by the Russians and the Chinese, in another attempt to extend Communist influence in the world by suppressing a free people. To a nation conditioned by half a century of obsessive anticommunism, it sounded plausible. One might feel that it had been a judgment of dubious value to decide to intervene so far away, or to be drawn into a land war once we had intervened, but it was hard to quarrel with the basic description of what had precipitated the war itself. The choice, it had seemed to many, was whether to spend American lives and money in the fight or to allow another free small nation to be absorbed by the Communists.

But the money and the lives both were pouring out at an alarming rate, and opponents of the war were saying some disquieting things. One was that the Geneva Agreement that had ended the French Indochina war in 1954 had provided for free elections in 1956, and that it had been our side—our hand-picked new President of South Vietnam, with our support—who had refused to hold them. Again the official answer, that you couldn't hope to have honest elections with half the country controlled by the Communists, sounded plausible, but with a number of question marks. How could anyone be certain that free elections were impossible before the procedures under which they would be held had even begun to be discussed? Why would the International Control Commission, appointed to supervise the elections, continue to urge that they be held if it could not assure their honesty? And why, at last, had the elections been agreed upon in 1954 if they were to be reversed in 1955?

But more disquieting than the unheld elections of 1956 were the developments within this "free nation" of South Vietnam since 1963. Opposition to President Ngo Dinh Diem from the Vietcong was understandable. They were the Communists who were the agents of the international conspiracy. But opposition from Diem's own people? And led by the monks of the country's dominating religious establishment, the Buddhists? What did this mean?

Reporting of the events of 1963, specifically the overthrow of Diem and the reaction of the people, was far from good in the United States. Diem had been picked out of his refuge in a New York monastery by an American expert on Southeast Asia, endorsed by the American Roman Catholic hierarchy, and put in power by our State Department. Diem was a Catholic, and his opposition was predominantly Buddhist. We understood Catholics (though very few of us knew much about the Vietnamese Catholics and their relationship with the French, or even that some of them also opposed Diem); Buddhists were an unknown quantity, a strange uncivilized sort of religion that didn't believe in Jesus Christ and did believe in reincarnation, with monks who went around in yellow robes collecting alms.

But one of those monks had burned himself to death to protest the Diem regime, and the photographs of Thich Quang Duc sitting in the lotus position of prayer while the flames consumed him, although horrifying, were sobering. The official insistence that Diem's opponents were not really monks but Communists in monks' clothing had few takers. A kind of resident common sense made it seem unlikely that even Communists would carry a charade to the point of setting themselves on fire for it.

The uneasiness increased as Diem was succeeded by one regime after another until the flamboyant Marshal Nguyen Cao Ky came to power in the spring of 1965. As Premier, strutting and preening in Saigon's night clubs with his beautiful wife, taking off periodically to fly his own fighter plane, and making admiring comments about Adolf Hitler and melodramatic statements of his intention to win the war in a hurry, Ky made good but unconvincing copy. What kind of democracy was it that put into power in South Vietnam a clique of generals from North Vietnam who had fought beside the French against their own countrymen and who took power by still another military coup?

The Buddhist-led "struggle movement" against the Ky regime increased the uneasiness, though not as much as if the role of the United States in suppressing that movement had been widely known. The Johnson Administration, worried by growing signs of Ky's unpopularity, wrote the script for the theatrical production and insisted that the young general accept it. Premier Ky obediently announced that there would be elections for a Constituent Assembly to write a Constitution, which in turn would provide for free national elections.

The script was followed religiously; the actors understood clearly that their audience was the great uneasy white nation across the sea. In Vietnam itself the production was a flop before it ever reached the stage. No Vietnamese, seeing the white expanses in their censored newspapers and knowing of the exclusion from registration of all voters considered "unreliable" by the Government, could do anything but snicker at the farce.

But across the sea the production was more successful. A Constitution—a *good* democratic constitution—was written, the elections were run and Generals Thieu and Ky were duly and properly elected to office, even if by a minority of the electorate. At the last minute the Great Stage Manager on Pennsylvania Avenue added his own touch of verisimilitude to the act by sending a team of twenty-two observers, his personal representatives, to assure that the elections were carried out fairly. The team was selected in consistent American political fashion: the proper number of clergymen, Negroes, Jews, intellectuals, politicians. They were led by Ky's principal American supporter, Henry Cabot Lodge, and lacked members who spoke

Vietnamese or had had any experience in observing elections in Asia. The team spent all of four days in Vietnam. It was taken where its hosts wanted to take it, principally the cities. It depended on interpreters chosen by the Government, listened to explanations of the election from officials of the American embassy, and returned to report with some modesty that the balloting, on the whole, had compared favorably with elections in this country.

The press dutifully though unenthusiastically reported these findings and dutifully ignored any contrary evidence. There was some. Professor Novak, sent by *The National Catholic Reporter* to Vietnam well before the elections, reported in careful, dispassionate detail all the ways in which the elections were being rigged in Thieu's and Ky's favor. A group of peace organizations sent Professor David Wurfel, then of the University of Missouri, another Southeast Asia expert who had spent much time in Vietnam, spoke Vietnamese, and had been an observer at three preceding Asian elections. He, too, went well before the elections and stayed much longer than four days, and his report paralleled and confirmed Professor Novak's. In Washington, Senator Ernest Gruening, who with Senator Wayne Morse had been the first to challenge the war, read into *The Congressional Record* my own analysis of the elections, and sent reprints to 150,000 American clergymen.

But the circulation of *The National Catholic Reporter* is small, peace organizations are perpetually without funds to distribute the information they have, and even 150,000 clergymen are a pretty minute segment of the country's population. Millions of Americans breathed a little more easily. The war was still escalating, the toll of lives and treasure was a bitter one, but at least we could be sure that little South Vietnam really was moving in the direction of a constitutional democracy, with a government in power that had been properly chosen in a properly conducted election.

The performance had been a smashing success.

3

The Pattern of Suppression

Some bright doctoral candidate in search of a thesis might do worse than to study the evolving American awareness of Vietnam. This country was deeply involved in the affairs of the little Asian nation long before most Americans could even locate it on the map. Decisions made with little opposition by Dwight Eisenhower and John Foster Dulles committed the United States to a tragic course from which it could have been deflected only by a President of great courage and wisdom who was also well-informed on the realities of politics and life in Vietnam, and we had no such President. Departments of Asian studies existed at some universities, but even they had little material on Vietnam, except for Michigan State College (now University), whose Professor Wesley R. Fishel had been instrumental in bringing Diem to the attention of the State Department and was now busily training Diem's police. It was almost impossible even to find a place where the language of the country could be studied. So pervasive was the ignorance about the area and the conflict in which it was involved that many good American liberals, including the incorruptible Norman Thomas, saw the accession to power of President Diem as a gain for democracy, and organized an American Friends of South Vietnam to interpret and support his regime.

For most Americans the reality of the Vietnamese conflict only began to become apparent with the "incident" of the Gulf of Tonkin, the subsequent shelling and bombing of North Vietnam, and the quick-tempo escalation of United States involvement in the war that followed. Since then Vietnam has become a nightmare for all of us, but one whose origins and nature are still surrounded by controversy and uncertainty.

My own enlightenment also began in 1965 with the trip that fourteen of us from the Clergymen's Emergency Committee made to Saigon. We had been appalled by the explosion of violence against a tiny, remote nation which our country had suddenly triggered, and had issued the strongest appeal from it to our own government that we were capable of writing.[1]

Now we wanted to see at first-hand what we could of the circumstances of the war, and to meet the leaders of the religious life of the country to see whether jointly we could find any way of speeding an end to the war. The most important of these, we knew, were the militant Buddhist group, headed by Thich Tri Quang, who had mounted the demonstrations that had unseated Diem and several of his successors. We were anxious to learn from them their thinking and plans, and, if possible, how we could help. It was at this point that we began in earnest to learn of the non-NLF opposition to the war and the South Vietnamese Government, and of the pattern of suppression that had developed to keep them silent.

[1] Though one incident that illustrates the intensification of feeling since then stands out in my mind. The Fellowship of Reconciliation's executive committee, presented with the initial draft of the *"Mr. President"* statement I had prepared (See Appendix 1), gagged at a sentence that read, "We are deeply ashamed of our country's actions." "Ashamed" was too strong a word to apply to the actions of our own government, members of the committee said, even though we disagreed with it. The sentence was changed to read, "We are deeply dismayed by our country's actions." It is inconceivable that the same objection would be raised in 1969.

The Vietnam war has been called the best-reported war in history. Television and the press have given us first-hand pictures and accounts of a quantity and intensity almost beyond bearing. But the reporting has been merely superficial. Body counts have been duly noted, along with occasional frank acknowledgment of the skepticism with which many American reporters greeted them. Pictorial records of bloody battles have been interspersed with equally candid notes of the difficulty of confirming the official briefings given out by the military in a war with no static front. But there has been very little reporting of what was happening beneath the surface, and no consistent interpretation of what it meant. The mass media, alert to governmental pressure and the sensitivities of their clients at home, even based their skepticism on the accepted rationale of the war—we against the Communists.

In the wake of the September, 1967, elections, any mass-circulation magazine or television network that wanted to could have broken open the whole ugly situation. In an earlier era of American journalism, when writers and editors joyfully dug beneath the surface rhetoric to expose the smelly mess, the job would have been done. But American journalism in the 1960's is big business, bland even in its melodrama, and the job was not done.

The arrest and imprisonment of Truong Dinh Dzu was an act of political suppression. That is, it was an act designed to avert a threat from the South Vietnamese people themselves to the Saigon Government. President Nguyen Van Thieu acknowledged freely to the study team in 1969 that Mr. Dzu was a "political prisoner," made so by the fact that his appeals for direct talks with the NLF, as a step toward a coalition government and peace, had almost won the election.

The arrest, imprisonment, and exile of Au Truong Thanh was similarly an act of political suppression, as was the subsequent arrest and sentencing of the Buddhist monk Thich Thien Minh. Thanh, a former cabinet minister who had resigned in protest at the continuation of the war and wholesale corruption in government, had attempted to run for President on a platform calling for a cease-fire; Thien Minh, second most prominent Buddhist leader in the country, had preached sermons calling for much the same thing.

All three arrests confirmed other, less publicized, evidence of a continued pattern of such suppression that had been emerging over the past several years. The elections of 1967 were further confirmation, and might have shocked the American people into more awareness of the real situation in Vietnam had they been adequately and honestly reported. But President Johnson's team of twenty-two "observers" effectively disguised that reality with their report that the voting had been generally honest. Or, as one of them observed, not much different from a Chicago election, a comment that may have returned to haunt him a year later. One Vietnamese, commenting on the shabby performance of the official observers, remarked: "We are planning to send twenty-two Vietnamese observers who don't speak English to the United States for four days to see if your elections are fair."

By late 1967 and early 1968 it had become apparent to anyone who cared to look that the Diem techniques for dealing with opposition had been re-established by Generals Ky and Thieu. Most of the country's political prisoners—75,000—had been released by the Government of Duong Van Minh after Diem's downfall, yet when President Thieu was inaugurated in November, 1967, it was possible to release more than 6,000 such prisoners, and for a high government official to acknowledge that they were "only a small proportion" of the total being held! Five thousand Buddhist monks, nuns, lay leaders, and students had been arrested after the 1966 uprising in Hue and Danang alone, and none of these were among those released at the inauguration. In May, 1968, the Buddhist monk Thich Nhat Hanh told an audience at a university teach-in at Bozeman, Montana, that "at least 20,000" non-NLF political prisoners were being detained.

Much earlier, *The Washington Post* had reported American officials as estimating that thousands of political prisoners were being held by the Ky Government in jails and detention camps throughout South Vietnam. According to a document issued by the United States Agency for International Development (USAID) in November, 1966, and quoted in *The York* (Pa.) *Gazette and Daily* on June 28, 1967, "vast numbers have never been tried . . . and have no idea when or how they will be released."

The practice of imprisoning, exiling, torturing, and even murdering those who disagree with the government is by no means confined to South Vietnam. An American familiar with Vietnam observed that such practices are "common to Asia." It is true. They are. They are also common to countries in every other part of the world, though admittedly in varying degrees. The International Commission of Jurists, which devotes its time to trying to free men and women who have been unjustly confined to prison, does not even bother to work in countries at war, since it is so much more difficult and there are enough cases in countries at peace to keep it occupied.

Even the United States, where the concept of free speech has been codified and traditionalized, has a much more serious record of suppression of dissent than most Americans realize. The uprooting from their homes on the West Coast of 110,000 Americans of Japanese descent and their confinement in what were euphemistically called "relocation camps" during World War II, with not a scintilla of evidence of any subversive activities or intent, was a large-scale indication of the willingness of the United States Government, in the passions of war, to set aside the most precious constitutional safeguards of some of its citizens. More immediately, the arrest, indictment, and imprisonment of young men whose outrage at the immorality of the Vietnam war leads them to refuse to serve in it is forcible suppression of political dissent, as are the harassment of young soldiers caught in the same crisis of conscience, the repressive acts of police and legislatures against demonstrators on streets and campuses, and the attempts to terrorize dissident groups of black Americans into submission by arresting their leaders. And if there remains, as there does in the United States, a judicial process that frequently, if often belatedly, restrains those who would most seriously breach the protective wall of civil liberties, the ugly fact still remains that even the first stages of national anxiety bring quick moves toward the isolation and punishment of those who do not share the official, or majority, view.

Yet most of us know that we do not like the fact that this is so. If freedom for many Americans has been debased into the materialistic notion that everyone should be free to acquire a maximum of possessions, for most of us there remains a nobler conception of freedom and a recognition of the wrongness of such suppression, and a sense of shock when some of its worst manifestations are made public, or when our own immediate crisis of apprehension has subsided a bit. The rhetoric of human brotherhood that clothes the case made by the Marxist countries is canceled out by memories of the Moscow show trials, the exiles to Siberia, China's liquidation of opponents, and the suppression of Czechoslovakia's tentative moves toward freedom. Our State Department's insistence on its devotion to the concept of a "free world" is tarnished and debased by the knowledge that it supports in office unpopular dictators in a score of countries ranging from Taiwan to Haiti. Most of us do not *like* the use of physical and psychological terrorism to silence those who disagree. We do not like it because of its sheer inhuman quality, and our instinctive awareness that mankind as a whole cannot survive the continued brutalization of its members, and we do not like it because we are part of a nation constructed, however imperfectly, on the belief that governments were made to serve their people and not vice versa.

This is why the repressive actions of the South Vietnamese Government are so revolting. Americans, feeling beset by a multitude of unmanageable problems, can often avert their eyes from the use of their taxes to prop up unpopular dictators and suppress their opponents; they have a harder time when more than 40,000 of their sons dead and 250,000 wounded are the price paid to keep in power a dictatorial junta that is detested by its own people. When this is done, not because our own country's safety has been in any way threatened, but on the ground that we are defending the right of the Vietnamese to choose their own form of government, as our various Administrations have claimed through the last fifteen years, then the revulsion for sensitive Americans turns to nausea.

No one knows how many political prisoners there are in South Vietnam. Even the Government of that country itself does not know, because there are so many agencies authorized to arrest and imprison and because so many individuals who have been imprisoned without trial have literally been "lost" so far as their records are concerned.

This does not inhibit either the South Vietnamese or American governments from minimizing the issue. When the Fellowship of Reconciliation published a full-page advertisement, headed "Is Eugene McCarthy Still Out of Prison? Truong Dinh Dzu Is Not," in *The New York Times* on December 29, 1968, asserting that there were between 20,000 and 200,000 such prisoners, an official of the South Vietnamese embassy wrote indignantly that the charge was false, that the prisons of South Vietnam could not hold that many prisoners. (He did not respond to a proposal, sent in reply, that his Government authorize an independent, unbiased investigation, with a promise of retraction if it indeed proved the charges false.)

When United States Senator Charles E. Goodell, apprised of the situation, sent his own inquiry to the State Department, William B. Macomber, Jr., Assistant Secretary of State for Congressional Relations, replied on May 9, 1969, that "the number of persons in prison—apart from common criminals and known or suspected Communists—is not only small but decreasing," and added that prominent Buddhists and "other political oppositionists" who had been put in "protective custody" had now been released and "presently, the Government of Vietnam is reviewing the cases of other, less well-known 'civil defendants' and is releasing those against whom there is insufficient evidence and remanding others for early trial." [2]

The official "line" was evident, too, when the Rev. Robert F. Drinan, dean of the Boston College Law School, reported getting the same information when he consulted a "highly placed official" in the State Department before deciding whether to be a part of the proposed study team.

"I thought for a time," Father Drinan wrote later, "of telling that State Department official that, on the basis of his assertions, I would cancel my commitment to go to Vietnam. . . . the official, by his claims, stated by implication that the religious groups were misinformed and were attacking a non-problem. . . . On June 11 I was back in Washington and at another meeting told one of the high White House officials . . . that a State Department official had lied to us." [3]

Later, learning that the State Department was still replying to inquiries with precisely the same assertions, Father Drinan wrote sharply to Acting Assistant Secretary Richard I. Phillips that "I do not think it helps the search for truth in this matter by deliberately placing outside the category of 'political prisoners' all of the persons alleged to be 'suspected' Communists. I found in South Vietnam that the South Vietnamese Government branded everyone in jail as a 'suspected' Communist. . . . I am afraid furthermore that I found no evidence whatsoever in South Vietnam for the statement in your letter that the government is now reviewing the cases of 'less well-known civilian defendants.' In fact high officials at the American embassy in Saigon informed us in a letter dated July 25, 1969, that the Saigon Government, in collaboration with the pacification program, is

[2] See Appendix 13.
[3] Robert F. Drinan, S.J., "The Ultimate Form of Corruption," *The New Republic*, July 19, 1969.

actually increasing substantially the number of persons who fall into the category of 'civilian defendants.' "

Indeed, there was overwhelming evidence that the spokesmen for both governments were lying. Some of the evidence could be plucked from the columns of the better American newspapers, though never assembled into a form that constituted a complete picture; some of it came to those of us who were in contact with the Vietnamese themselves.

Soon after the inauguration of the Thieu Government in November, 1967, *The New York Times* reported (December 18, 1967) that the South Vietnamese Senate had begun debate on a bill to mandate release of "all the thousands of political prisoners" taken into custody in the past years *with the exception of the Vietcong*. Nothing further has been heard of the bill.

Two months later the National Assembly (successor to the Constituent Assembly) was reportedly "stunned" when President Thieu's new budget included an item of $670,000 to feed 12,000 citizens whom the Government expected to have under temporary detention on a daily basis. The Washington Post News Service (September 18, 1968) reported that at the same time arrests in Saigon alone were proceeding at the rate of 2,000 a day. (This was a report that, interestingly enough, reached the American public ten months later.)

On February 24, 1968, The Associated Press reported the arrest of Vu Huong Khanh, a candidate who had finished eighth in the presidential election, and of the labor union leaders Tran Huu Guyen and Vo Van Tai, along with several Buddhist monks. At least twenty persons were thought to have been arrested in the preceding three days. "No reasons were stated by the Government for the arrests, but officials mentioned a list allegedly compiled by the Vietcong of persons who might figure in a coalition government."

Others among those arrested at the same time and not identified by the AP were Tran Thuc Linh, a juvenile court judge and author of ten books on the law, citizenship and individual rights and responsibilities, and Thich Tri Quang, the Buddhist leader. Indeed, since 1966 Tri Quang has been under a form of arrest, either actually detained or under so rigid a surveillance as to constitute detention. The representative of the Fellowship of Reconciliation in Saigon wrote that two policemen preceded the *bonze* and four followed him every time he left An Quang Pagoda, ostensibly to protect him. Linh, according to John Sullivan,[4] was arrested because some papers allegedly found on a dead Vietcong said that Linh would govern Saigon in the event of an NLF victory.

Sullivan, an experienced journalist who had left his profession to work for the American Friends Service Committee, returned from Vietnam in May, 1968, with a detailed report of developments that went largely unreported in the American press. Thanh, Linh, and Dzu, he noted, had been released only after they had engaged in a 15-day hunger strike. Dzu was subsequently removed from a hospital bed, where he had been confined with a heart attack, and taken to National Police Headquarters.

Sullivan quoted numerous informants to the effect that the rate of arrests had doubled since the Tet offensive, including many important officials evidently feared as potential challengers to the Thieu-Ky authority in the event of another NLF offensive. The number of prisoners in Hue, he was told by a Catholic priest, had increased from 3,000 before Tet to more than 9,000 after. Even the Lower House of the Assembly, Sullivan reported, had become "quite noisy" on the subject of illegal arrests by the police after the Tet offensive, and voted, 49 to 39 to ask the Internal Affairs Committee to investigate.

Nothing, however, seemed to stop or even slow the increasing pace of arrests and suppression. President Thieu, *The Vietnam Guardian* reported on July 11, 1968, signed a "decree law" that authorized the Government to carry on unannounced

---

[4] *A Report to the Peace Education Division of AFSC* [the American Friends Service Committee], May 9, 1968.

searches day or night; to assign "specific locations" for persons considered dangerous to the national security; to ban all demonstrations or assemblies that "threaten security and public order" and possession or circulation of publications, documents, and leaflets considered harmful to the national security; to control and limit movement and transportation of all citizens, and to declare martial law wherever it thought fit. All violators, moreover, were to be brought to trial before the infamous Military Field Courts (See Chapter 4.)

At about the same time *The Saigon Daily News,* also an English-language newspaper, was reporting that there were 100,000 persons in South Vietnam's jails, and that they lived under incredibly difficult conditions of overcrowding and lack of sanitary facilities. "The Can Tho provincial jail," *The News* reported, "was built by the French for 500 prisoners, is now used to keep over 2,000. Detainees have no room to sit. Legs of most prisoners have been swollen from having to stand on their feet to sleep. . . . They are also trained to live without washing like hyppies [sic], although the Mekong River which flows across Can Tho never dries . . ." [5]

Other reports flooded in, some of them letters officially prepared by Buddhist or student associations; others were notes smuggled out through Singapore or Hong Kong to give the latest reports on the arrests and, when possible, supplying names. "But we cannot supply many names or the locations of prisons," one student wrote sadly. "They are arrested secretly, when no one is around; we know only that they have disappeared. Then, later, one whispers to another that it was a police raid, but no one can ask without risking his own liberty."

Late in 1968, the Fellowship of Reconciliation received a letter bearing a November date from the 25,000-member General Association of Saigon Students, summarizing the things that had been happening to them during the past few months:

[5] Quoted in *News/Views from the Field,* published by the United Methodist Church, Washington, D.C. Issue of Sept./Oct., 1968.

Shortly after [the April election of the students' executive committee], Saigon was faced with the second wave of offensive by the soldiers of the National Liberation Front, and we found ourselves devoting most of our time working to alleviate some of the victims' plight. At the beginning of June was born *Student,* published by the executive committee of GASS to serve as the official voice of the association. Half a month after the periodical came out (having been duly submitted to the censors as required by the authorities), the Government of Saigon suddenly declared us to be pro-Communists, Communist stooges, etc. On July 11, 1968, the police abducted our friend Nguyen Truong Cong, the publication's editor-in-chief and searched for co-ed Nguyen Thi To-Lien, its secretary general. Threatened with violence, other students went into hiding. Among them was Nguyen Dang Trung, the Chairman of the Executive Committee of GASS.

On July 25, 1968, a special tribunal (this so-called tribunal has no legality) sentenced Cong to five years of forced labor. . . . On July 28, the National Police threw out a public call to Chairman Trung. Promising lenience, it urged him to present himself without delay at its headquarters. . . . Trung ignored the urging, and on August 2, the same tribunal sentenced him to ten years of forced labor in absentia. GASS convened a press conference the following day to protest against this unjustified act, but police forces arrived to surround its headquarters in strength. On August 9, the police again arrested co-ed Dao Thi Nguyen Thanh and student Duong Van Day, both members of the University & High School Students for the Relief of War Victims. But they were soon released after 20 other students protested by fasting. . . .

On September 14, 1968 . . . the National Police searched our office at 4 Duy Tan Street. Wreaking havoc amidst our documents and papers, they did not find whatever they looked for and instead arrested Nguyen Thanh Cong, Chairman of University & High School Students for the Relief of War Victims and Secretary General of the Representative Council of Saigon Students.

On October 4, 1968 . . . Cong was tried by a military tribunal, convicted of disturbing the peace and given three years of suspended sentence. The truth of the matter is that Cong has simply worked closely with the executive committee in organizing, on July 13 and September 8, sessions of discussions whose topic was "peace" . . . and that he, among other representatives from other departments of the University, has signed the June 13, 1968, Appeal for Peace.

Although Cong was given a suspended sentence, he was not released as required by the law. At the Chi Hoa prison, Cong protested this by fasting, the first time from October 10 to October 12, the second time from October 14 to twenty days later. . . . Various individual students, members of GASS, workers, religious faithfuls, and even some congressmen publicly demanded that Cong be permitted to go free. . . . Instead, [he] was brought to an army induction center where he presently still remains, even though his draft deferment runs until December 15 of this year.

The letter goes on to say that on October 30, the Representative Council of Saigon Students released a statement demanding a cease-fire and peace negotiations. "This statement was signed by the representatives of the seven departments of the University. Three of the signers were arrested on the morning of November 9. . . . Other students, looked for by the police, have gone into hiding. Student leaders are presently living under constant threat and harassment, not knowing when their turn will come to be incarcerated."

A letter forwarded from Hong Kong by another correspondent reported the arrest on June 12, 1968, of Pham Phi Long, chairman of the Buddhist Students Association, with a number of his colleagues; another in October carried the word that "many Buddhist high school students are being locked into jail without charge. It is said that they may have belonged to Mat Tran Lien Hoa Binh Dan Tec, a new peace group which is popular among high school and university students."

The lists of arrest were endless, made doubly impressive by the difficulty of obtaining them, but they were not the only indication of the suppression that was gathering all South Vietnam in its grip. Dozens of newspapers were warned and suspended or suppressed; editors and columnists jailed; foreign correspondents expelled for writing anything that the censors felt might reflect division in the country, or the presence of a peace sentiment among the people, or any kind of criticism of the Government itself.

Inquiries brought the reply that most of those imprisoned in 1966 or before were still in prison or had been completely lost track of. Indeed, the only significant group of political prisoners released during this period were a large number of cadres of the old Diemist Can Lao party and other reactionary former Diem supporters who had been jailed after his collapse. At least one of the Can Lao leaders, Ngo Trong Hieu, was then approved as a candidate for election to the Senate.

In February, 1969, another letter from the Association of Saigon Students continued the recital of meetings and demonstrations broken up, literature destroyed, and student arrests, and added the story of a peace demonstration by Catholic students that had suffered the same fate:

On Christmas Eve, 1968, more than 2,000 students participated in a procession held in the spirit of the message transmitted by the Pope, during which the torch of peace was borne aloft. This [procession] was clamped down on by the Government, and resulted in the arrests of hundreds [including a well-known Redemptorist priest and peace advocate, the Rev. Nguyen Ngoc Lan, who was later released but subjected to repeated "interrogations" in the weeks that followed].

In the next few days, the Government, with the aim of rooting out all those holding the support and trust of the students, had kidnapped: Miss Huynh Quan Thu, General Secretary of the Saigon Students Union; Miss Dao Thi Nguyen Thanh, General Secretary of the Students Committee for the Relief of War Victims; Mr. Truong Van Khue, Mr. Tran Van Chi, and Mr. Tran Minh Duc, all representatives of Student Teachers; Mr. Pham Hao Quang, Chairman of the Central Executive Committee of the Faculty of Science.

More recently, the Government has interfered with elections of student representatives. Some examples of proof are: that Mr. Nguyen Dinh Mai was arrested within the Faculty of Science itself as he was campaigning for his own election; of the four groups up for election in the Faculty of Law, the whole of the fourth group was arrested.

There are many other examples of individual students who have been arrested, exiled or tortured for their patriotism, and now the Government proceeds with its campaign of student arrests in Universities all over South Vietnam.

In face of such a grave situation, we students of South Vietnam earnestly appeal to you—students, humanitarian movements, and people throughout the world—to continue in your support of our patriotic aspirations: that is, to bring independence, liberty, national sovereignty, and peace to Vietnam.

Caught in the wave of repression and terror, too, was the Buddhist School of Youth for Social Service, founded in 1965 by Thich Nhat Hanh. The school had quickly proved to be a remarkable success, thanks to the imaginative leadership of Nhat Hanh, his associate director, Thich Thanh Van, and their colleagues. It combined the training of young social workers who, Nhat Hanh saw clearly, would be sorely needed after the war ended, with immediate work in the villages, helping with the war-inflicted damage and injuries and lifting the spirits of the bewildered and frightened villagers. Its teachers and directors themselves had moved long and easily through the villages, and knew their people well. It was clear to them at once that if they were to succeed, the school's workers must be known to be volunteers, completely supervised by members of the Buddhist Church and unconnected with the Government in any way.

"The government relief workers," explained a Buddhist worker, "did everything wrong. Better paid than the villagers could hope to be, they came dressed in uniforms and carrying guns, and with money to construct things that the people knew had come from the hated government. The people knew, too, that what these workers wanted, in most cases, was information about the Vietcong." He added, "The government workers never stayed after the sun went down. They knew they would be killed if they did."

The school's workers, on the other hand, were young Vietnamese volunteers, with monks as their leaders and supervisors. The total cost of their maintenance and work, whether in classes or in the villages, averaged about $15 per month, and not a dollar came from either the South Vietnamese or United States governments. The consequence was that they could move with relative freedom across the lines that divided South Vietnamese forces from Vietcong, and could work in villages largely controlled by the Vietcong because the villagers themselves were their protection.

It was inevitable that such an institution would draw to it the very young people who were the core of the peace sentiment in Vietnam, and with them the antagonism of the Government. In February, 1967, I visited the school's new campus, with attractive, low white buildings constructed by the students themselves. It was a nervous trip, but the Fellowship of Reconciliation had raised some money and medicine for the school in Europe and America, and they wanted me to see it. The campus was situated on the edge of Saigon, in the Cholon section, and we traveled to it in a tiny French car through sections of the city euphemistically termed "insecure" for Westerners. My hosts had calculated carefully, so that we drove through the hottest part of the day, when the markets were closed and many people were indoors, but they were still nervous. Because of the danger, I was the first white person they had invited to visit their campus.

The school was attractive and its 200 students charming and friendly. There was a hole in the bright white new wall where a mortar shell had broken through the preceding week, but everyone was willing to call it a mistake. A few weeks later a group of masked and uniformed men raided the campus and threw grenades into two classrooms, killing a teacher and a student and wounding twenty-one others, some of them seriously. (A young girl whose foot was blown off was somehow sent to Japan for remedial surgery after initial hospitalization. She spent her convalescence learning to operate simple knitting machines so that she could help set them up in the refugee camps where the student-workers were operating.)

Soon after, five workers (including two monks) making up one of the school's teams were forced at midnight from the village hut where they were sleeping and taken to the bank of a river for execution. One monk was left for dead but survived.

At about the same time a team of eight workers was kidnapped and never heard from again. All incidents were attributed by the Government to the Vietcong, but knowledgeable students and others in Saigon suspected that the attackers could just as reasonably have been from the Government's side.

Ultimately the school had to abandon formal classes, since any young men who showed up were immediately grabbed by the Government, their student exemptions were canceled, and they were sent off as soldiers to the most dangerous fighting. Instead the school organized into self-contained units the workers it had already trained and sent them into the cities and refugee camps, where each small team recruited young boys and girls from among the refugees and trained *them* in the social work procedures they had learned, while carrying on relief work on a remarkably large scale, a procedure which the institution still follows.

The steady flow of reports, letters, petitions, and pleas was making it evident that something was taking place in South Vietnam that might be significant in bringing the war to a close and that was not getting adequate attention in the West. Clearly there was more than a civil war going on between the military forces of two contending parties; within the areas controlled by Saigon there was an undercurrent that disturbed that government very much and had led it to impose a cruel pattern of suppression on its own people. Whether or not the phenomena that lay behind that suppression could have political significance, Americans have the right to know if their taxes are helping to pay for the imposition of such tyranny. Since any official inquiry would certainly be self-serving, it seemed like the opportune moment for an unofficial, dependable investigation. The United States Study Team on Religious and Political Freedom in South Vietnam was ready to be formed.

4

The Study Team
in Vietnam

The Vietnam war has probably stimulated the creation of more ad hoc groups of citizens concerned about a single subject than any other incident in American political history. The traditional peace groups, with their membership of a few thousand, have been dwarfed by committees of women, mothers, businessmen, doctors, lawyers, university faculties, religious leaders, neighborhood groups, and all kinds of quasi-political formations designed to express the popular opposition to the war and somehow to end it.

In the fall of 1968 another one came into existence—the Hoa Binh ad hoc committee of churchmen. "Hoa binh" means "peace," and has been a dangerous word to use in South Vietnam. The churchmen, mostly directors of the social-action divisions of various denominations or other religious organizations, had been prompted to come together as the result of a conversation some of them had with Tran Van Dinh, a former diplomat who had resigned from the South Vietnamese embassy in Washington, where he now lives in exile. On a speaking trip for the Disciples of Christ in Indiana, Dinh had raised the question with some of his hosts whether some new moves by American and South Vietnamese religious leaders together might move the war closer to its end. The result was the Hoa Binh Committee, which ultimately was to include leading personalities from the American Jewish Congress and the Synagogue Council of America, the United States Catholic Conference, and such Protestant groups as the Church of the Brethren, the Disciples, the Episcopal, Methodist, Presbyterian and Unitarian-Universalist Churches, and the United Church of Christ, as well as the National Council of Churches, the Fellowship of Reconciliation, and Clergy and Laymen Concerned about Vietnam. Several of its meetings coincided with an American speaking tour by Vo Van Ai, of the Overseas Vietnamese Buddhist Association, and Masako Yamanouchi, a young Japanese woman who had worked closely with the Buddhist School of Youth for Social Service in Vietnam for two years. They were brought in as consultants, along with several Vietnamese living in the United States.

The committee's early discussions revolved around the possibility of a statement or action that could be taken by Buddhist and other religious spokesmen in Vietnam jointly with Christian and Jewish leaders in the United States, but it soon became wryly evident that any Vietnamese who signed such a statement, however prominent his position, could count on immediate imprisonment or worse.

Similarly, a proposal that a number of Buddhist leaders be brought to the United States for a major speaking tour and conversations with government and press personalities was aborted when it developed that they would not be permitted to leave Vietnam.

Two things had emerged in the discussions, however, that began to assume primary importance to the committee. One was the mass of evidence that there existed in South Vietnam a substantial body of opposition to the Thieu-Ky Government and the war that was not identified with the National Liberation

Front. The second was that any South Vietnamese who dared to speak in these terms was immediately imprisoned, if he did not disappear entirely, and that there seemed to be reason to believe that the prisons of the country were crowded with thousands of such prisoners. The Hoa Binh Committee decided that it could serve the cause of peace best if it could send to South Vietnam a study team to ascertain the facts. The team would have to be composed of sufficiently prestigious and respected Americans to enable it, if possible, to break through what was assumed would be the hostility of both the South Vietnamese and United States governments, and to be listened to by the American public when it reported.

So was born the United States Study Team on Religious and Political Freedom in Vietnam, a private group of citizens organized to learn for themselves the facts of a situation about which dependable facts were not otherwise available, and in the process implicitly—and later explicitly—to challenge their own government's version of those facts. It was a development, I believe, that ought to be the forerunner of many similar actions. With human survival hanging on every major political decision or military action, and the heavy weight of evidence that the officials who make such decisions cannot often be trusted to share the truth of the situations, private citizens must find ways of determining for themselves where the truth exists.

The committee had difficulty both in determining the goals of the team and in defining the terms it was using. Most members were clear that they wanted to determine whether there were in fact such a thing as the Third Force, which had been described to them, and whether it seemed to have any potential in the making of peace and, second, to learn the truth of reports that scores of thousands of political prisoners were being held in the jails and detention centers of South Vietnam. At the same time, in its search for a possible Third Force it did not want to be seduced into "discovering," as one member repeatedly warned that it might, an alternative to the Thieu-Ky re-

gime that the Nixon Administration could seize on as an excuse
for continuing the war. Few members of the committee thought
that such a thing was likely or even possible; there seemed little
point to the abandonment of Thieu and Ky, after the heavy investment that had been made in them as a "constitutional government," by a United States that was determined to pursue the
war. Besides, the argument advanced by Third Force spokesmen included the insistence that the United States must withdraw from Vietnam and could under no circumstances count on
their help in continuing the war.

Something of the same ambivalence was attached to the definition of "political prisoners." The South Vietnamese Government and the American State Department had already made
their line clear: There were no more than a handful of political
prisoners in South Vietnam, only "common criminals and Communists or suspected Communists." [1] The committee had no
difficulty with that; as a member of the team was later to write
to the State Department, "I found in South Vietnam that the
South Vietnamese Government branded everyone in jail as a
'suspected' Communist. Clearly the Saigon Government is not
going openly to admit that they have imprisoned the political
opponents of the Thieu regime."

As early as 1964, South Vietnam had written into its statutes
a "decree law"—that is, a law handed down by decree rather
than adopted by a legislature—outlawing "any individual,
party, or organization that acts by whatever methods to realize
directly or indirectly the goals of communism or a pro-Communist neutralism." The Constitution adopted in 1966 specifies
succinctly that "The Republic of Vietnam opposes communism
in any form," and that "every activity designed to publicize or
carry out communism is prohibited."

For a government that identifies calls for peace or for a neutralist foreign policy as "designed to publicize or carry out
communism," as the South Vietnamese Government does, it was

[1] See Appendix 13.

inevitable that imprisoned opponents would be identified as "Communists or suspected Communists."

But there was a more difficult problem when it came to proven agents of the National Liberation Front. What should be the study team's attitude toward them? Most of the committee thought it obvious, however regrettable, that a government at war would imprison or otherwise isolate persons actually found to be helping to set ambushes for its troops, or ferrying supplies to its enemy, or in some other fashion directly and unmistakably allying themselves with hostile actions of the enemy forces. The reported use of torture on such prisoners would be a legitimate area of inquiry, but for a study team to report that active enemy personnel were being imprisoned would be to labor the obvious. The committee's concern was to demonstrate the truth or falsity of what many of its members already believed to be the case: that the allegedly free society of South Vietnam being "defended" by the United States was in fact a form of police state that maintained itself in power only by the wholesale arrest and imprisonment of opponents who were *not* allied with the enemy and whose offense was to ask for a genuinely representative government and peace.

Ultimately the committee defined its purposes in sending the study team as:

First, they will seek to identify the variety of religious forces in South Vietnam and the range of political expression existing there. They will seek to investigate the situation of religious groups and the extent of the imprisonment of leaders of nonaligned groups who represent potentially important political sentiment. The team will be interested, for example, in visiting both Mr. Dzu and Thich Thien Minh. Second, the team will seek to investigate the situation of all prisoners in South Vietnam. Recognizing the difficulties of doing this in a wartime situation, the team will nonetheless attempt to obtain realistic information.

The committee throughout was clear about its motivation in sending the team—to contribute something to ending the war. The study team itself would be chosen to represent a variety of attitudes on the war. The committee, fairly certain that its suspicions were well founded, hoped that a public revelation in the United States of the dictatorial character of the South Vietnamese Government would fortify the growing public demand that this country stop supporting it and get out. Some members, appalled at fragments of specific information about the nature and extent of torture involved, remembered the revulsion among the people of France when they learned of the torture French troops and their allies were using in Algeria, and hoped that Americans would be similarly revolted.

The study team was chosen with great care. A United States Congressman, a churchman, and a noted civil libertarian, all lawyers: Representative John Conyers, Jr., of Detroit, the Rev. Robert F. Drinan, S.J., dean of the Boston College Law School, and John de J. Pemberton, national secretary of the American Civil Liberties Union. A man with military experience: retired Admiral Arnold E. True. Three representatives of the religious establishment: Mrs. Anne McGrew Bennett, a distinguished churchwoman and the wife of John C. Bennett, president of the Union Theological Seminary, Methodist Bishop James Armstrong, and Rabbi Seymour Siegel, professor of theology at the Jewish Theological Seminary. The Fellowship of Reconciliation, with the experience of having already sent one such team to Vietnam, was asked to supervise and direct the venture, and my associate secretary, Dr. Allan Brick, was added to the team as its executive director. Later another lawyer-churchman, the Rev. Peter Jenkins, British Congregational clergyman and general secretary of the Fellowship in Britain, was added to provide a non-American element.

Three capable young people with extensive experience as volunteer workers in Vietnam were sent there weeks in advance to set up accommodations and appointments. The team left for Saigon on May 25, 1969, via Paris, where I had arranged meetings with two former Vietnamese cabinet members, the journalist Pham Tam, who had escaped from Vietnam after four years in its various prisons, and several other exiles, all of whom had "done time" as the prisoners of Diem, Ky, or Thieu.

The team had also decided to try to talk with some representative of the National Liberation Front, and I had arranged a meeting with Mme. Nguyen Thi Binh, the second-ranking member of the NLF delegation to the Paris talks and since elevated to Foreign Minister of the Provisional Revolutionary Government. But en route to NLF headquarters at Verrières-le-Buisson some members of the team had second thoughts about the visit. Their first interview had been with an exiled South Vietnamese statesman of considerable eminence, and those members who had had some lingering misgivings about the authenticity of their venture were suddenly convinced that they were, as one of them put it, "on to a big thing." The visit to Mme. Binh, about the purpose of which there had been questions all along—"I'd love to talk with her, but how can she help us on the subject of political suppression in South Vietnam?" said one—was being re-examined in the light of its possible effects on the team's mission.

"Let's not kid ourselves," one member said as we parked by the side of a highway to discuss the matter, "it will play right into the hands of those who want to discredit our report. Hawks in and out of Congress will try to evade whatever we have said by accusing us of having gotten our materials from the other side's propaganda machine, and they'll 'prove' it by pointing to this visit at the very start of the trip."

The argument carried the day, and the team reluctantly canceled the visit. Mrs. Bennett and I, who had met Mme. Binh before, went on alone to explain and to chat for a while with her and some of her colleagues, while the rest of the team mulled over the materials they had begun to accumulate. (The abortive visit was later to be the subject of a different kind of attack by a critic who incorrectly described the incident as having occurred on the team's return from Vietnam, "even though they had had many contacts with representatives and officials of the Saigon regime in South Vietnam." The fact is that on the return trip, while the team paused in Paris to finish its report, the same members who had decided against the visit ten days earlier now asked if I could arrange a new one. "I'd like very much to talk with her," said the group's spokesman, "and now that the Vietnam trip has been completed and our report written, I think it would not provide an opening for attack." Unfortunately, it was a summer Sunday and the appointment could not be made.)

Saigon, astonishingly, was alight with excitement over the impending visit, which had been widely reported in the city's more than forty newspapers in spite of the censor. One editorialist called it "an unwarrantable interference in the internal affairs of the Republic of Vietnam," and both the Thieu-Ky Government and the American embassy were reported to be predictably unhappy, but the eminence of the team's members, and notably the presence of a United States Representative, canceled any possible thoughts of excluding or openly hindering it in its operations. On the other hand, men and women who had been terrorized into silence for years were waiting eagerly to talk to the visiting Americans and their British colleague.

"It is astonishing," wrote Gene Stoltzfus, one of the advance men, "what is happening here. Men who *know* that to talk to the team could be their death warrant or at least their return to prison, and who are watched all the time, insist that they must talk with it. A prominent lawyer, only recently released from prison, said, 'Of what use is freedom if I do not use it.'" Stoltzfus was obviously deeply moved himself. "These people are taking great risks," he wrote, "and we have a responsibility to make the most of it. The team must not let them down."

Later the team was to report that it had met with the leaders of "five old-line political parties no longer able to function as recognized entities," and that all these men had been "active in the resistance movement against the French and were ardent nationalists." (Marshal Ky and General Thieu had also fought in that struggle—on the other side, with the French, against the "ardent nationalists.") "A retired general present," the report added, "had been in prison eleven times."

The team's arrival was heralded and its mission explained in front-page articles illustrated with photographs in the English- and Vietnamese-language newspapers, as was its almost immediate appearance as guests of honor at a celebration of Vesak —Buddha's birthday—before several thousand people at the An Quang Pagoda. Indeed, public attention was so heavily focused on the visitors and their activities, as a Buddhist correspondent subsequently noted gleefully, as to crowd out of the papers entirely a conference set up by the Government-sponsored Buddhist splinter group led by Thich Tam Chau.

A schedule had been skillfully arranged for the nine-member team to make maximum use of the week it had available. It made some visits and interviews as a body; more often it split into groups of two or three to multiply its effectiveness. As a result, it was able to report that it had "met with President Thieu, Minister of Interior Tran Thien Khiem and members of his staff, Ambassador Ellsworth Bunker and members of his staff, national religious leaders, lawmakers, intellectuals, attorneys, students, a variety of persons of different political persuasions and talked with scores of political prisoners. It visited prisons at Thu Duc, Chi Hoa, and on Con Son Island, as well as the National Police Headquarters."

Its conclusions were clear, dispassionate and devastating. Anticipating the thirty-page report it was to make, the team sent a telegram, over the name of its Congressman member, to President Nixon on the eve of his flight to Midway to consult with President Thieu:

SAIGON
JUNE 5, 1969

PRESIDENT NIXON
WASHINGTON, D. C., USA

THE INDEPENDENT STUDY TEAM ON RELIGIOUS AND POLITICAL FREE-DOM IN VIETNAM HAS COMPLETED ITS STUDY HERE AND IS PREPARING A DETAILED REPORT. THE TEAM MET WITH SOUTH VIETNAMESE AND

UNITED STATES OFFICIALS, VARIOUS BUDDHIST AND ROMAN CATHOLIC LEADERS, REPRESENTATIVES OF OTHER PRINCIPAL SECTS, MEMBERS OF THE NATIONAL ASSEMBLY, ATTORNEYS AND OTHER SPECIALISTS IN JURISPRUDENCE AS WELL AS NUMEROUS PRIVATE INDIVIDUALS, INCLUDING SOME PRISONERS.

THE TEAM INSPECTED PRISONS IN SAIGON, THU DUC AND CON SON. OUR FINAL REPORT WILL BE RELATED TO THE FOLLOWING FIRM IMPRESSIONS:

THE GOVERNMENT OF SOUTH VIETNAM DOES NOT PRESENTLY EXEMPLIFY AT LEAST ONE OF THE GOALS SET FORTH IN YOUR MAY 14TH STATEMENT. (QUOTE) THERE SHOULD BE AN OPPORTUNITY FOR FULL PARTICIPATION IN THE POLITICAL LIFE OF SOUTH VIETNAM FOR ALL POLITICAL ELEMENTS THAT ARE PREPARED TO DO SO WITHOUT THE USE OF FORCE OR INTIMIDATION. (UNQUOTE.)

RELIGIOUS AND POLITICAL SUPPRESSION IS WIDESPREAD. SPEAKING FOR PEACE OR IN ANY OTHER WAY OPPOSING THE GOVERNMENT EASILY BRINGS THE CHARGE OF COMMUNIST SYMPATHY AND SUBSEQUENT ARREST. LONG DETENTION WITHOUT TRIAL IS FREQUENTLY THE RESULT.

THE NUMBER OF POLITICAL PRISONERS CONTINUES TO INCREASE.

THERE MUST BE NO ILLUSION THAT THIS CLIMATE OF POLITICAL AND RELIGIOUS SUPPRESSION IS COMPATIBLE WITH EITHER A REPRESENTATIVE OR STABLE GOVERNMENT.

WE RESPECTFULLY REQUEST THAT YOU CONSIDER THIS IN WEIGHING ANY COMMITMENTS TO THE THIEU GOVERNMENT.

> ON BEHALF OF THE STUDY TEAM
> ON RELIGIOUS AND POLITICAL
> FREEDOM IN VIETNAM,
>
> HON. JOHN CONYERS, JR., M.C.

A few days later the study team summarized its full report in four only slightly less cryptic paragraphs:

1. Many thousands of persons being arrested in South Vietnam are denied all procedural protection. Arrests are made by a variety of local and national officials—by District police, special security forces, military forces and intelligence units—each exercising "relatively unfettered discretion."

2. The Thieu-Ky Government's widespread and increasing use of the extra-constitutional Military Field Tribunal has been responsible for the sentencing and imprisonment of additional thousands of persons, denying them the fundamental elements of a fair hearing and often failure to serve prior notice of the charges against them. Many of these prisoners remain without trial in the hands of the arresting authorities while the remainder have been removed to prisons by administrative action without charges or trials.

3. The study team agrees with those who say that repression, though not as obvious and violent as under the Diem Government, continues to be pervasive and brutal. While some prisons visited appear to reflect modern notions of penal administration and certain prison officials seemed sensitive to the needs of inmates, the sheer weight of witnesses' statements concerning physical abuse seemed overwhelmingly conclusive. It became clear that whatever amelioration appeared in the formal correctional institutions, torture and brutality are widespread in the arresting and interrogation process.

4. Without question the Thieu-Ky Government uses the words "communism", "neutralism" and "coalition" to silence dissent and weaken political and religious opposition. Student peace movements, Buddhist pleas for nonviolence and a "third solution," and the freedom of the press have been systematically suppressed by an insecure government that relies more on police state tactics and American support than upon true representation and popular support. As one Vietnamese attorney phrased it: "One cannot fight for freedom without insuring freedom at home." [2]

The Hoa Binh committee, having defined the team's mandate, had left to it all decisions as to its procedures. The members had gone with open minds, some disposed to agree with the Hoa Binh assessment of the situation, some more skeptical, unwilling to believe the inferences about the United States' role that such conditions would warrant, but all determined to examine and report the facts as honestly and fairly as possible. So the report conceded that South Vietnam's Constitution is only two years old, that the country is in a state of war in which some excesses and violations of constitutional rights might be expected to occur, and that some of the penal authorities were

[2] For full text see Appendix 14.

obviously trying to do a commendable job under difficult conditions. Yet the report on the whole was to be called "the most devastating indictment of the Thieu regime yet published," and not only confirmed but also exceeded the worst that had been said of conditions in the unhappy little country.

The team "will seek to identify the range of religious forces in South Vietnam and the range of political expression existing there . . ." its mandate had said. The team reported that although only one-tenth of the country's population is Catholic, "Catholicism has played a dominant role in the Vietnamese political life" since the time of Diem, and that, since the largest number of Catholics were those who had fled North Vietnam with their French supporters in 1954 and 1955, that dominant influence had been a strongly anti-Communist one. "President Thieu reminded the study team that, although he had trouble with the Buddhists, Catholics had supported his administration." (Thieu himself is a Catholic.) Yet there are also Catholics who "want a closer tie with the Buddhists and who are seeking what some call a 'third solution,' " that will "find answers between communism and corrupt militarism." One of these is the famous Rev. Hoang Quynh, an active leader in the All-Religion Citizens' Front.

Among the Buddhists, the team reported, there are two major factions, "the 'moderate' government-authorized faction of Thich Tam Chau and the 'activist' faction of Thich Tri Quang and the An Quang Pagoda." The "moderate" wing, the report noted, had resulted from the Government's attempt in 1967 to fragment the Buddhists by withdrawing the charter of the Unified Church and recognizing the Tam Chau group as "the church." Yet the An Quang Pagoda, the team noted, "continues to be a major factor in the religious and political life of the country," and observed the presence at the Vesak service not only of leaders of both Mahayana and Therevada schools of Buddhism, but also of ranking leaders of Cao Dai, Hoa Hao and Catholic forces, along with a former Chief of State, Phan

Khac Suu, the General Secretary of the House of Representatives, and other members of that body, "indicating a broad base of support among disparate groups."

White doves of peace had been released at the ceremony, the team noted, as more than 3,000 people heard the Buddhist Supreme Patriarch, Thich Tinh Khiet, say, "Every hostile tendency of the world has jostled its way into the Vietnam war in order to exploit it and seek for victory, whereas all the Vietnamese people, either on this side or on the other side of the 17th parallel, are mere victims of this atrocious war. Our nation is thus forced to accept ready-made decisions without having any right to make our own choice."

"President Thieu and pro-Government supporters," the team noted, "may insist that such peace talk is 'political.' If so, it is an obvious expression of that freedom essential to an emerging democracy."

Were there other evidences of the "existence of nonaligned groups who represent potentially important political sentiment"?

Yes, said the team's report, there is a "genuine political opposition," though "most of it has been driven underground." Its leaders, whose parties have been outlawed and requests to publish newspapers rejected, "reflect a vast middle position in South Vietnam." They are the ardent nationalists who "struggled against the French and consider the Americans their new colonial masters." They have endured many sacrifices over the last twenty-five years, been in prison many times, but still maintain their integrity and courage.

Their most visible allies are the students, who survive the most extreme retaliatory acts to continue their demonstrations, strikes, and petitions. "Van Hanh [Buddhist] University was the chief target for attack," a professor of law told the team. "If students go to meetings, the police follow them, and they can be arrested at any time. Many times they are drafted before the legal age or before their deferments as students expire."

But the students at Van Hanh University are not alone. A peace meeting at the Saigon University Student Union in September, 1968, in which students, professors, deputies from the Lower House, and some monks participated, was broken up by the police and thirty persons, mostly students, were arrested. At about the same time a student in Saigon University's Medical School who had been accused of "leftist tendencies" was found dead outside the school with his hands tied behind his back, having been thrown from a third-floor window. Police called it "probable suicide" and dismissed the case as closed!

Yet the student resistance continues, the team noted, recalling the 2,000 who had marched in a Christmas Eve peace procession—many of them Catholics—that was predictably broken up by the police, with hundreds arrested. And the report recalled also the Buddhist student who "stepped out of a sullen mass of prisoners at Camp No. 7 on Con Son Island and addressed members of the team. The translator said: 'He is here because he refuses to be drafted. He says he doesn't want to serve the United States. As a Vietnamese citizen he will go into the army only when we have independence.' "

Even in the National Assembly the team found evidences of political opposition to the Thieu-Ky policies, including criticisms of Operation Phoenix (pacification program) and of the practice of imprisoning political opponents. And on the other hand, a "new alliance" of political parties created by President Thieu and to which he "proudly points" as indicating the breadth of his support, included only splinter groups that, together with the Thieu-Ky vote, "had failed to capture half of the popular vote in the 1967 elections."

There is clearly a suppressed political opposition reflecting a "vast middle position," the team declared, and added its conviction that "there will be no truly representative government in South Vietnam until voices such as these can be legitimized and participate in the democratic processes of the republic."

What happens to these political opponents of the Saigon Gov-

ernment? the Hoa Binh committee had asked. *What is the extent of the imprisonment of leaders of nonaligned groups?*

"Without question," responded the team, "the Thieu-Ky Government uses the words 'communism,' 'neutralism,' and 'coalition' to silence dissent and weaken political and religious opposition. Student peace movements, Buddhist pleas for nonviolence, and a 'third solution,' and the freedom of the press have been systematically suppressed by an insecure government that relies more on police state tactics and American support than upon true representation and popular support."

The team focused its attentions on three particular representatives of a "political and religious opposition": Truong Dinh Dzu, the attorney and peace candidate who had been runner-up in the 1967 elections on a peace platform; Thich Thien Minh, second-ranking official of the Unified Buddhist Church, who had been sentenced to ten and five years (concurrently) for allegedly "harboring rebels, concealing weapons and illegal documents . . . harboring deserters and supporting draft dodgers"; and Nguyen Lau, publisher and owner of *The Saigon Daily News,* who had been arrested and imprisoned on April 16, 1969, for "having maintained private contacts with a Vietcong political agent." All three were in prison, the first two under sentence, Mr. Lau being held still, almost two months after arrest, without trial or sentence. The team was able to meet with Dzu and Thien Minh, but were not permitted to see Lau nor, it noted, "thirteen other prisoners they had made specific requests to visit."

"These three cases have not been isolated because they are more important than others," the team noted, "but because they are more well known. They are symptomatic of a climate of intellectual, religious, and political repression that has led to the imprisonment, exile, or silencing of thousands of loyal Vietnamese nationalists, persons who are not pro-Communist, but who are critical of the Thieu-Ky Government and who insist upon the right to think for themselves."

Mr. Dzu, a prisoner on Con Son Island, had been moved from that "Devil's Island" to the more humane Chi Hoa prison in Saigon only days before the team's arrival. His case was clear. He was arrested on May 1, 1968, "on charges of urging the formation of a coalition government as a step toward peace." He has never been accused of being a pro-Communist. President Thieu, discussing the case, acknowledged freely that Dzu was a "political prisoner," and the team's report adds that "The fact that, running as a peace candidate and advocating direct talks with the NLF he ran second only to the President, accounts more than anything else for his imprisonment." Since peace and direct talks with the NLF are the *sine qua non* of significant political opposition to the Thieu-Ky regime, the Hoa Binh question could be considered answered on the basis of Truong Dinh Dzu alone.

Thich Thien Minh had been arrested on February 23, 1969. His "trial" was before one of the notorious Military Field Courts and he was sentenced to serve terms of ten and five years at hard labor, and the Buddhist Youth Center which he directed was seized. A short while before the team's arrival, his sentence was reduced to three years; while the team was in Saigon, the Youth Center was returned to the Buddhists.

"It is assumed by many," the team noted, "that Thich Thien Minh was arrested not because of the specific crimes with which he was charged but for his public criticism of the Thieu-Ky Government and his strong advocacy of peace." In February he had been summoned to the Ministry of the Interior (then headed by General Tran Thien Khiem, now the Premier) and warned to tone down his sermons because they were disrespectful to the Government of President Thieu. He had said in one of his sermons that the people of South Vietnam could accept neither the "terrorist regime" of North Vietnam nor the "corrupt government" in Saigon, to which Thieu had responded publicly that "My government can die because of those pacifists, but before we die, they will have to die first."

The team also noted that when it had been taken to visit the Buddhist monk, who was held in a military compound two doors from the house of an American military adviser, the government officials who had conducted them there "pointedly left the room that the discussion might be private." However, since the members had already determined that a government agent was sitting behind a thin wall less than four feet away, and since Thien Minh was required to speak only in Vietnamese rather than English or French, "the interview was necessarily inhibited." The monk, who was nearly killed when a grenade exploded under his car in 1966, said simply, "My only offense is that I believe in peace."

Nguyen Lau, whom the visitors were not permitted to see, is a well-known Vietnamese and an avowed anti-Communist. A member of an old and wealthy family, educated at Oxford and the Sorbonne, he both respected the old traditions of his people and despised war profiteers and corrupt government officials. As a publisher he insisted on freedom of the press. "If people are free to walk the streets," he had said, "they are free to talk to me." He was unambiguous about the state of freedom in 1969 Saigon:

"Diem said bluntly that he was not going to tolerate freedom of the press. There were no illusions then. We are living a lie now. People say they are giving you freedom and someone without experience in journalism may be innocent enough to believe that this is paradise. Now you may be carried away by your illusions and land in trouble" (as reported in *The New York Times,* March 24, 1969). Less than a month later Lau was in prison.

Clearly the team believed the reports it had that Mr. Lau was framed. A visit to Lieutenant Colonel Nguyen Mau, chief of the Special Branch at the National Police Headquarters, disclosed that the only piece of evidence the Government had produced was a photostat of a press card allegedly issued by the publisher to one Tan That Dong, which the Government al-

leged was the alias of a Vietcong agent, Tran Ngoc Hiem. But
the team also learned that two days after Lau's arrest the police
had brought to his home photographers and a "so-called Vietcong," whom they photographed in various locations around
the house. When Lau's two sons, aged 10 and 14, protested,
they were handcuffed and the picture-taking continued.

"Without question," Bishop Armstrong was to tell Senator
Edward M. Kennedy's subcommittee on refugees a few weeks
later, "there are thousands of prisoners in South Vietnam who
have been denied all procedural protection during the time of
their detention and interrogation, who have been erroneously
classified as 'Communist,' who have been physically mistreated,
and who represent a broad middle ground of nationalism and
progressive political sentiment." [3]

The team tried to find out how many political prisoners there
were. It had heard many estimates, from the State Department's
"diminishing few" to Vo Van Ai's 200,000 and the assertion
by an anonymous former prisoner of "several hundred
thousand." [4] The wide variation arose in part from the simple
fact, the team found, that no one really knew how many there
actually were. So many agencies have the power of arrest, so
many prisoners have been sent to prison without charge or trial
and their records lost, that there is no central location at which
the total is registered. But part also was a matter of definition:
the larger figures included all those arrested as "suspected
Communists or Vietcong" as a result of the sweeps through
whole villages; the smaller number referred to those who were
consciously opposed to the regime and the war and whose arrests marked the attempts of the Government to suppress their
opposition.

Members of the team questioned assiduously and came up
with some answers. Whatever the larger total, it seemed appar-

[3] See Appendix 8.
[4] Nguyen Van Minh, "Jail Notes of a Young Vietnamese," *The Nation,*
March 24, 1969.

ent that there were even more political prisoners in the strict sense of that term than had been guessed. The Director of Correctional Institutions, Colonel Nguyen Psu Sanh, acknowledged that 69 per cent of the 35,000 prisoners in the country's forty-one "Correctional Centers" alone were classified as "Communists" or "civilians related to Communist activities" —euphemisms for neutralists, peace activists, and government critics generally. (The Correctional Centers are only one of several varieties of civilian prisons in the country. None of these figures includes prisoner-of-war camps.)

Don Bordenkircher, Colonel Sanh's senior American adviser, estimated that, in addition, 10,000 are held in the infamous "interrogation centers." (See Chapter 4.) "Doubtless," the team reported, "the total number of political prisoners in South Vietnam . . . far exceeds the official statistics and estimates." And then, having in mind the State Department's bland assertion that the number of such prisoners was diminishing rapidly, the team added: "Ambassador [William E.] Colby, General [Creighton W.] Abrams' Deputy for Pacification, said that the number of prisoners had gone up and will continue to go up as the pacification [Civil Operations and Revolutionary Development Support] program develops." And lest there be any ambiguity, the report added, "the large majority of those imprisoned in South Vietnam are held because they oppose the government; they are 'political prisoners.' "

Led by its four lawyers, the visitors probed into the standards for deciding who is subject to arrest, and the procedures for determining those standards. It found "both the standards and the procedures to be loose by any measure, even by the most generous measure of allowance for the exigencies of civil and guerrilla warfare." The evidence was more than adequate, the team concluded, to sustain the conviction "that this looseness is used deliberately to suppress political dissent and to oppress some religious groups."

"Second," the Hoa Binh committee had written, *"the team*

will seek to investigate the situation of all prisoners in South Vietnam. Recognizing the difficulties of doing this in a wartime situation, the team will nonetheless attempt to obtain realistic information."

The difficulties were, to some extent, insurmountable. Anyone who has had any experience with prisons knows that an inspection visit by any group likely to be critical or hostile is known far in advance, and preparations are made for its reception. This happens even in countries with functioning democratic societies in peacetime; how much more difficult was it then to escape it in wartime South Vietnam. Arrangements to visit prisons had to be made with officials of the very government that was under scrutiny; to submit the names of any but the most widely publicized known prisoners was to endanger that person's life. Fortunately, although no member of the team spoke Vietnamese, both of its accompanying staff members did. One of them, by refraining from exhibiting his fluency in the language to prison officials, was able to make the visits more than the "whitewash" the officials devoutly hoped for.

Even so, the team learned enough to horrify it. At the Thu Duc prison for women, the team found one "crude building" about forty by thirty feet inhabited by fifty women, some nursing babies. Sanitation was "primitive and inadequate," and the members saw evidence that some prisoners had not received needed medical attention. They also found many prisoners who had not been sentenced after many months of detention and others with what struck them as inhumanly long sentences, as in the case of a "slight old woman who, according to her dossier, had passed Vietcong letters," and who was in the eleventh year of a fifteen-year sentence.

Fifty children up to thirteen years of age and almost as many between the ages of thirteen and seventeen were crowded into Thu Duc, many of them also unsentenced. "Two students who were called 'Communist' were found to be unsentenced detainees . . . held because they had exhibited 'leftist tendencies' and had written for a Saigon University paper which was later suspended. In another building 20 per cent of the women said they had not been tried or sentenced."

Chi Hoa, the "showcase prison" of Saigon, was another the visitors were allowed to see. They were given an attractive brochure about the prison "with pictures of prisoners in classes, at worship, and enjoying recreational activities." But they also learned that the 5,500 inmates included 400 children under eighteen, half of them below fourteen. When the team asked to see the "separate children's section," it was shown two cells. In one room, forty feet long and slightly more than half as wide, they found forty-seven children under eight years of age. A four-year-old confided when questioned that he had been arrested for stealing a necklace. In the next cell, approximately the same size, were sixty-seven more children, averaging slightly older but all under ten. In each room, the team noted, the children, even the four-year-old, assembled in line when they entered and stood at attention, and did not move or speak. "Only their eyes followed the visitors' moves!"

The final visit was to Con Son Island, site of South Vietnam's "escape-proof" prison and the largest concentration of political prisoners.

"The tour had been carefully arranged by prison officials," the report stated. "The only time the team members deviated from the prepared pattern, successfully demanding to see Camp No. 4 instead of the camp that the prison authorities had scheduled, they saw something of significance. There were large dark dormitory cells (three out of about ten such cells were inspected) in which there were from 70 to 90 prisoners each, all of whom (as determined by a show of hands) were condemned to life in prison. None had had lawyers or any trial other than a judgment by a military tribunal."

The team had been told by a number of former inmates of the "tiger cages" at Con Son, small barred concrete cells in which prisoners being disciplined were chained to the floor on all fours, and they asked to see them, but their guide, Major Tran, denied their existence. They had once been there, he said, behind Camp No. 4, but now the only disciplinary cells were the ten that had been shown. But the staff member who spoke Vietnamese sauntered over to where a prisoner stood looking out the window and, with his back turned to the room, asked whether the prisoner knew of the tiger cages.

"Yes," said the prisoner, "but you looked in the wrong place. They are here, behind Camp No. 2 and Camp No. 3." The team had looked behind Camp No. 4. As the members were about to leave, they asked a group of about eighty prisoners one last question:

" 'Ask anyone who has ever been in or has ever seen the tiger cages to raise his hand.' The group fell silent. Not a move. Not even the blink of an eye. The prisoners stared into our eyes in utter silence. We thanked the Major for his cooperation and returned to Colonel Ve for final farewells." [5]

[5] Tom Fox, "Devil's Island Off Vietnam," *Commonweal,* July 11, 1969. (Mr. Fox, a doctoral student in Asian Studies at Yale, was one of the team's staff.)

5

Prisons
and Prisoners[1]

The Vietnamese rooming house where I stayed in Saigon was set back one hundred yards or so from the main street that runs to the center of the city. To hail a taxi or pedicab, however, I had to walk not only the hundred yards to that street, but also another hundred to the right or left until I reached a place where a taxidriver would stop. The same thing happened when I returned; the driver would shrink visibly when I gave him my destination and either proceed hurriedly into the driveway that led to the rooming house or, more frequently, stop well before we had reached it and let me out. On two occasions, when I was riding on one of the frightful contraptions in which the passenger sits on an open benchlike seat on wheels driven at breakneck pace by a man on a motorcycle behind him, the driver stopped a good quarter-mile away and begged me to walk the remainder.

[1] For a fuller account of the detailed proceedings against the political prisoners of South Vietnam and the manner in which their imprisonment is carried out, readers are referred to the booklet "Torture and Imprisonment in South Vietnam," by Pham Tam, who spent four years in these prisons. It is available from the Fellowship of Reconciliation, Nyack, New York, for 50 cents.

The reason was that directly across the main road from the rooming house was the entrance to Saigon's dreaded National Police Headquarters, protected by guards who, my drivers assured me, would immediately "go boom" at any car that stopped in front of them without waiting to check on its intentions.

National Police Headquarters occupies a sprawling walled compound spreading over several acres and includes, as one would suppose, offices, barracks, and the usual other facilities of such an institution. The entire place is dreaded by Saigon's population as the center of the Government's suppressive power, but there is one building that is regarded with particular loathing and fear. Set off in a far corner of the compound, it is Tong Nha, the building euphemistically called the "interrogation center." At any time it has a population of only 100 or so prisoners, but they are political prisoners, and the business of the interrogation center is their torture.

On the corner of Ngo Quyen and Le Quang Liem streets, elsewhere in Saigon, stands a large villa, also surrounded by a wall topped by an intricate lacework of barbed wire, with heavily armed guards and snarling dogs occasionally visible behind its closed gates. Those Saigonese who know what it is avoid this area, but most do not know, since many villas in Saigon also have walls around them and many, in wartime, are topped with barbed wire. But the villa at Ngo Quyen and Le Quang Liem streets is special. It is Mat Vu, Interrogation Center No. 8, and like its seven counterparts in the city, it is also the focus of torture for political prisoners. All eight, along with twenty similar places in South Vietnam's other cities (Dalat, Can Tho, Danang, Hue, etc.) are operated by the Hoat Vu, or Active Service Police, which functions as a secret police force to "repress all popular movements struggling for peace and neutrality, all organizations whose policy is opposed to that of the Government, and to wipe out secret NLF bases within the capital." The Hoat Vu, writes Pham Tam, receives its orders directly from the President, the Vietnamese Chiefs of Staff, and from American intelligence services and Special Forces.

The study team visited the National Police Headquarters, but it did not get into the Interrogation Center, nor did it see any of the eight villas, or the wing set aside in the Ngo Quyen (Cho Quan) Hospital down the street from Villa No. 8 where the vic-

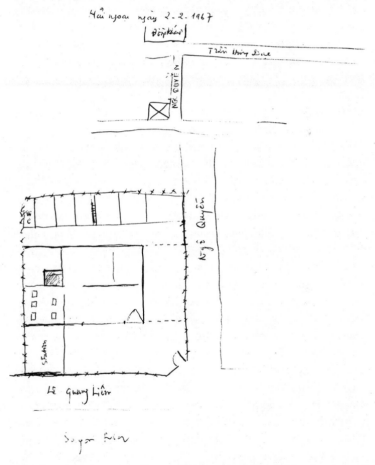

Mat Vu, Interrogation Center No. 8—the villa at Ngo Quyen and Le Quang Liem streets—a sketch drawn by a former prisoner.

tims of torture are taken when they can no longer endure their injuries.

A former high government official who had experienced Tong Nha himself had predicted that the team would not get in. He was looking at the sketch of the center's interior he had just drawn for me.

"The prisoners are kept in these rooms," he said. "There are about twenty persons in each, men and women together. Usually they are shackled by the legs to steel bars set there for that purpose. Here"—he pointed to another square—"is the interrogation room, where the prisoners go to be questioned."

He smiled. "Your team will not get in to see these things, and if they did, there would be nothing to see. You would have to apply for permission to the Minister of the Interior. Your request is almost certain to be denied, with one excuse or another, but let us suppose that it is granted. Just processing it would take at least twenty-four hours, and that is plenty of time to remove the prisoners who have marks of the torture, or who might possibly talk, and replace them with others—prisoners who have not yet been tortured or actual government agents. But let us suppose, even, that they did not remove prisoners who had been tortured. Most of the marks of what happened to them would not show, and those that did would be explained as having happened because of a fall or for some other innocent reason. The prisoners would not talk to you even if you spoke Vietnamese. They have to remain there, you see, after you go. Besides," he added gently, "their experiences with Americans have not led them to feel much trust for your countrymen. Forgive me for saying this."

(From the study team's report: "The team members were told that only ten out of the 7,021 prisoners [on Con Son Island] were under discipline. On request, the visitors were shown two of the ten. They had been in solitary for six months because of their refusal to salute the flag. One said he would never salute it. His legs were deeply marked; the Colonel in charge explained this was the result of a past disease. Questioned directly, the prisoner said it was the result of a long period in leg irons.")

"Then," continued the former government official, "suppose you asked to see the interrogation room, which you would know about because I have told you of it. They would take you to see it and you would see nothing. The rack and the thumbscrew are a thing of the past; we are simpler and more sophisticated now. In that room you would see"—ticking them off on his fingers—"the desk and chair of the interrogator, a wooden bench sloping down slightly to one end, and a heavy iron hook in the ceiling. And, of course, the usual electric outlets in the walls.

"If you asked about the sloping bench, the official would explain that it sometimes puts prisoners at their ease to lie down, and the raised end for their heads makes conversation easier. You might not believe him, but how would you know, or how would you prove, that the prisoner is bound to the bench, face up, with his head at the lower end rather than the higher? How would you know that this is the modern version of the 'water cure'? Until recently the water cure meant forcing the prisoner's head under water and holding it there until he very nearly strangled, then pulling it out and letting him recover for a while, then forcing his head under again, and so on until he yielded or died. Now it is simpler. A gag is placed on the prisoner's face—remember he is bound—so that it covers his mouth and nose completely. Then water is dripped on the gag, a drop at a time. As the gag becomes soaked the prisoner has a harder and harder time breathing and after a while he cannot breathe at all. It takes longer, of course, but it has the advantage of giving the prisoner more time to reflect on what is happening to him." He smiled again, without humor. "Besides, it's economical; it saves water."

(From the study team's report: "A disturbing aspect of the

prison situation in Vietnam is physical abuse of prisoners. U.S. officials—there are American advisers at every level of Vietnamese bureaucracy—agree that there is torture, but insist that it does not take place in the correctional centers but in the interrogation and detention centers where the prisoners are taken first. Accounts by ex-prisoners verified the fact that torture in detention and interrogation centers is general procedure. Another type of water torture in which a soaked cloth is placed over the nose and mouth of a prisoner tied back-down to a bench is said to be very common. The cloth is removed at the last moment before the victim chokes to death, and then is reapplied. In a related form, water is pumped into the nose.")

"Or suppose you were to ask about the iron hook in the ceiling," the Vietnamese exile went on. "It is only a hook, after all, and the official would explain easily that it usually holds a large ceiling fan of the type widely used in Saigon, but that the fan stopped working and is out for repairs. Would you have any way of proving that when a prisoner is being interrogated, the official's desk is sometimes pulled under that hook and the prisoner, with his arms tied behind him, forced to stand on the desk? Or that a rope is then tied to the bonds on his arms and looped over that hook so that he is dragged up onto his toes? Or that he is forced to stay in that position for literally days at a time, except for brief periods when he is taken down to go to the toilet? And of course you would have no way of knowing that he stands there with a naked 500-watt electric light bulb suspended some fifteen inches behind his head. When they are taken down," he said reminiscently, "the prisoners often have totally lost the power of speech and the control of their movements."

(From the study team's report: "Although team members were allowed to visit the National Police Headquarters in Saigon, it was an arranged visit. There was no evidence of the forms of torture here described. Colonel [Nguyen] Mau said that modern interrogation techniques ruled out the need for physical violence. Team members saw the interrogation rooms but no prisoners were being questioned. The team's evidence for the tortures described come from interviews with ex-prisoners testifying to what they had endured and seen, together with the statements of doctors and others who had treated the victims. While the testimony of prison officials and the appearances of the National Police Headquarters cannot be lightly dismissed, the sheer weight of witnesses' statements seemed overwhelming and conclusive to team members.")

"That is one use of the electrical outlets," the former official said thoughtfully. "Another is almost too hackneyed to mention, but of course it goes on and it continues to be effective. Bare wires are placed to a male prisoner's testicles or to the tips of a woman's breasts. It is excruciatingly painful. Most prisoners faint and many suffer heart attacks and die."

"Ordinarily they don't actually use the electrical outlet for that, though," said another former prisoner. "It is too powerful. Instead each interrogator carries with him a small hand generator that he cranks like an old coffee mill after he has fastened the wires to the prisoner's testicles or nipples, so that the harder he cranks the greater the current.

"Then the water cure comes in different forms, too, though it was usually as it had been described. But sometimes they bind the prisoner beneath a bucket suspended from that hook in the ceiling. The bucket has a hole in the bottom. The interrogator puts ice in the bucket and as it melts the water drips through the hole, one drop at a time, on to the prisoner's head. Until you have experienced it you cannot imagine what agony it can be. After quite a short while each drop of water makes the whole body vibrate like a drum."

"Of course, they are not the only forms of torture, though," the second said. "If you looked at the desk he talked about, you would see that it is splintered along the edges, as many old desks are. If you thought anything of it, you would probably think it an admirable example of economizing. Actually, the splintering comes from beating prisoners on the hands as they are held palm up on the desk's surface. The beatings usually are with wooden clubs about two inches thick, though sometimes they are metal. They beat them so hard that the bones break, the desk splinters, and the victims cannot use their hands for many weeks, if ever.

"Of course they beat them also on other parts of the body, too. Beatings are especially what happens to intellectuals somehow; they don't get the other types of torture as a rule."

"If we hope to deal with the Communists later on," the young professor had said to me in 1967 when she insisted on the publication of her name as a signer of the students' peace petition, "we must be able to match them in their dedication. If we are afraid to go to prison, we cannot match them. Besides" —wistfully—"they do not often beat professors in prison."

(From the study team's report: "An intellectual who was arrested in 1966 and spent the first six months of his two and one-half years term in an interrogation center described what he called the typical case of a woman law student in a nearby cell. She had been in the interrogation center for six months when he arrived and stayed for the next six months during his own imprisonment there. Throughout this year, she was tortured mostly by beating. When she was finally called before a tribunal to hear the charges, she had to be carried by two fellow prisoners. The tribunal, apparently because of her status, heard her case carefully and determined that it was a case of misidentification. Someone in Zone D had reported a VC returnee or spy who looked like her.")

Electric wires to the testicles or nipples are not the only common form of sexual torture. Repeatedly former prisoners have told of Coke and beer bottles, and even live eels, being forced into the vagina of a prisoner, adding excruciating pain to the personal outrage, and often leading to fatal or near fatal hemorrhages.

(From the study team's report: "A respected physician told team members that recently police brought a dead girl from an interrogation center to a city hospital and asked the doctor there to certify to death from natural causes. On examination of the cadaver, the doctor found signs of beating and sexual violation. He refused to certify. Pressure was brought on the head of the hospital to issue the certificate. Such incidents are not unusual.")

There are three explanations for torture: the quest for information, intimidation by terror, and sadism, though information is the only one given any kind of official credence.

Prisoners are tortured in order to force from them any information they have about the Government's enemies or its opponents. Mostly the information sought is names—names of actual or suspected NLF agents or supporters, names of "unreliables" who may not support the NLF but definitely do not support Saigon, names of students and professors and editors and neighbors in any way suspect. Sometimes, of course, where the prisoner actually is an NLF agent, the hoped-for information may include important details concerning plans or personnel of the enemy forces, though the ability of the Vietcong to launch surprise attacks on South Vietnamese cities and forces suggests that relatively little valuable knowledge of this sort is acquired.

There is a limit to any man's capacity to endure such suffering, and whether he is peasant or professor, farmer or student, the prisoner usually breaks down and gives his interrogators "information." But then, of course, questions arise. Is the information accurate, or is he still strong enough to attempt to mislead them? Perhaps a little more torture will determine. Or has the prisoner given accurate information, but not all, and perhaps not even the most important? Give torture the benefit of the doubt; apply some more and see what comes out!

If the prisoner has been captured in battle or in the vicinity of suspected enemy forces, the torture is usually done by soldiers seeking information about hidden weapons and the location of the Vietcong unit to which the prisoner is assumed to belong.

"The methods used in such situations," writes Pham Tam, "are direct and unsophisticated. Prisoners are beaten, slugged with gun butts, strangled with leather belts or barbed wire, their heads plunged under water and held there, the flesh of their bodies sliced or stabbed, while threats are made to cut open their stomachs. This torture may last for hours. If the peasant is a member of the NLF, he can end the torture by one of two alternatives: confession or death. If he is *not* an NLF member, he has no choice but death. (This explains why the peasants, whether or not they belong to the NLF, must either take flight or hide when the U.S. armies and their allies arrive.) If by chance, the prisoner emerges alive from the torture, he is classed as an NLF member. Weapons found any place in the area of his arrest will likely be identified as his, and the man will be considered part of the last NLF unit to have passed that way, perhaps even its leader."

Torture for the sake of terrorizing the opposition into silence and inactivity is directly linked to the search for information. Not only is the prisoner himself terrorized; all who know of his plight and his experiences similarly must be tempted to silence or flight. The knowledge of the treatment being inflicted on one's friend or associate and the likelihood that one's own name may be given when he finally breaks down is enough to weaken the strongest will. All Vietnam knows of the terrors of the interrogation centers; many Vietnamese have friends or relatives who have experienced them or who have disappeared without explanation and who may be assumed imprisoned in one of the dreaded centers.

And finally there is sadism, not included in any official rationale for such activities, but inevitably a factor in them. Normal men are sickened by orders to do such work and find excuses for transferring away from it. The sadistic, on the other hand, are attracted to it, and soon make up most of the personnel of the torture centers. They bring to their work not only their delight in making other people suffer, but a perverse ingenuity in finding new methods of inflicting the suffering, often, as those with any knowledge of the psychology of sadism will know, sexual in nature. So one interrogator at the Central Bureau of Investigation, writes Pham Tam, is known to have his own special version of the heavy club all interrogators carry, carved in the shape of a penis, which he calls "the penis of Heaven." He himself has been nicknamed Than Ong Cac Troi —Mr. Heavenly Penis-Stick.

Thus, too, many forms of torture involve naked prisoners, male and female, who may be beaten on the chest or the soles of the feet or the genitals, or have pins thrust into them, or be suspended by the feet from the ceiling while serving as a punching bag for the interrogators. The prisoner is naked, too, in another form of treatment that has become "popular"— immersion to the neck in a large metal drum full of water, which is then beaten heavily with cloth-covered cudgels on the outside.

"The pain is indescribable," said a former prisoner, who had experienced it. "The water transmits the force of the blows to every inch of the body, so that it is as though you are being beaten everywhere simultaneously. I have seen prisoners leap clear out of the drum when subjected to this treatment."

Whatever the immediate consequences in terms of information secured or opposition silenced, torture in the longer run is counterproductive, to use a favorite Washington expression. The torturers and their superiors are despised by everyone who knows of their work; the ranks of the Government's own agents are increasingly permeated by the most brutal of the population; and the determination to overthrow the regime that perpetrates such actions becomes fixed and fanatical.

"It is the never-ending cycle of hate that is so terrible," said a former official. "I saw a mother tortured in the presence of her six-year-old daughter. The mother was a young woman whose husband had been killed when American planes bombed their village. In her anger and hatred she turned to the Vietcong and became a liaison person for them. Ultimately she was captured, and her little daughter had to watch her tortured. Then the little girl was sent to one of the government orphanages, where she will live with that memory in overcrowded conditions, without enough to eat or decent medical care and, of course, without the presence of her family. Imagine how her hatred will grow! And this is how it is with tens of thousands of our people. Sometimes I fear that we shall never be able to break out of the cycle of hate that this war has produced."

(From the study team's report: "Several ex-prisoners testified that it is not unusual to torture family members, including children, before the eyes of the prisoner. 'Then,' explained a woman teacher who had been imprisoned twice, 'the prisoner will tell anything.' ")

Brutalization by police or army, arrest without warrant or warning, imprisonment without trial or appeal, torture and brutalization in prison—these are the prospects of any South Vietnamese who dares to speak out for peace or ask for a new government, and the actual experience of scores of thousands of them. So many agencies and forces operate prisons or detention centers of some sort that it is nearly as hard to determine how many prisons there are in South Vietnam as how many prisoners are in them. Secret and semiofficial prisons and detention centers have been set up by the South Vietnamese army, by local military officials, by the intelligence services of both the South Vietnamese and American armies, by Special Forces of both armies, and by local administrative bodies.

The "official prisons" are under the Ministry of Interior (until August, 1969, the Minister was General Tran Thien Khiem, now the Premier). There are five "big" prisons, ranging in size from three thousand to thirty thousand prisoners each, and fifty-eight smaller ones in the provinces and cities of the country and housing from 500 to 2,500 inmates each. "Secret" prisons in the compound of the National Police Headquarters house from two thousand to three thousand. Similarly, semiofficial detention centers are operated in every province by the National Police, the Special Police, the Hoat Vu, the Military Security Forces, and the local army units. Others are scattered through the cities and provinces, often known only to the particular forces that operate them.

Most inmates, even in the big official prisons, are designated as "Communists" or "political." Large numbers have never been tried; the warden of Con Son Island prison acknowledged to the study team that 2,316 of his admitted 7,021 prisoners were detainees who had never been tried or sentenced. (He was the only official who admitted statistics on this category; on the other hand, his figure of 7,021 is less than half what other informed Vietnamese assert is the total population of Con Son.)

Chi Hoa prison in Saigon holds from six thousand to eight thousand; Phu Quoc, another island prison, as many as thirty thousand, almost all political prisoners; Thu Duc, reserved for women arrested in Saigon or the immediate vicinity, houses three thousand to four thousand; and Tan Hiep, near Bien Hoa, has about the same number, almost exclusively limited to political prisoners who have not been tried and those who have served prison terms but have not yet been released.

A young Vietnamese who had served a "political" sentence, Nguyen Van Minh, wrote in the March 24, 1969, issue of *The Nation* ("Jail Notes of a Young Vietnamese") that some of his fellow inmates had been held "for investigation" for two, five, even ten years. "Political tendencies varied greatly," he wrote, "from those who had been jailed for crying out for peace to those who refused the draft, refused to carry weapons, or wear a military uniform. Some had been grabbed while demanding that Vietnam recover its national sovereignty, others while demonstrating in favor of free elections. Beyond these were cadres from the traditional nationalist political parties, people caught paying taxes to the NLF, a girl suspected of being an enemy liaison agent, a man believed to be a high-ranking spy for Hanoi.

"In the end the authorities looked on *all* opposition types as VC, suspected VC, or at very least as having pro-Communist, neutralist or 'peacenik' inclinations. Get them! Grab them! Toss them all in jail! Actually, I think if all the people of South Vietnam were allowed somehow to express their inner opinions, some 95 per cent would fit into at least one of these categories."

The charge of "Communist" is, of course, a device to disguise the naked violation of the rights of any citizen who is unwilling to give total subservience to the regime, and is not even credited by the officials themselves. It is interesting, thus, to contrast the "official figures" given to the study team with the really official figures submitted by the director of a large prison to his superiors.

The "official" figures were given by Colonel Ngueyn Psu Sanh, Director of Correctional Institutions. In the country's forty-one Correctional Centers, he said, the prisoners are classified as follows:

Criminals	16.98%
Communists	64.25%
Civilians related to Communist activities	4.16%
Military	11.91%
Political activities harmful to the national interest	.21%
War Prisoners	2.49%

Pham Tam quotes a copy of a *really* official report, sent daily by prison administrators to their superiors. This copy, smuggled out of Chi Hoa Prison in September, 1968, listed only 50 of a total of 1,665 political prisoners in one section of the institution as "Communists." Of the rest, 1,315 were Buddhists, and 163 Catholics, with the balance made up of Protestants, Cao Daiists, and Hoa Haoists. The same report disclosed that the 1,665 political prisoners were part of a total population of 1,870 in that section, and that 1,062 of them were peasants. It should be noted also that at a time when both Vietnamese and American officials asserted there were few if any Buddhist monks still in prison, the study team found 120 of them in Chi Hoa alone.

Optimistic assessments of South Vietnam's progress toward constitutional government are frequent by spokesmen for the State Department and White House, and by their supporters in the press. They have no substance in fact, unless one believes that the existence of a piece of paper in itself is significant. Although protections for the citizen are written into the Constitution, they either are accompanied by escape clauses or have been abrogated by subsequent legislation.

South Vietnam's State of War Law, No. 10/68, adopted by the National Assembly and promulgated by the President on November 5, 1968, is one example. It authorizes, among other things, the "search of private houses, both by day and night," and "fixing the place of residence of those elements judged dangerous to the national security."

Since "fixing the place of residence" in fact means assigning people to one or another of the national or provincial prisons for a period of up to two years without trial—with the "assignment" renewable—this clearly makes a mockery of the most elementary rights of citizens in a democracy. "Such a standard," observed the study team, "patently abdicates to the judging body the determination of who is to be subject to such imprisonments, with little, if any, legislative control. In fact, it was determined that students with nothing more than the notation in their files that they exhibited 'left-wing tendencies' were being incarcerated in national prisons whose administrator classified them in his census as 'Communists'; i.e., in the same category with individuals found to have assumed leadership roles in organizing warlike activity for the NLF."

"Procedural protections," wrote the team at another point, "are essentially nonexistent at the arrest and interrogation stage. Arrests are made by a wide variety of local and national officials, by district police, special security forces, military forces, and intelligence units—each exercising a relatively unfettered discretion."

Since it is immediately after arrest that the interrogation and its accompanying torture occur, lasting often for many months, it is of little value to the prisoner to suppose that he might, if he is lucky, be able to have a lawyer when he has finally been lodged in a prison. For despite the constitutional provision that "a defendant has the right to a defense lawyer for counsel in every phase of interrogation, including the preliminary investigation," the study team was assured by Lieutenant Colonel Nguyen Mau, Chief of the National Police Force's Special Branch, "that no one within his knowledge ever saw a lawyer at this stage—certainly never when detained at the Interrogation Center of the National Directorate of Police in Saigon." To which the team added: "All of the team's information tended to confirm that this generalization applied to other places of interrogation, both in Saigon and in the provinces."

Many prisoners are "assigned residence" by the Provincial Security Councils, though again dependable figures are lacking. One member of the team was able to sit in on one of the regular weekly sessions of such a Provincial Council as it considered a list of nearly one hundred cases, its quota for a single afternoon. Each council member, he reported, had a typewritten list of the cases, which he consulted as information about the case was read from a file by an officer.

"Without notice to the arrested person," the team's report noted, "without his presence or that of witnesses to the facts relevant for determination, without confrontation or opportunity for rebuttal, to say nothing of rights of counsel or to appeal, the liberty of each of the hundred persons listed was summarily determined and detentions in prison were ordered for periods—renewable by like procedure—of up to two years!"

The State of War Law of November, 1968, also violates the

Constitution in its revalidation of the infamous Military Field Courts created by preconstitutional decree in 1965. To these courts, which the team flatly declared "are not really courts at all," are committed "all violations of the law related to national security," which the courts are authorized to try "in accordance with emergency procedure." (It should be noted that these Military Field Courts have nothing to do with the tribunals which exist in the South Vietnamese armed forces for trial of offenses committed by military personnel.)

Like the Provincial Councils, the Military Field Courts do not bother with such niceties as judicial process, the rights of evidence and confrontation, or appeal. The judges are military officers, and their judgments are final, not subject to appeal. Their power was evidenced in the arrest and sentencing of Thich Thien Minh, one of the country's best-known Buddhist leaders. Their growing power and the constantly increasing number of cases coming before them, the study team reported, have had a "devastating effect on the people of Vietnam and . . . a chilling impact on all political activities."

Secret arrests, interrogation by torture, intimidation of political and religious freedom, imprisonment without trial or after only a travesty of a trial—these are the characteristics of the American occupation of South Vietnam. It is a description from which United States officials, in Saigon and Washington, dissent angrily. The Republic of Vietnam is a sovereign state, they insist; the United States gives it economic and military aid but does not attempt to dominate decisions, even where ugly things like torture are involved, that are the internal affair of the South Vietnamese Government. "Moreover," a junior officer in the American embassy said wryly, "they wouldn't let us if we wanted to. They're tough babies, and they know they have us over a barrel."

But they are "tough babies" only because the United States has given them the means to be tough. The Vietnamese have not chosen the ruffians and tyrants who rule them; the United

States has. And if they "have us over a barrel" it is because the United States chooses to support the Saigon regime for one reason only: because it will go on fighting a war that its people desperately want stopped. Thieu, Ky, and Khiem are still America's alternatives to peace, and if keeping them in power requires condoning the most repulsive violations of human rights open to the imagination, then the United States has chosen to condone them.

Many political prisoners in South Vietnam's interrogation centers, though by no means most, actually have been apprehended by Americans in such actions as Operation Phoenix, the pacification program. The United States Mission explains that although American advisers do take part in such arrests, they are involved only with Vietcong or suspected Vietcong sympathizers. But "Vietcong sympathizers" in South Vietnam can be a euphemism for peace activists and neutralists, as well as for those who genuinely assist the NLF, and United States intelligence agencies work hand in glove with South Vietnamese to identify and capture such political "unreliables."

American advisers operate throughout the whole bureaucracy of South Vietnam, and it would be straining credulity to argue that they do not know of the obscene things that happen in prisons that have sometimes been built or are currently being enlarged with American dollars.

"U.S. officials," the study team noted, "agree that there is torture, but insist that it does not take place in the correctional centers but in the interrogation and detention centers where the prisoners are taken first."

But interrogation centers, detention centers, and prisons are part of one system, and when the Director of Correctional Institutions, Colonel Nguyen Psu Sanh, said that there were 35,-000 prisoners in the correctional centers, it was his "senior American adviser" who added the estimate that there were 10,000 in the interrogation centers.

In all, it seems likely that the total of 200,000 or more political prisoners insisted on by neutralists, peace leaders, and former prisoners themselves, is accurate. How many have endured or will endure the torture of Mr. Heavenly Penis-Stick and his associates, or the stench and humiliation of the "tiger cages," will never be known, but they must number high in the thousands.

Some Americans, reading this account, will react with the angry insistence that their country is not directly involved, that in time of war sadists come into positions of power but do not reflect more than the sorry accident of such a time. But however they attempt to rationalize the situation, what Americans need to face is that these horrors in fact are being perpetrated with American assent, by a government kept in power solely by American military might, by men paid for by American dollars, and in a system permeated by American advisers. This is part of the black and spreading stain of shame that the Vietnam war has cast on this country's reputation. To win a war, or to end it "with honor"—*honor,* no less—we condone and finance a totalitarian government in the total suppression of individual rights, and in a pattern of imprisonment and torture that should be turning our stomachs with revulsion.

6

Why Do
They Struggle So?

It was the middle of my two-week visit to Saigon early in 1967. Since Americans may stay in Vietnam for only seven days without a visa, I had separated the two weeks with one in Hong Kong in order to avoid drawing attention to myself. I had spent the first week, which was Tet, in the Hotel Majestic, where no Vietnamese would visit or even meet me, since they were sure that the place was "bugged" by the CIA. The second week I stayed in a Vietnamese boarding house in an area more vulnerable to the Vietcong but also far safer for my friends. This night several leaders of the student underground peace movement were in my room, telling me of their plan to shock the American people into realizing the agony of their country. The plan was simple: Twenty of them were going to burn themselves to death at the same time on the steps of the University of Dalat.

That they would trust me even to tell me of such an idea was due, I gathered, first to the letter of recommendation I had brought with me from Thich Nhat Hanh, the monk whose disciples most of them considered themselves to be, and second to the dramatic confrontation I had had with their movement's top leader, Thich Tri Quang.

The two were very much tied together. Nhat Hanh, exiled in Paris because of his own peace mission to the West, had urged me to make this trip. He felt that I should have personal contact with those who were also working, under far more difficult circumstances, for peace in Vietnam. And he wanted me to talk with Tri Quang, communicating as letters could not his own thinking after almost a year in the West, and some evaluations and ideas that we shared concerning new peace efforts that might be jointly arranged in Vietnam and the United States.

Tri Quang was living quietly in the An Quang Pagoda. A Western correspondent wrote that he was "sulking" in the aftermath of the unsuccessful "struggle movement" of the previous spring and his own 100-day fast, which also, in terms of political movement, had been a failure. My contact, Miss Cao Ngoc Phuong, a young Saigon professor, returned from An Quang and told me uneasily that Tri Quang was sorry, but the press of Tet visitors and functions made it impossible for him to see me just then.

"But," she said hopefully, "I will go back tomorrow. Perhaps it will be different."

But it was not different. Miss Phuong was stricken. Tri Quang sent his best regards, with appreciation for the work for peace being done in my country, but he had no time to see me.

I asked why, and she answered quite directly. Tri Quang had vowed not to talk to another American so long as the war continued or General Ky remained in power. He had felt assured that Ambassador Henry Cabot Lodge had indicated a willingness to stand aside if the uprising in Hue resulted in the toppling of the Ky Government, as the Americans had stood aside when the Vietnamese had toppled Diem three years before. Instead, at the crucial moment, when the momentum of the Hue developments seemed likely to succeed, the Americans had rescued Ky by refusing gasoline to the dissident troops and then by flying Ky's marines and special forces and their tanks to Hue to suppress the uprising.

Miss Phuong added that the students were deeply concerned and unhappy about Tri Quang's apparent decision to take no further action. Hue had failed, they agreed. Anything new would be even more difficult, now that they could be sure of the Americans' hostility. But they must do *something*, and Tri Quang was their leader. Without him they were powerless.

I could understand Tri Quang's bitterness, if that was what it was, and I sympathized with the students' feelings, but my immediate concern was my own mission. I had come 12,000 miles, three weeks after an operation for a double hernia, at the request of Tri Quang's friend and associate, Nhat Hanh, and I was damned if I was going home without seeing him.

All this I put laboriously into a letter addressed to Tri Quang. I wrote that I could understand his feelings about what had happened, but I did not think that he should hold against me the fact that both Lyndon Johnson and I were Americans any more than I could feel hostile toward him because both he and General Ky were Vietnamese. I ended by saying, with all the deference my limited French could manage, that I felt sure he would understand why, having come halfway around the world to see him, I could not possibly return without doing so and why, consequently, it would be necessary for me to undertake a *grève de faim* outside his door until he *did* see me.

It must have been some sort of a record for sheer gall to have threatened with a hunger strike a monk who only weeks before had ended his own 100-day fast, but it worked. A few minutes after Miss Phuong, with two other students crouched giggling and apprehensive nearby, had pushed my letter under the door of Tri Quang's apartment, he opened the door and, with a big smile, invited me in. Since then we had met, in all, three times, for a total of almost five hours of talk.

But my impulsive gesture had done more than get me into the inner sanctum of the An Quang Pagoda; it had won the instant trust and affection of the student radicals. Meeting was dangerous for them, but we had met and were meeting, and this discussion, with the news of the proposed mass immolation, was one such occasion.

It is not easy to face a group of young people who have just told you they plan to burn themselves to death in order to communicate with your own countrymen. In a few days I had come to feel great respect and deep affection for these kids. They were tremendous in their courage; they had to dodge about the city, sometimes having to sleep in a different location every night to avoid the police, sometimes escaping three jumps ahead of the police raiding a meeting, but never giving up. Never, either, losing their sense of humor. I had been brought up on a diet of stories about the inscrutable, expressionless Oriental, and that particular myth would recur to me from time to time. These youngsters were full of humor, quick, sharp, and subtle. I could not bear the thought of their self-destruction, not simply because it seemed to me their country would need them so desperately in the future, but because of the sheer, indecent waste of such lovely humanity.

And, of course, for a Westerner brought up as a Christian, the whole idea of suicide was repulsive. Suicide is cowardly, an unwillingness to fight on; suicide is sin. I no longer consciously believed either of those things, but presumably they were still deep in my subconscious. I had seen the photographs of Thich Quang Duc, the monk who had burned himself to death in 1963, remaining fixed in an attitude of prayer until he was dead, and I recognized *something,* a quality of courage and concentration that I could never hope to attain, in this willingness to sacrifice oneself for one's people, but still—suicide!

Then, too, I did not really want to believe that only such drastic means could attract the attention and understanding of Americans. These people had suffered so much already. There was not a person in the room who had not lost at least one member of his immediate family killed in the war; one or two had long since lost touch with their families and did not know whether any of them were alive or dead; one had brothers fighting on both sides. Surely there must be more that we in the United States could do to change our government's policies without requiring such added suffering from them.

So I argued with them, reasoned, persuaded, cajoled, pleaded. Surely, I said, we had not reached such a point of desperation; the American people could be reached with less extreme means of communication. I had an idea. One hundred students on American campuses had recently addressed a letter to President Johnson protesting the war. It had been a moderate communication, but it had been a protest. Why did not my Vietnamese friends, campus leaders from the five universities of South Vietnam, who were the counterparts of the one hundred Americans, address a letter to their fellow students in the United States, thanking them for their action and pleading with them for additional understanding and help?

They were willing to be persuaded. We talked for a while about what should be in the letter, and then they drafted it, and made copies, and set out, on bicycles and on foot, through the quiet of the after-curfew city, illegally searching for the right signers. I still have that statement, in the original Vietnamese, with the signatures of eleven faculty and fifty-nine student leaders, which they brought back a few nights later, on the eve of my departure.[1]

We talked about other plans, too—a series of peace demonstrations which they would launch on Easter Sunday and which I would try to persuade students in Europe and America to complement, and we worked out the code by which they were to confirm the arrangements.

I was wrong, unfortunately. Most of the young people who signed that statement are still alive, and I am grateful for that, but about everything else I was wrong, and I suspect I may have been wrong to dissuade them from their original plan.

[1] See Appendix 3.

Perhaps twenty students burning themselves to death in 1967 would still have carried enough shock value to turn America from its terrible course. It's too late for that now, and I'm afraid it was probably too late in 1967, but it might have worked, and scores of thousands of other lives that have been lost might have been saved.

I took the message back to New York with me, and the Fellowship rented a room for a press conference at the Hotel Commodore; we sent out word, and nobody came. Nobody, that is, except one representative of a peace magazine, of impeccable goodwill but very limited circulation. We took the students' statement around from editorial office to editorial office; nobody printed it but James Wechsler, who did a column about it in *The New York Post* and *The Boston Globe* because, he wrote, his conscience bothered him about his not having gone to the press conference.

We sent the plea, with an explanatory letter, by registered mail to each of the one hundred student leaders, and received not a single reply. I had an opportunity to talk directly with a score of them at a meeting in New York. They listened politely and attentively, and I thought they seemed moved, but then they sent me from the room while they discussed what they should do. Soon one of them came out to communicate their wish that I should write to the Vietnamese students and tell them how grateful for their peace efforts the Americans were, "but," he said, "without any publicity, please." He asked if we thought the Vietnamese would be pleased. No, we said, we did not, and asked why they wanted no publicity, and he explained that they did not wish to damage the credibility of their moderate position. They had just come from a meeting with Secretary of State Dean Rusk, and thought they were having an effect on him.

Then we bought space in *The New York Times* for April 9 and printed the letter, along with a plea from Thich Tri Quang, who pointed out that the Americans were making Communists in Vietnam by their actions, but we had a poorer response than from any such ad we ran.

Five weeks later, on May 16, Phan Thi Mai, one of the girls who had signed the statement, invited some of her friends to meet her on the steps of the Tu Nghiem Pagoda in Cholon, the Chinese section of Saigon. When they arrived, Phan Thi Mai was kneeling, facing two statues, one of the Virgin Mary, the other of the (Mother) Bodhisattva Kwan Yin. She had with her a basin, presumably for the ceremony of "washing the Buddha," but in fact filled with gasoline, which she poured over herself as her friends were arriving. Only when she had ignited herself did they realize what she had done. Like Thich Quang Duc, she remained in her kneeling position while the flames consumed her and until she was dead. The police quickly gathered up and destroyed the poems and messages she had left, including pleas to both North and South Vietnamese to stop murdering one another, and to President Johnson to stop the war. But Phan Thi Mai had anticipated them and had had photocopies made the night before and left them with friends, so they were published in many parts of the world. In the United States the poems were read in many a pulpit and, in many cases, through an almost blinding haze of tears.[2]

What is the explanation? Why are these young Vietnamese willing to struggle so and to give up their lives in a fashion far more difficult than the random chance of death in battle? Above all, my Western friends ask, if they are so dreadfully opposed to the United States' military presence in their country, why do they not join the Vietcong and fight the United States and its "puppets" directly?

And indeed on several occasions, including the night when they handed me the statement and the signatures, my young Vietnamese friends would say to me solemnly, "If something does not happen *soon* to end the war, we shall have to join the Vietcong." Some of them have, as did some of those directly in-

[2] See Appendix 4.

volved in the Hue uprising, but in most cases only when they were about to be caught by the police and faced with the stark choice of either fighting in the South Vietnamese army or with the Vietcong. But most have not, and even when confronted with such a choice, they have instead chosen prison, or a hunger strike, or a desperate attempt to escape through the flaming jungles. Why?

The answer to that question is the key to understanding the conflict in Vietnam and may be the key to ending it. Millions of Americans are profoundly disillusioned about the war while continuing to be as profoundly uninformed about its nature. More than 40,000 young Americans have been killed and 250,000 wounded, and their angry and worried parents and relatives do not understand why the interests of the United States should require such a sacrifice. They want out, but they will not get out, and the casualties will not stop until there is a more widespread comprehension of the history, the culture and the religious beliefs that have shaped Vietnam.

A valuable two-paragraph primer for Americans might read like this:

Peace in Vietnam is inseparable from independence for Vietnam. Independence for Vietnam means freedom for that country from domination by foreign troops. The Americans—and the Australians, Koreans, New Zealanders, and Thais who are their allies—are foreigners. The North Vietnamese are not foreigners.

The strength of the National Liberation Front and of the North Vietnamese derives from the authentic nationalism that expresses itself in this drive for independence. The Communists, who control both the NLF and the North Vietnamese, are Vietnamese, not Russians or Chinese, and are authentic nationalists themselves. Their control has been steadily strengthened by the very visible fact that their adversaries, who have brought far the greatest amount of suffering to the country, are either foreigners or Vietnamese who are dependent on those foreigners.

Vietnam has a national history that dates back more than two thousand years. A great deal of that time has been marked by stubborn resistance to attempts by stronger nations to conquer and dominate it. The people take great pride in that history, whether they come from the North or the South; the leaders of the various resistance efforts are the folk heroes of the people, including Ho Chi Minh, the most dramatically successful of them all since the forces of Genghis Khan were pushed back in the thirteenth century.

Nearly one thousand years of Vietnam's history was dominated by the Chinese, marked by the sporadic and often tragically unsuccessful attempts of the Vietnamese to eject them. But through this whole period, though the Vietnamese absorbed much from Chinese culture, they refused to be assimilated, and understandably accumulated a pervasive national hatred for the Chinese. (One of the more acutely ironic aspects of the American military enterprise in Vietnam, which at one point was described by Secretary of State Dean Rusk as designed to hold back a threatened onrush of the Chinese, is that it has had precisely the opposite effect. A North Vietnamese ambassador observed to me sadly in 1965, "You Americans are forcing us into the arms of the Chinese, where none of us want to go, by making us dependent on them for arms and technical help. I wonder sometimes if anyone in the United States knows anything about Vietnamese history!")

But this sense of national identity and pride is not the same as that experienced by Americans. Vietnam for the Vietnamese is not what the United States is for Americans, but a more mystical relationship, not with the government but with the people and their culture. The reality of daily affairs has always been the reality of the village, composed of several hamlets. Vietnamese regard their central government with suspicion as performing primarily such functions as collecting taxes that go to Saigon and conscripting young men for unknown and irrelevant ventures. For much of the country's history, the central government has been aware of such feelings and acted with circumspection in dealing with the villages. Taxes, usually the most abrasive factor in the government-people relationship, were often left to the village councilors, who were elected by the villagers, to collect. When there were disagreements about the amount due, they were usually resolved in favor of these village authorities.[3] Democracy in Vietnam was a genuine democracy, but it was centered in the villages, not in the central government.

Hence another of the great ironies of America's involvement in Vietnam was Washington's satisfaction as Ngo Dinh Diem, its hand-picked President, replaced most of these elected officials with his own men, often fellow Catholics, and sometimes, especially in high offices, refugees from the North. Washington saw this as the consolidation of the central government's authority over a basically disorganized and even anarchic people. The villagers saw it as an intolerable intrusion on their self-government, confirming their views about the essential uselessness and exploitative nature of central authority. The Vietcong saw it as a heaven-sent opportunity to disrupt Saigon's whole structure of government through assassination, since the villagers usually felt no great sense of loss at the murder of a stranger who had been imposed on them in the first place. Since the Vietcong ordinarily replaced the chief with one of their own people in the village, they were thus able to build the widely reported "infrastructure," which has turned out to be so elusively indestructible despite Saigon's best efforts.

Until the escalation of the war after 1965 sent millions of refugees flooding into the cities (Saigon, not long ago a lovely city of 500,000 called the "Pearl of the Orient" is now a vast slum of some three million), most Vietnamese were peasants and villagers, nonideological because they were non-national in

[3] For much fuller accounts of the history of the Vietnamese, see *Vietnam: Lotus in a Sea of Fire* by Thich Nhat Hanh (New York: Hill and Wang, 1967), or *Vietnam, the Origins of Revolution* by John T. McAlister, Jr. (New York: Alfred A. Knopf, 1969).

their orientation except in the mystical sense already described. Thus while tens of thousands of recruits could be secured to expel the French or the Japanese, the political parties that combined to organize such resistance and set the pattern for independent government were minuscule in size. When the first Indochinese war ended in 1945, McAlister writes, one of the three leading nationalist political groupings was estimated to have no more than 1,500 members, another 8,000, and the Vietminh itself only about 70,000, many of them also nonideological. These out of a population of some 24 millions! McAlister quotes the late Professor Paul Mus, an outstanding authority, as writing at the time that "The Communist party is an élite of shock troops, but even in this case they are more like a clandestine group than a normal party. The masses are still lacking. No party exercises over them an immediate and profound hold. The parties then lack an essential thing: a pact with the people."

All of this meant that the masses of the Vietnamese peasants, largely sympathetic to the struggle for independence from the French and Japanese, identified undiscriminatingly with all those nationalists who led and articulated that struggle, without distinguishing among them on the basis of the real issues that divided them. The Communists, well-organized, with many of their leaders having been politically trained in the Soviet Union, were skillful enough to unite nationalists of all parties in the open struggle against the French,[4] and ruthless enough to exclude all but their own from the governments that were created when the military struggles ended. In 1945 the non-Communist nationalists had outside support only from the Chinese, who had been authorized by the victorious Allies to occupy North Vietnam, an alliance that had at least as many disadvan-

[4] Milovan Djilas, former Vice President of Yugoslavia, notes in *The Unperfect Society* that although ideologically "Communists consider nationalism as the deadliest sin, yet the irony is that, with the passing of time, nationalism has imposed itself as the surest way for the Communists to get to enjoy the fruits of power." (New York: Harcourt, Brace & World, 1969.)

tages as advantages considering the general Vietnamese attitude toward the Chinese. In 1954 they had no outside support.

In 1946 the struggle for participation in the government between Communist and non-Communist nationalists came to an abrupt end when the French, having allowed their puppet, the Emperor Bao Dai, to abdicate, decided to restore him and themselves to power. The Vietnamese contestants at once set aside their own struggle and reunited against the foreign invader, another incident that might well have impressed policy-makers at the State Department if they had thought about it.

Post-Geneva 1954 was a replay of 1945, except that the Communists now had support from both the Soviet Union and the People's Republic of China, and the non-Communists in North Vietnam had no one. The non-Communists' struggle for participation in Ho Chi Minh's Government did not last long. A combination of political skill and ruthlessness rapidly subdued all dissent to the Communist regime, and the surviving non-Communist leaders fled to the South.

The South, they thought, would be more hospitable. It had no significant Communist organization, and what Communists there were operated under severe restrictions. A variety of political or quasi-political groups existed and could contend for their separate ideas. The non-Communist nationalists were not opposed to a reunified Vietnam—on the contrary, they favored it—but they hoped that by the time reunification occurred they might have established a political base in South Vietnam strong enough to assure their significant participation with the Communists in the emergent government. The United States, of which they had great hopes, had brought to the Presidency from self-imposed exile an authentic nationalist, Ngo Dinh Diem. Their chances seemed good.

When, in 1955, Diem announced, with American support, that the elections agreed upon at Geneva would not be held in 1956 as stipulated, many of the non-Communist nationalists, while recognizing the clear violation of the agreement that had ended the war, secretly rejoiced. They were not under the illusion promulgated by Diem and the American State Department that the elections were not held because "it would be impossible to hold free elections in the part of the country [the North] dominated by the Communists." On the contrary, they knew that even in a completely free and fair contest, Ho Chi Minh, the hero of the entire country, would sweep right over any opponents. It was because the non-Communist nationalists thought that in such an election there would not be even discussion of some important issues concerning preservation of the democratic freedom of dissent in the new Vietnam that they welcomed the chance to have a "little more time" to build the political base they needed in a better-informed and more politically conscious citizenry.

They did not get what they hoped for. Diem brought to the Presidency a monolithic determination quite as ruthless as that of Ho Chi Minh and socially much less progressive. Non-Diemist political forces were suppressed and eliminated, their leaders imprisoned, assassinated, exiled, or terrorized into silence. Land reform measures introduced by the Vietminh were reversed, village democracy was overridden, and the hopes of the nationalists were cruelly destroyed. Not until Diem, having eliminated all other organized opposition or potential opposition, took on the powerful Buddhist Church, was the process of suppression slowed.

So the politically conscious nationalist forces of South Vietnam are ambivalent. Few of them have joined the National Liberation Front. The NLF is not the genuine "front group" that the Vietminh was—a coalition of organized forces with at least one common interest—but a synthetic front supported by a facade of individual Buddhists, Catholics, Socialists, and labor and youth leaders, with emphasis on the relatively small number of Communist party members that make up its executive committees. But the fact is, of course, that three members of a committee backed by a well-organized political party outweigh any time twenty-two committee members with no strength except their own persons.

Yet while they are reluctant to join the NLF, they find themselves in the same rapport as in pre-1954 times with its stubborn battle for national independence, and are completely opposed to the present government of South Vietnam, the domination of their country by the Americans, and continuation of the war that is destroying their country.[5] So the Buddhist monks and laymen, the students and professors, the writers and poets and labor leaders and politicians say wistfully that if "something does not happen soon, we will have to join the Front," but do not join it.

Their position is so dangerous, unsatisfactory to either side in the war and a threat to both, that they dare not talk publicly about it. To those they trust, however, and through their representatives in Paris, their explanation of their refusal to join the NLF is a four-point combination of pragmatism and principle:

1. They are repelled by the dogmatism and suppression of dissent that characterize Communist regimes even while they are attracted by the NLF program for the economic and social development of the country.[6] Buddhism has played a major part in molding their characters, and Buddhism is a nondogmatic re-

[5] Any such generalization must be qualified, of course. Some non-Communist Vietnamese are also strongly anti-Communist in a sense familiar in the West. The largest single group is comprised of the Catholics who migrated from North Vietnam in 1954 and 1955. Living together in the North, in their own villages, beneficiaries of French discrimination in their favor, they had generally sided with the French, and had even fought beside them, in the struggle against the Vietminh. Their expectation of reprisals, whether or not justified, was understandable when the French relinquished the North to the Vietminh in 1954 and were exacerbated by the shrill warnings of some leading American Catholics. Their flight impoverished them, since they had to leave behind virtually all their possessions, and simultaneously embittered them. They remain, nearly a million of them, the strongest and most unwavering supporters of the Saigon Government in Vietnam.

[6] The national program proposed by the Buddhist Socialist Bloc of South Vietnam and released by the Overseas Vietnamese Buddhist Association in Paris bears a close resemblance to the national program proposed by the NLF.

ligion, seeking in all areas and from all persons the truths it believes exist in them, seeking to assimilate new insights rather
than to suppress them. No monks are ever expelled for heresy;
on the contrary, monks are free to form their own schools of
thought within Buddhism and recruit their coteries of disciples,
and many do so. Thich Nhat Hanh describes Buddhism as "a
search for truth with the knowledge that when you find it, it
will be a lie." Or, as he said to a student at Santa Barbara, Cal-
ifornia, who had asked "how one finds the Buddha," "the only
way to find the Buddha is to kill the Buddha whenever you find
him." Then, to the puzzled listening students he explained,
"Buddha is truth, and the search for the Buddha is the search
for truth. The only thing that is certain to prevent your search
for truth is the conviction that you have found it."

For the followers of such an enlightened philosophy, the notion that a particular group of ideologues has determined on *the*
truth and may not be questioned or challenged, is unacceptable.
Both Communism and anti-Communism, declared Nhat Hanh,
are Western fanaticisms, and Buddhism is the enemy of fanaticism of all forms.

2. Practically, the Buddhists want to end the suffering of
their people, and they believe it to be self-evident that it will
not be ended through the military victory of either side. They
do not believe that either side can win a military victory, and
have been saying so long before that fact became widely accepted in the West.

The entire history of Vietnam dictates that the United States
and its "puppet government" in Saigon cannot win it. No people who have fought over one thousand years to expel the
Chinese are going to throw up their hands in acceptance of a
hated occupation after only fifteen.

Short of using its nuclear weapons to annihilate the entire
population, the United States can never hope to impose peace
on Vietnam. Even if the NLF should decide that the immediate
punishment being suffered is too heavy and allowed the fighting

to die away or accepted some kind of compromise settlement —both unlikely—guerrilla warfare, sniping from hidden coverts in the jungle, sporadic shelling of American bases, terrorism against outlying agents of the "foreigners," would resume soon after the overwhelming presence of American force had been reduced. And the NLF and North Vietnamese leaders, possessing a high degree of political sophistication, know that the United States cannot maintain a high level of occupation forces for a long period in the face of political opposition at home.

On the other hand, say the people of the middle group, it is equally impossible for the Vietnamese to win a complete military victory over the United States. Political victory perhaps, but military, no. The Americans simply possess too much firepower and too much wealth, and they have invested too much in their rationale of the war to expect them to withdraw totally within the foreseeable future. Sometime, perhaps, they acknowledge, the United States may grow so weary of the war that it will do as its adversaries demand and simply withdraw, lock, stock, and airbase, in spite of the major political defeat which American politicians and strategists feel such a move would represent in the eyes of the world. But such a prospect is far away, they say, and before such a thing happens millions more Vietnamese will be killed, wounded or uprooted from their rice paddies and villages, and the price is too high to pay.

3. The war, the Buddhists know, is not being fought in a political vacuum. Had there been nothing more at stake, or apparently at stake, than two groups of Vietnamese contesting for the power to rule their country, the United States would never have become involved, nor would China and the Soviet Union, and the United States would have no difficulty in withdrawing. It is because both sides interpreted Vietnam as happening within the context of a world struggle for domination between the "Socialist powers" and the "free world" that the war has become the monster that it has.

The Buddhists do not want to become vassals of either side, tricked into participation in a division of the world that they regard with horror. In the present circumstances they are unwilling members of the "free world" camp. A victory by the United States would confirm that status and perpetuate the uneasiness of their society; a victory by the NLF and the North Vietnamese would mean their absorption into the Communist camp and their consequent isolation from the rest of the world.

What they long for is a neutralized South Vietnam, leading hopefully to a similar status for the whole Indochinese peninsula, friendly to all other nations and perhaps serving as mediators and reconcilers in a world whose own existence depends upon reconciliation.

4. Many of them also reflect their Buddhist background in their rejection of violence in favor of nonviolent means of dealing with conflict and adversaries. Although the press emphasized the incidents of violence in such resistance manifestations as the 1966 "struggle movement" at Hue, they point out that their efforts have been almost entirely nonviolent, and that the most dramatic incident at Hue was the bringing out on to the streets by the people of their family altars, their most precious possessions, in a classically nonviolent tactic to try to stop the tanks of General Ky.

In February, 1969, at the time when a renewed Tet offensive by the Vietcong was widely expected, the Venerable Thich Tinh Khiet, patriarch of the Unified Buddhist Church, made public a message whose spirit was summarized in this paragraph:

We do not consider the powers that create suffering to Buddhism and to our people as enemies. But we should do our utmost to stop their unenlightened schemes and activities that make us and them suffer. The words "aid, help" as well as the word "liberation" should be correctly re-examined. True help does not consist in using help to bypass those who receive help and compel them to do our bidding. Liberation does not mean using rifles to kill those who do not share the same ideology. Liberation in modern times cannot tolerate violence, even for the sake of emancipating human beings and nations. Because, as long as violence is used, it will be challenged by violence. True liberation means liberation of the mind from unenlightened scheming and activities. So we could not share in any kind of fictitious help or any kind of bogus and violent liberation. From beginning to end, we support a nonviolent campaign aiming at happiness for the individual self, strength for peoples and progress for the world. Liberation by nonviolent methods is true liberation: to liberate oneself and the unenlightened forces from all cravings that are the root cause of suffering to oneself and to mankind.

A year earlier a group of young Buddhists, working at relief and community development in the villages under the direction of the Buddhist School of Youth for Social Service, made public its own message. It followed several attacks on them and their school—shelling, murder and kidnapping—by unknown persons, though officially attributed to the Vietcong. Facing this kind of danger daily, the student volunteers wrote:

Now, once again, we solemnly promise never to hate those who kill us, above all never to use violence to answer violence, even if the antagonists see us as enemies and kill till they annihilate us. We recall our pledge that people, no matter what their origin, never are our enemies. . . . Help us to keep steadily this nonviolent mind in our social work by love which asks for nothing in return . . ."

It is hard to persuade people with such attitudes to engage in killing and terrorism even in the best of causes!

7

Third Force—
Fact or Fancy?

Is there a Third Force in Vietnam?

Many people recognize that such a force could be important, both in ending the war and in shaping postwar South Vietnam. But does it actually exist, or is it a product of wishful thinking? The question was asked of a young American who had worked for several years in Vietnam with a relief agency before his resignation in angry protest at the way in which his efforts were co-opted by his country's war machine.

"I wish there was a Third Force," he answered. "It would be tremendously helpful in ending the war. But there isn't." Then, sourly, "There is a Vietnamese Third Force everywhere in the world except in South Vietnam!"

"No Third Force exists in South Vietnam," says an American peace movement leader, "and if it did it would be only another ploy by the United States in order to maintain its presence and power in Vietnam. The only legitimate organized political force in South Vietnam is the National Liberation Front."

Such comments prompt some Vietnamese to unaccustomed irony.

"So there is no Third Force in South Vietnam," says Vo Van Ai, secretary-general of the Overseas Vietnamese Buddhist Association. "It brought down Ngo Dinh Diem in 1963. It deposed General Khanh. And in 1966 it would have overthrown Marshal Ky if the Americans had not intervened with their military strength. It was not the Front that did those things, fighting in the jungles. It was this nonexistent Third Force, operating in the cities in the very centers of power of the Saigon Government. It is quite a record for something that does not exist."

"The trouble is," says Thich Nhat Hanh, "that we talk of a 'third solution' and those who would welcome and support it, and you Westerners translate it as a 'third force' contending for power with the other two forces. For you a 'third force' makes it into a three-sided war instead of a two-sided one. If there is a 'third force,' and there is, it is the whole Vietnamese people."

Is there a Third Force?

It is a critically important question for Americans who would like to end the war and really make it possible for the Vietnamese people to "determine their own future," but the answer is not easily come by. A politically significant Third Force would presumably have a self-conscious coherence, a leadership and a constituency, and a program for ending the war and governing the society after the war. Do those exist in South Vietnam? Are they detectable by ordinary methods of reporting, and especially by strangers, and more especially by white strangers? It is an important question for Americans to consider.

Americans who visit Vietnam carry with them, inevitably, the conditioning of their own background and environment. The United States is a free society with a two-hundred-year history of constitutional government and political freedom. Considering its size and the tensions under which it operates today, it is probably the freest society in the world, even though it is a very long way from perfection. But Americans who visit Vietnam under their own steam, as opposed to those who are transported there involuntarily in military servitude, are people who have been accustomed to speaking their minds forcefully when they oppose actions of their government, and to expect protection in their right to do so. And that right still exists and is protected, even though young Americans who refuse military service may wind up in prison; older men and women who destroy draft board files in protest to the war are likely to find themselves behind bars; and others who engage in civil disobedience to what they regard as "unjust laws" recognize the probability that they will have to pay for their action with a term of imprisonment. The President and his aides can be and are freely accused of lying; scandal in government makes headlines and frequently retires high public officials to private life, and the open, voluble opposition to the Vietnam conflict approaches what some indignant citizens regard as treason, without much fear of legal suppression. We have a tradition of irreverence for political structures and office-holders, and the expectation that we can speak, write, and organize to accomplish their change or replacement without fear of undue punishment.[1]

South Vietnam—the Republic of Vietnam—on the other hand is a police state. Criticism of the Government, let alone overt opposition to it, is punishable by imprisonment, exile, or death. Arrests are often secret and may be made, as

[1] Young Americans who have been clubbed, tear-gassed, and arrested for demonstrating for peace or some other laudable objective will reject this caustically. The United States, many of them have concluded, is already a "police state." Without in the least minimizing the shame of the violent repressions used by Mayor Richard J. Daley's police in Chicago, on various university campuses, and in other places, or the *danger* of increasing repression in the future, I would observe that their judgment illustrates how little they know of what a police state really is. Many black Americans, on the other hand, and particularly those who have struggled for equality within the context of legalized violent repression in the Deep South, are justified in using the term, and by the same token would be likely to understand very well the realities of life in South Vietnam.

Pham Tam observed, by "anyone with a gun." Those trials that are held are mockeries of justice, and thousands of men, women, and children are imprisoned for long terms without even the formality of charge or trial, much less the right to a legal defense. Physical torture is a part of the prison experience, assassination is frequent, and there is no authority concerned with bringing the assassins to justice. The Government simply announces that the killing was by the Vietcong and jails anyone who suggests a different explanation.

South Vietnam is also an occupied country, and a corrupted one. Tens of thousands of white strangers, some in uniform and others not, pour millions of dollars into propping up the structure of an unpopular and detested government. The Central Intelligence Agency is everywhere, its American agents disguised as relief workers, advisers, and journalists, with numberless Vietnamese who also have been seduced by the CIA's dollars to be its agents and betrayers. Suspicion and distrust are pervasive in the South Vietnamese atmosphere. To confide in the wrong person is to jeopardize one's liberty or even one's life.

In such an atmosphere, Vietnamese who constitute however loosely organized a political opposition to the Government are understandably reluctant to discuss their activities and plans with anyone except their most intimate associates. They are not paranoid. They know that there are many Westerners who are genuinely on their side and thoroughly trustworthy, but except in rare cases, they do not know how to tell them from the CIA's people. They are appreciative of the work that the more than thirty foreign-financed and staffed relief agencies in Saigon do for the war-ravaged Vietnamese people, but they know that even relief agency representatives meet with government officials in the same over-all organization in which the CIA participates, and they know or suspect that the agencies themselves are infiltrated by CIA or South Vietnamese government agents, all seeking information that will lead them to opponents of the regime.

It is difficult for Americans and other Westerners to believe this, knowing the dedication and courage that many of their representatives on relief agencies exhibit, knowing, too, that many of them are operated by church-related organizations. Yet they must recognize that no foreign-operated relief operation can do anything or go anywhere in South Vietnam without the permission and, indeed, the active assistance of the South Vietnamese Government and of the United States Military Assistance Command in Vietnam. Its operatives cannot move far from Saigon without using government or American military transport, cannot function in any area without permission from local authorities, and consequently must be continuously in contact with government and military agencies and officials. Inevitably such contacts provide many opportunities for intelligence agencies to pump the young men and women involved for information. (Or worse. Some of those Americans who resigned from relief posts in South Vietnam did so after they had realized the extent to which they were being counted on by the military to "clean up" after a "pacification raid" had destroyed a village and uprooted its inhabitants. On one occasion such a worker in a supervisory capacity was called one morning to prepare to handle 600 new refugees who were "about to be made.")

In 1967 I discussed the Vietnamese suspicions with a friend who was directing one American relief effort. He and many of his associates were pacifists, and the larger number of his volunteer workers were conscientious objectors. It was unthinkable that they would consciously betray the Vietnamese, even the Vietcong, to the CIA.

"Not consciously, of course," my friend replied when I had said as much. "But the Vietnamese are right nevertheless, I'm afraid. Our workers are young, without experience in intrigue and poor liars. CIA and other intelligence operatives, on the other hand, are very clever, well-trained individuals skilled in the art of extracting information from people who do not even realize they are giving it. It is not an even match, especially when you remember that the kids usually have no idea who are the CIA people present." He reflected a moment and sighed. "I hate to say it," he concluded, "but I really have no doubt at all that every American-based relief agency in the country is infiltrated by the CIA and probably those from other Western countries as well."

Americans and West Europeans read of such conditions and wag their heads and think they understand, but a full realization is hard to come by. Saigon is crowded, but people seem to move about freely, newspapers are published, no one seems to be looking over his shoulder apprehensively. Perhaps one should not expect to find a storefront labeled "The Saigon Third Force Political Club," but there must be *some* way of finding out, *some* person to talk to. Surely it cannot be as bad as it has been described. So an American government official of impeccably dovelike disposition and incorruptible personal integrity, fresh from dire admonitions to proceed with great caution in following an indirect means of making contact with a student Third Force leader, asked the American embassy in Saigon to make the appointment for him, with the result that the student had to sleep in a different locality every night for two months. So, too, an earnest official of another government, agonizedly concerned about peace, asked at a luncheon of voluntary agencies in Saigon for directions to meet another such person whose name he had acquired, but only after swearing great oaths to be circumspect. So the Vietnamese who are the theoreticians, organizers, and potential office-holders of the Third Force movement, recognizing how much their cause would profit if they could announce themselves and their actions freely, still must operate in secret and depend on their exiled representatives abroad to interpret their actions and Aesopian language in terms the West will understand.

But the question persists: Is there a Third Force?

There is obviously a "first force": the Saigon Government.

Officially, the Government of the Republic of South Vietnam, successor to the regime of Ngo Dinh Diem established by a referendum in 1955 over the discredited French puppet, Emperor Bao Dai, having come to power through military coup in 1965 and "confirmed" by the elections of 1967. It consists of President (General) Nguyen Van Thieu, Vice President (General) Nguyen Cao Ky, and Premier (General) Tran Thien Khiem.

The Thieu-Ky-Khiem Government is supported by the military junta that deposed the neutralist Premiers Duong Van Minh and Phan Huy Quat and installed Generals Ky and Thieu in 1965, by civil servants whose jobs are dependent on the government and businessmen who have turned rich profits as a result of the war, and by a substantial minority of South Vietnamese, mostly Catholic, whose anti-Communism stems from their own flight from North Vietnam in 1954–55 and resembles the obsessive variety that panicked the United States during the era of Senator Joseph R. McCarthy.

Politically the Thieu-Ky Government is constructed on a very narrow base. Rumors throughout the spring and summer of 1969 that it was to be broadened in order to seek a more moderate policy were effectively squashed in August with the forced resignation of Premier Tran Van Huong. Huong, a respected civilian who had come in third in the 1967 Presidential race, had accomplished relatively little during his tenure as Premier, but he *had* ordered the release of some 6,000 political prisoners during Thieu's absence from the country and had tried to reduce some of the pervasive corruption in the government.[2] He was replaced by Khiem, top-ranking army general,

[2] Huong was himself a political prisoner at one point during his career, a fact of which he was reminded by a representative of the International Red Cross who was pleading for permission to provide clothing and other necessities for political prisoners as well as prisoners of war. He recalls that Huong, who is a poet and former teacher, became lost in memories. "I will never forget the dawns," the Premier said, "and the listening for the sound of the guard's footsteps in the corridor, and then the door of the cell opening and the guard beckoning me out, to the interrogation room—where you know what happened to me." Then he gave the asked-for permission.

already Deputy Premier and head of the National Police. Khiem was also President Thieu's closest personal friend and devoted to an equally hard line on the war.

A new cabinet, announced immediately after Khiem's elevation, consisted of four generals, two lesser military officers, and a miscellaneous collection of civil servants and technicians who were political unknowns. Even a constricted new "party" created by Thieu a few months earlier in a transparent attempt to create the appearance of a political opposition was not represented, let alone the genuine opposition centered in the Buddhists of the An Quang Pagoda and their allies. The key posts —the Premiership and the Ministries of Interior, Defense, and Rural Development—are all occupied by military men, while four ministers and one deputy minister, according to *The New York Times* of September 2, 1969, are former supporters of the late President Diem.

Chosen by less than 20 per cent of South Vietnam's electorate in an election it organized and corrupted, openly detested by its own people, governing from a narrow political base while carrying on an unpopular and losing war, the Thieu-Ky-Khiem Government has one powerful supporter—the United States of America. Without it, Saigon would collapse; with it, it retains a precarious hold on power by the device of terrorizing its own population into a sullen silence.

Openly arrayed against the Saigon-Washington alliance is the "second force," the National Liberation Front of South Vietnam (Vietcong), its ally, the Democratic Republic of (North) Vietnam, and its supporters, the People's Republic of China and the Soviet Union.

The NLF was officially organized in 1960 after sporadic outbreaks of guerrilla fighting against the Diem regime had marked the two previous years, especially in the Mekong Delta. From the start, the NLF had the support of North Vietnam; indeed, its organization was announced by the secretary-general of the North Vietnamese Labor (Communist) party, Le Duan, at the party's third convention, where he described the NLF as led by the party with the aim of overthrowing the Diem regime, revoking the South Vietnamese Constitution, and realizing the reunification of North and South Vietnam.

Yet from the start the National Liberation Front was much more than a tool of the Communists, North or South. In a real, if ironic sense, it was the creation of Diem and his American supporters. After 1954 the Vietnamese were tired of war, and even Diem's American-backed refusal to permit the country-wide elections that had been agreed upon at Geneva, while outraging the Vietminh, would not by itself have been likely to spark a renewal of the fighting. The North Vietnamese were preoccupied with the task of building a workable society and were having their difficulties. Unification remained a firm objective, but it could be postponed, to be achieved, it was hoped by political means.

Though Diem's action in returning to the rich landlords land that had been taken from them by the Vietminh and distributed to the peasants who had been tenant farmers aroused much bitterness, it did not affect enough of the population to bring about a renewal of more than localized fighting. Had Diem developed a strong coalition of non-Communist nationalist forces in the South, it is unlikely that he would have been overthrown or that the NLF would have become a significant force.

But Diem was a mandarin who saw himself as the "mother and father of the people" ("dan chi phu mau"), destined to rule by decree and entitled to absolute fidelity from his subjects. Such a conception of government could tolerate neither the village democracy of the past nor the developing sophistication of modern political parties of the opposition. Diem alienated the villagers by supplanting their chosen leaders with his own agents, often military men. In doing so he opened the way to terrorism and assassination by the NLF, since its victims frequently were seen by the villagers as their enemies.

At the same time, Diem ruthlessly suppressed all other political groupings of nationalist forces that had cooperated in the struggle against the French and that now sought an opening to participate in the new South Vietnamese government. In the aftermath of the long war against the French, some of these groups controlled significant military forces and some areas of the country. Among these were the Binh Xuyen in and around Saigon, the Cao Dai in Tay Ninh and other provinces in south and central Vietnam, and the Hoa Hao, the Dai Viet and the Quoc Dan Dang in various parts of the country. These groups, ousted from participation in government by Ho Chi Minh in 1945 and 1954, saw their military and political strength as a means of bargaining for places in a South Vietnamese government that would represent them all. But Diem and his American advisers would not have it! Diem's mandarin concepts of government dovetailed with the American strategists' conclusion that toleration of these independent nationalist forces would constitute an impossible condition of "states within a state." Trickery and treachery were used to suppress and eliminate all possible organized opposition or potential opposition. Even when Cao Daiist and Hoa Haoist leaders indicated a willingness to end their open resistance and cooperate, they were tricked. The Cao Dai general, Nguyen Thanh Phuong, was murdered by being shot in the back, and the Hoa Haoist leader, Le Quang Vinh, was arrested and executed when he came to discuss cooperation. (Two of the best-known of these leaders, Nguyen Bao Tam and Vu Tam Anh, were "liquidated" at Mat Vu, Interrogation Center No. 8.)

So the actions of Diem, supported by his American advisers, designed to strengthen South Vietnam against a Communist take-over, in fact strengthened the Communist-controlled NLF by eliminating the political options for Diem's non-Communist opponents. Unable to participate in the political life of their country, unable, indeed, to survive, they found their choices reduced to silence, exile, prison, or the NLF. So, too, by demonstrating a willingness to tolerate and even solicit large-scale foreign intervention and war in order to suppress all opposition, Diem reinforced the Communists' accusation that he was simply an American puppet and their claim to be the genuine defenders of Vietnamese independence. The consequences should have been predictable, but to the leaders of a United States preoccupied with its own version of the Communist threat in Europe and unfamiliar with reality in Southeast Asia, they were not, so that Thich Tri Quang could say to me bitterly in 1967: "In 1945 there were two important Communists in South Vietnam. Today there are thousands, and they were all made by your country."

Yet Diem was overthrown not by the NLF but by his own people, from whom he had demanded absolute fidelity while crushing their own aspirations for independence, and in the period 1963–65 the strength of the NLF in what was still a civil war was only the other side of the Saigon Government's weakness and its inability to win the support of its own people. In 1965, when the United States began heavy bombing of North Vietnam and escalated its own troop strength from 16,-000 to 160,000, the guerrilla fighters of the National Liberation Front were still fighting with weapons left over from the war against the French or captured from the inept and unenthusiastic army of South Vietnam. Even so, it was clear they were about to win, which is why Americanization of the war began.

After that the character of the war changed. Vietcong guerrillas were reinforced by trained North Vietnamese regulars; captured and outmoded rifles were replaced by Chinese-made AK-47 automatic rifles superior to the Americans' own M-16; Hanoi and other heavily bombed areas of North Vietnam were ringed with the most sophisticated Soviet-made air defenses the world has ever seen; and similarly sophisticated weapons began to appear in the fighting in South Vietnam, bringing a new vulnerability to American bases and South Vietnamese cities alike.

So the two principal contending forces are known and identified. One, the Thieu-Ky-Khiem regime, is seen by its support-

ers as the official government of the embattled Republic of
Vietnam, imperfect and guilty of many undemocratic practices,
but deserving support because it is involved in desperate resistance against Communist aggression, and by its critics as a
shameless collection of corrupt Vietnamese generals willing to
serve as the tools of United States imperialism even though
their country is destroyed, traitors to their traditions and people
in order to achieve riches and power for themselves.

The second, similarly, is seen by its supporters—and its
own propaganda—as the "sole authentic representative" of
the South Vietnamese people, carrying on the centuries-long
struggle for independence against foreign invaders, and by its
opponents as the instrument of Communist aggression against a
new small nation seeking freedom, cloaking its true nature
under a mantle of nationalist claims.

Millions of non-Vietnamese, of the right and the left, understand the war's alignments in this way, and see the choice of
support as being between these two forces. Millions of Vietnamese, on the other hand, are unwilling to accept either of
these groups as the sole architects of their national future. It is
they, and their spokesmen, who constitute the Third Force.
Their existence and their actions have both been visible for the
last six years and can be recognized at once by observers who
bear in mind four attributes that characterize the Third Force:

1. It has operated in the cities, where it is most vulnerable
to police and other government reprisals.

2. It has been heavily committed to nonviolent tactics not
only because rejection of violence is basic to Buddhism but because to use violence would inexorably force alignment with
one of the two warring forces.

3. It is not a force in search of power for itself, but of a solution that would end the war and make possible a Vietnamese
society that would permit the full participation of all Vietnamese.

4. It is pitted against not only the Vietnamese who rule the

country, but also the military, political and economic strength of the most powerful nation on earth, the United States.

In such circumstances, given the conditions of Vietnamese society described earlier, the search for the Third Force and its strength and meaning must be conducted with imagination and understanding, reading statements with regard to the context in which they were written, rather than as they would appear in a Western democracy, seeing actions as they are measured against the potential punitive measures they incur.

The full emergence of the Third Force occurred in 1963. Ngo Dinh Diem had become master of the political forces of his country. Other nationalist parties and their military and organizational strengths had been dissipated and destroyed; their leaders had been assassinated, exiled, imprisoned, or had surrendered into silence. (At Diem's overthrow, 75,000 political prisoners were released!)

One potential rival to his power remained—the Buddhist Church. Not only representing the religion of the great bulk of the Vietnamese people but also historically identified with their nationalist aspirations, the Buddhists had done little overtly against the Diem regime, but their apprehensions and anger smoldered. Diem, a Catholic who had appointed his brother Archbishop of Vietnam, was heir to the Catholics who had been favored by the French and—many of them—fought on the side of the French. The Buddhists, correspondingly repressed by the French, identified overwhelmingly with the forces that had fought and defeated the French. Clearly it seemed to Diem that the Buddhists, however politically inactive at any given moment, constituted the sole remaining threat to his power and must be subordinated to it. Increasingly their publications and spokesmen openly criticized the feudal autocracy the Ngo family had imposed on the country, and its incompatibility with the freedom of thought and action representative of Buddhism.

Direct confrontation began when Diem refused permission to

the Buddhists to fly their flag on Vesak Day (Buddha's birthday), an act roughly comparable to an order forbidding Christians to observe Christmas and one that was recognized immediately by the Vietnamese as the beginning of the same kind of
attack that had previously been made on the smaller religious
sects. The Buddhists refused to surrender. Their flag flew; and
massive resistance to attempts at government suppression
began. Perhaps the climactic point of the movement occurred
on June 11, 1963, when a highly venerated 70-year-old monk,
Thich Quang Duc, lowered himself into the lotus position on
Saigon's busy Phan-dinh-Phung Street, poured gasoline over
himself, and burned himself to death.

The act sent shock waves throughout the country and, to a
lesser extent, throughout the world, and the Diem regime's fate
was sealed. One death of a saintly old man had demonstrated
more than any words could the popular revulsion against the
Diem regime. Strikes swept the country, demonstrations demanding a new government and peace rose in every city. Ultimately elements of the army joined the revolt, and the struggle
ended in the tragic murders of Diem and his closest associates.

(There is a dramatic parallel between the circumstances in
1963 and those of 1969. Thieu, like Diem a Catholic, also like
Diem was put into power and sustained there by the United
States. Like Diem, he clearly sees the Unified Buddhist Church
as the principal threat to his power—in January, 1969, he
said, "My government can die because of those pacifists, but
before we die, they will have to die first"—and has sought to
contain and suppress the church. Thieu has operated with
somewhat more sophistication than did Diem, revoking the
church's charter and attempting to set up a rival Vien Hoa
Dao—Secular Affairs Institute—under Thich Tam Chau
and depose the church's Patriarch, Thich Tinh Khiet. But again
the Buddhists have reacted as they did in 1963, recognizing the
threat to their charter as the political act that it was, and setting
themselves firmly, and successfully, to resist it.)

Diem's fall brought a wave of popular rejoicing. The Vietnamese thronged the streets, laughing and singing. Peace was in the air. The newly appointed head of state, Duong Van Minh, outlined a neutralist policy looking toward an early cease-fire and negotiations. The prestige of the Buddhists and the political and intellectual forces mobilized around them—the Third Force—was at a high point, while the NLF which had built its case on the need to depose the Diem regime, floundered uncertainly and in silence.

The good feelings lasted for three months until General Nguyen Khanh, a hard-liner backed by the United States embassy and the CIA, deposed "Big Minh" and announced that the war against communism would be resumed.

Five months later Khanh himself fell from power and into exile, pushed out by a new popular wave of protest led by students and Buddhist protesters in Hue and Danang. Once again the Third Force had demonstrated its strength. But it was up against not only South Vietnam's own corruptible military leaders, but also the power, wealth and determination of the United States.

The last real chance for peace came with another popular, Buddhist-led coup that put into power Phan Huy Quat. Quat lasted a month, just long enough to announce his intention to free the thousands of political prisoners who had been reaccumulated and to seek a coalition government with the NLF. Then he learned that United States economic aid, by now essential to his hungry people, would not be available to a "defeatist" regime, and was encouraged by a junta of generals, most of them Northerners, to call in Air Marshal Nguyen Cao Ky to succeed him.

Ky came on to a scene rife with peace agitation. Early in 1965 the Buddhist La Boi publishing house issued a book of peace poems by the popular Thich Nhat Hanh entitled *Chap Tay Nguyen Cho Bo Cao Trang Hien* (*Let Us Raise Our Hands to Pray for the Appearance of the White Dove*). The poems spoke of the popular hatred for the war and desire to bring it to an end. The Government declared it contraband and ordered all copies seized, but in the week before it did so, all 4,000 copies of the first printing had been sold. (The Saigon regime publicly announced that the author of the poems was obviously a Communist; a few days later Radio Hanoi and Radio Peking denounced Nhat Hanh, saying that "his soul and body have obviously been entirely bought by the Pentagon and the White House.")

In February, 1965, a group of South Vietnamese intellectuals called on Saigon and the NLF to declare a cease-fire and enter into negotiations. Within three days the sponsors of the petition were able to secure more than 4,000 signatures. The movement was violently suppressed by the Government. Almost a hundred of its leaders were arrested, and the three initiators were exiled into North Vietnam by being thrust across the Ben Hai Bridge at the 17th parallel.

One of the three, Dr. Pham Van Huyen, formerly a member of two governments and now exiled in Paris, recalled to me how it had been. Himself a 1954 refugee from North Vietnam, he was under sentence of death *in absentia* in that country, a fact of which he was vigorously reminded by his captors.

"My wife and our young daughter were in South Vietnam," he related. "They offered me a post in the Government. At one point they suggested that I might be Premier. But it would have been Premier of a war government, and I was determined to work only for a peace government. So I left, but it was hard, especially with the knowledge of that North Vietnamese death sentence waiting for me."

But the North Vietnamese had no notion of punishing a man who had been exiled from the South for advocating peace. "They made me a Hero of the Republic," he smiled reminiscently. "They entertained me royally and wanted me to stay. But I couldn't stay there and work for peace, so I left."

Also in early 1965, another manifestation of the popular desire for peace came with the organization by a Buddhist monk and university professor, Thich Quang Lien, of the Movement to Protect the Peace and Happiness of the People (Phong Trau Bau Ve Hoa Binh Va Hanh Phuc Dan Toc). Again it had a quick, warm reception, and again the Government moved in swift suppression. Quang Lien was exiled to Thailand under the supervision of the South Vietnamese embassy in Bangkok.

Deeply committed to the avoidance of more violence in their war-ridden country, the students, labor unions, intellectuals, and Buddhists continued their protests through demonstrations, petitions, appeals, and through dramatic actions such as that of the faculty members who shaved their heads as a mark of protest. The protests were directed even more to the United States than to their own government, since the multiplying pressure of scores of thousands of American troops made it increasingly evident that no change of government could occur if the Americans were determined to prevent it.

The accession to power of the flamboyant, bellicose, Westernized Ky, who had fought with the French against the Vietminh before 1954, stimulated the people to new efforts. When the new Premier announced his formation of a "war cabinet," thousands of Vietnamese paraded through the streets of Saigon with signs demanding a "peace cabinet." Some of the signs were addressed directly to Americans, saying that the people wanted the United States as "friends in peace, not allies in war."

Although Ky's glamour and melodrama may have fascinated the Western press, in South Vietnam they were overshadowed by the increase in the number of protesters arrested and lost to sight, of newspapers forced to suspend publication, by the obvious intention of the new government, with American help, to continue the war to an elusive victory.

By the spring of 1966 so many demonstrations had provided evidence of Ky's tenuous hold on his people that President Johnson pressed the Premier into agreement to provide for a new constitution and "free" elections. The South Vietnamese, aware of the manner in which the Government would manipulate any such election to perpetuate its own power, made another strenuous effort to form a government for peace. The "struggle movement," again initiated by the Buddhists and their student allies, burst forth in massive demonstrations against the Ky Government in central Vietnam, particularly in Hue and Danang. Tens of thousands of Vietnamese poured into the streets in anti-government demonstrations that spread rapidly throughout the country. Radio stations in the Hue-Danang area were taken over, students set fire to the American library in Hue, and the South Vietnamese army units under the popular General Nguyen Chan Thi, joined the revolt.

The rebellious Buddhists and their allies felt that they had been assured by Ambassador Henry Cabot Lodge that the United States, as in 1963, would not interfere with any attempt to replace Ky with a more representative government, and they were not worried when Saigon sent high-ranking officers to Hue to persuade the dissident army units to rejoin the Saigon forces. On the contrary, three successive groups of officers, sent for such a purpose, themselves defected to the rebels!

But Ambassador Lodge had changed his mind, or had received new orders. The United States had invested too much in the war and in the Ky Government; it was not prepared to see Ky's replacement by a new administration that would make peace its first order of business. As the Ky regime trembled on its base, as had Diem's three years before, the United States came to the rescue. Supplies, including vitally needed gasoline, were ordered withheld from the I Corps defecting troops; United States planes and helicopters were mobilized to fly Ky's marines and paratroopers to suppress the struggle movement. Without gasoline, the defecting soldiers were helpless. Many of them took refuge in the pagodas, from which they were rooted out by Ky's forces, an operation which some segments of the United States press described as demonstrating the violent nature of the Buddhist-led movement!

The rebels' chances of success were gone, but still they struggled on. In one of the most dramatic incidents of the rebellion, thousands of Buddhist families in Hue, Danang, and even Saigon, in a classic example of nonviolent resistance, brought their family altars, the most precious possession of a Buddhist family, into the streets to stop Ky's oncoming tanks!

But the overt rebellion was over; its leader, Thich Tri Quang, was arrested and taken to Saigon, where he undertook his 100-day hunger strike and wrestled with the bitterness that flooded him at the "treachery" of the Americans he had thought his friends.

Since then the struggle has gone on persistently, even with highly visible drama, as when the funeral procession for the martyred student Phan Thi Mai became a peace march through Saigon's streets with so many participants—estimated at 50,000—that it took five hours to pass a single point.

"We do not worry about getting our Saigon government out of power," a student leader assured me earnestly. "That will take a week at most. It is the Americans who stand in the way of our having a government of our own choice that would make peace." In this he had confirmed Ky's Foreign Minister, who, in 1965, had said to a group of us, "Without American support this Government would not last five days," an estimate that seemed optimistic when in 1967 Marshal Ky himself, in one of the unexpected outbursts of candor that distinguish him, put the survival potential of his Government without United States support at three days!

A call for a boycott of the 1967 elections by the Buddhists and their allies was frustrated by the fraud introduced into the procedures by the Government so that no one could tell how many actually had voted, and by the intimidation of the voters, who were warned that unstamped registration cards would lead to the assumption that their holders were Vietcong sympathizers and would also deny them food rations. But the election itself was both preceded and followed immediately by serious protests.

Seventy of the best-known leaders of the five universities in

South Vietnam (Saigon, Van Hanh, Dalat, Can Tho and Hue) in March, 1967, addressed an appeal to American student leaders who had protested the war, thanking them for their efforts and calling for more. They excused their failure to sign their letter—"We have made petitions and appeals," they wrote, "but we cannot let our names be made public, because we would be arrested and imprisoned. That is the kind of society we live in here today."

Actually they had all signed the letter, in their own handwriting, and I have their signatures today. James Wechsler, writing in *The New York Post,* said, "Only two of the signatories authorized publication of their names but, for purposes of authenticity, Hassler permitted me to see the full roster of handwritten names. They have my assurance that I neither copied nor memorized it."

Two of the signatures were made public, in this country and in Europe, where the statement was much more widely publicized than here, at their owners' insistence. The two were those of a young woman, a professor of botany at Saigon University, and a young man, the former president of the student body at Dalat University and a fugitive from the police. The young professor explained why they had to insist that their names be made public. "If you cannot identify any of the signers," she said, "people will believe you made the whole thing up. Besides, the fact that we may be imprisoned when they are made public must not deter us. Communists are willing to suffer for their cause, and we will never be able to hold our own in setting up a government with the Communists later if we are less willing. Anyway," she smiled to reassure me, "even in Vietnam they don't often beat professors in prison!" Two days after the statement was published in *Le Monde* in Paris, she was arrested.

An extract from the statement follows:

. . . American power has become so great in support of the Ky government that no one can speak against the war without risking his life and liberty. If it were not so, millions would speak out. The people of South Vietnam desperately want the war to end, but they are losing hope. . . . The present government . . . is not our government and does not represent our people. It was imposed on us by the United States, and is controlled by military men who fought for the French against the Vietnamese before 1954. If we were free to vote freely, that government would not last one day. . . . Do not believe that the danger of a Communist takeover justifies continuation of the war. We believe we are strong enough to form an independent government. The decision, however, should be ours, not yours, when it is our lives and our country that are being detroyed." [3]

At the same time, two ranking members of the Unified Buddhist Church, Thich Tri Quang and Thich Quang Do, sent a brief message to their American coreligionists:

It is because of the religious conscience in us that we cannot accept the war which is going on in our country, that we cannot accept the presence of foreign troops and of troops whose actions are influenced by foreign governments, for this massacre of our people and of each other.

The more the war goes on, the stronger communism becomes, the more Americans become colonialists, and our people are destroyed.

We pray that the religious conscience will guide humanity to stop a war that has reached its utmost in atrocity.

Done in Saigon, February 18, 1967
THICH TRI QUANG
and
THICH QUANG DO

Before writing their statement, they had discussed with me whether it should be longer, a fuller explanation, as I suggested, of their position and actions in terms that would be comprehensible to millions of confused Americans. Tri Quang eventually had shaken his head decisively, with a reply that silenced me if it did not convince me. It was inconceivable to him that the

[3] For full text see Appendix 3.

American people could be in any doubt about the terrible things their country was doing to his—"You are doing far worse things than the French ever did"—and if they did not approve of these things, let them stop the war. Why should they need a message from him?

"You are a democracy in the United States," he said, "not like here. The people must approve of the colonial policies of their government, or they would have ended them."

He would not accept an account of the obsessive anti-Communism in the United States, or fear of China, as an explanation. How could the most powerful country on earth be so ruled by fear?

On April 9, 1967, the Fellowship of Reconciliation, having failed to get the American press to make any mention of either of these two appeals, published them as a full-page advertisement (which costs about $6,500) in *The New York Times*. With them we included excerpts from an editorial from the Catholic newspaper *Song Dao:* "There is no military solution to the problem of Vietnam (as Mr. Johnson himself acknowledges), because the prolongation and escalation of this war cannot but treat Vietnam as a pawn sacrifice on the international chessboard, entrap all of humanity in the tragic abyss of a third world war, and destroy all spiritual values of religion."

If the generals and their American advisers had hoped that the 1967 elections would quiet the opposition, they were not long in being disabused. Five days after the election, on September 8, twenty-five newly elected members of the upper chamber of the National Assembly signed a letter demanding that the elections for President and the legislature be abrogated. Addressed to the Judge of the Supreme Court of Appeals, the letter declared that the Government had outrageously distorted the proportion of voters to falsify the results of the elections, that a large number of citizens had been unable to vote because the Government had refused to give them voting slips, and that many had been denied the vote because ballot boxes were closed after a few hours. (In some cases, polling stations opened at 9 A.M. and closed at noon on government orders.)

The following day, September 9, the 25,000-member General Association of Saigon Students held a special meeting to discuss the elections, to which they invited the Presidential candidates. Three of them, Truong Dinh Dzu, Hoang Co Binh, and Vu Huong Khanh, attended and heard the association's vice president in charge of current affairs, Binh Kien, declare that "the elections of September 3 were nothing but a farce conducted by foreigners." The association issued a statement (published in *Tin Tuong* in November, 1967) declaring that it considered the elections to have been a "scandalous misrepresentation . . . a result of foreign intervention." It added that the association "utterly rejects the election results and denounces the deceitful acts of the government before national and world opinion."

Three days later thirty students called on the thousand candidates of the preparatory class of the Faculty of Sciences to join their struggle, and with the professors looking on approvingly, the candidates tore up their papers by way of protest and joined faculty and students in a strike and a massive demonstration in the university's yard which was broken up by security police. After the students had been dispersed, the police broke into the university buildings and destroyed banners and communiques of the rebellious students.

The university was in a ferment of protest. One school after another announced its unanimous and unconditional support of the General Association's stand. On October 2 a huge demonstration, completely nonviolent, was broken up by club-swinging policemen, and thirty-three of its leaders were arrested, while other policemen simultaneously raided the Bo De secondary school on charges that pupils there were planning a demonstration in support of the university students. The strike spread to Hue, where in the face of ominous police warnings, pupils at two secondary schools stayed out, merchants refused to open their stalls or shops, and local transport was paralyzed.

In Saigon students of the Faculty of Sciences held a silent sit-in with banners reading "October 2 was a black day: September 3 was a day of shame," and 600 students mounted a demonstration that they called "The vigil of shame." A day later a press conference of the General Association of three universities (Saigon, Van Hanh, Can Tho) was broken up by the police, and the students in charge, Ho Huu Nhut and Nguyen Van Tu, were arrested. A few days later fifteen more student leaders were arrested and placed under military discipline at the Lam Son draft center, where they promptly began a hunger strike. From Lam Son they smuggled out an appeal to American students, attributing their arrests to "our activities in demonstrating against the undemocratic and unrepresentative elections of September and October."

"We know how much some of you have struggled to ease the sufferings of our country," the plea added politely, "and we thank you for your efforts. Yet the disaster continues and can only be ended when we of South Vietnam are free to choose a government that will genuinely represent our aspirations. To deny us the right to such a government, as the present Saigon government has done with the help of the United States, is to deny democracy." [4]

Precise information is hard to get from a police state, but it is known that the student actions continued and spread throughout the country even after the arrests. Twenty leaders, mostly students, were arrested in Dalat, charged with "major crimes" and sent to various prisons for long terms, where one of them, a twenty-year-old girl, immolated herself in protest.

The students were not alone. With the turn of the year sixty-five of Saigon University's leading professors released a state-

[4] See Appendix 6.

ment calling on both sides to institute an immediate cease-fire.[5] The embattled generals responded quickly and harshly. The deans of Saigon University received a message from Tran Luu Cung, Vice Minister of Education:

> By order of the Ministry, all the professors who signed the Appeal for a Cease-Fire on 16 January 1968 must immediately reconsider their position, before severe sanctions are applied. The Deans will kindly assemble the signatories to the above-mentioned Appeal and ask them to sign the enclosed declaration [renouncing the Appeal] in case they signed the Appeal of 16 January 1968 absent-mindedly, without looking at its contents.

The deans were unable to find any professors willing to acknowledge that they had signed the statement "absent-mindedly, without looking at its contents," and on February 7 all sixty-five were summoned to the Ministry of Education and ordered to sign a retraction. Most of them refused and were immediately imprisoned.

The 1968 Tet offensive, launched on January 30, and its sequel beginning May 5 burst over the South Vietnamese cities. Some observers believe that the National Liberation Front expected the populations of the cities to rise in open revolt with them against the Thieu-Ky Government; others suspect that the NLF sought only to demonstrate to the United States how far it was from victory and to wring concessions from it in Paris. Whatever the hopes, the city-dwellers did not join the NLF. Vietcong members moved freely among them; few betrayed them, but few joined them. The offensives toppled Lyndon Johnson from the Presidency, but they did not affect the determination of thousands of South Vietnamese to find a different means of extracting their country from the war. (On the contrary, the Vietcong's murder of some hundreds of civilians in Hue persuaded many Vietnamese that dissenters would have little to choose from between Saigon and the NLF.) The resistance and the appeals continued. Newspapers, vulnerable both at

[5] See Appendix 5.

the point of personal prosecution for "supporting communism" and through their dependence on the Government for supplies of newsprint, still continued to belabor the Administration for its corruption, its unrepresentative character, and for its rigidity on the war, and were suspended or closed one after another.

In September the Student Union at Saigon University was closed by the police because of a peace meeting in which students, professors, deputies from the Lower House, and some Buddhist monks had participated, and thirty persons were arrested.

With the beginning of 1969, the Supreme Patriarch of the Unified Buddhist Church openly joined the struggle, calling the war "the outcome of the confrontation and clashes between international ideologies," summoning both sides to negotiations for an immediate cease-fire and his own people to continued resistance, always nonviolent, to the war.[6]

Buddha's birthday, May 30, saw 3,000 Vietnamese thronging into the An Quang Pagoda, headquarters of the "militant Buddhists" and called by President Thieu "the CIA of the Vietcong," for a peace meeting. Present not only were a former Chief of State, Phan Khac Suu, and the General Secretary of the House of Representatives, Tran Ngoc Chau, but also representatives of the Cao Dai and Hoa Hao sects and of the Catholic Church, including the noted Rev. Hoang Quynh. Their presence emphasized the growing collaboration of the various peace forces, already noted in their participation in the Committee for the Release of Thich Thien Minh.

Buddha's birthday saw also a strange form of immolation when a young monk, Thich Thien Dieu, in his own insistent call for peace and after weeks of prayer and meditation, stood before several thousand people and held his finger in a candle flame for almost two hours, never moving a muscle, until it was charred to the bone. A month later, on July 1, a 40-year-old South Vietnamese marine, Vo Van Be, became the first man

[6] See Appendix 9.

from the armed forces to immolate himself in protest against the war, dying only a few yards from where Thich Quang Duc had burned himself to death in 1963.[7]

And on the same day that thousands prayed for peace at An Quang Pagoda and Thien Dieu burned his finger, a member of the South Vietnamese House of Representatives, Pham The Truc, was issuing an appeal from Tokyo to the people of the United States and Japan.

The Thieu-Ky Government, he said, "is still, in its basic nature, a military dictatorship . . . only able to maintain its status by the continuation of this war." The United States, by supporting the Thieu-Ky regime and advocating the "Vietnamization of the war," was making the solution to the war all the more difficult, he asserted, so that leaders of the United States Government "have proved again that there is not the slightest improvement in their basic understanding of Vietnam and Asia." The United States, Pham The Truc said, should immediately stop supporting the Thieu-Ky military regime ("All the treaties which have been concluded between the United States Government and the military regime of Vietnam have no value to the Vietnamese people whatsoever"), withdraw all military forces from Vietnam, and make peace the first priority in the Paris talks.[8]

A few days later Vietnamese Buddhists from their exile all over the world, including leading monks and professors of both the Mahayana and Therevada congregations, met in conference in Paris, designed both to make contact with religious leaders of the West and to announce the establishment of a Buddhist "delegation" at Paris. Neither side at the talks, they said, really

[7] Westerners are often understandably repelled by the spectacle of persons who burn themselves to death or mutilate themselves as a political or moral protest. An explanation of the cultural traditions and meaning of such acts, in which the individual assumes suffering for the sake of the people, not unlike the Christian conception of redemption, is given in Thich Nhat Hanh's letter to the Rev. Dr. Martin Luther King, Jr., in "Vietnam: Lotus in a Sea of Fire."

[8] See Appendix 11.

represented the people of Vietnam. Both sides set victory, or partial victory, as their first priority, rather than peace. In Paris, as in Vietnam, the Buddhists were driven by their religious commitment to be a voice for the harried, voiceless people.

Their plans were frustrated by the refusal of the French Government to allow them to meet in Paris or to have a press conference (French security police barred entry to a Dutch television crew that had come to film the conference), but several of the leading monks have remained in Paris and are in constant communication with their friends in Saigon.

Is there a Third Force in South Vietnam?

In a country where demands for a cease-fire, or for a neutralist foreign policy, or for negotiations with the National Liberation Front are equated with communism, and where "support of Communist aims" is a crime punishable by torture, imprisonment, exile, or death, it is hard to see in what other ways the Third Force could make its presence felt. Political parties are banned, speech is censored (at least twenty-five newspapers and two magazines were closed in the twelve months since censorship was declared ended in the spring of 1968), demonstrations are suppressed. Yet with thousands of their most articulate leaders in prison or exiled, Vietnamese students still hold huge peace meetings and send appeals to their fellow students around the world, Vietnamese professors risk their lives and livelihoods to join them, Vietnamese editors and columnists persist in their criticism, and thousands of Vietnamese citizens throng to marches and meetings calling for a cease-fire and peace.

Is there a Third Force?

The Nixon Administration responds with a depth of inanity rarely achieved even by its predecessor that indeed there is and that its right to exist must be safeguarded by supporting the existing "constitutional government." [9] But of its potential for ending the war the Administration says nothing.

[9] See Appendix 10.

Is there a Third Force?

In the summer of 1963 the American civil rights movement mobilized 300,000 people for a demonstration in Washington. Four years later, the American peace movement produced 400,000 people for a demonstration in New York.

Both were political events of great importance. The Washington demonstration marked the emergence of a political constituency committed to full equality for black Americans and of a black self-consciousness and pride that would never again be prepared to accept subservience. The 1967 demonstration in New York and a somewhat smaller but still very large companion piece in San Francisco made visible a political constituency determined to get the United States out of the Vietnam war. They were followed by a series of other major political events that flowed from the existence of that constituency, among them the toppling from office of a powerful, egocentric President and the near-nomination of a political outsider with consequences for the political structures of our society that are still in the process of development.

Both were triumphs of a determination that triumphed over a lack of coherent organization and a multitude of obstacles. Months of organizing and publicity preceded the events themselves. Committees were set up in hundreds, perhaps thousands, of cities and towns across the United States. Chartered buses, trains, and planes brought participants from every section of the country. In hundreds of communities instant carpools were created when bus companies reneged on contracts at the last minute, moved by their managers' "patriotism" or concern for the well-being of their vehicles, or by the refusal of bus drivers, who come largely from the same stratum of society as do the police, to "drive those Communists." And if the partisans of the respective efforts criticized the press for inadequate or inaccurate reporting, it nonetheless was the newspapers that helped to create the successes with their millions of words of publicity and underlined the political significance of the events with their observation that in each case the overwhelming majority of the participants were "respectable," middle-class people.

In January, 1969, the peace movement in South Vietnam produced a demonstration in Saigon that involved an estimated total of half-million participants. No chartered trains or buses or planes came in. The railroad in South Vietnam has not run for years, bus trips are few and dangerous, and although there are an immense number of planes in South Vietnam's skies, they are not under the operation of people sympathetic to peace demonstrations.

So that the Saigon demonstration was made up almost entirely of Saigonese—500,000 demonstrators out of a population of three million, one out of every six, in the capital city of a country where even speaking for peace is a crime! Granted that no police can arrest or gun down a half-million people; still fear is an individual matter, and each Vietnamese who joined that mass outcry for peace must have been aware of the risk.

Like Washington and New York, the Saigon manifestation, along with all the others that had preceded it, was visible evidence of the political reality of what has been called the Third Force. If one were to extrapolate from the size of the respective demonstrations relative to the populations from which they were drawn, to the size of the constituency represented, it obviously bespoke an immense supporting public.

So the Third Force goes about demonstrating its existence and potency.

It has a leadership, most of it in prison, exile, or hiding, but always with a handful of bold souls to speak out in the center of enemy territory.

It has a political program—a procedure for ending the war and arranging for the withdrawal of foreign troops; a foreign policy based on neutralism vis-à-vis the power blocs and an insistence that no political strings be attached to economic help in rebuilding the country; a domestic policy that foresees a structure based on democratic socialism, with immediate re-opening of trade and travel with North Vietnam; and a method of arranging with the NLF the genuinely free elections, with all citizens and factions participating, to create a coalition government to implement such a program.

And it has a constituency, obviously very large, that has manifested its presence in every conceivable way open to it, under conditions of great hazard, on numerous occasions over the last six years. As in the West, its vanguard is the student population, but as in the West also, the students clearly speak for a mass of their fellows running right across the age spectrum.

Leadership, a coherent political program, and a mass constituency. What else should a Third Force need?

Yet much of the Western peace movement, trapped in its own devil theory of the war, understandably impressed by the courage and persistence of the NLF and fearful of doing anything that could conceivably be used by the NLF's enemies against it, says, No, it would be nice if there were, but there isn't. An American movement built on the disorganized determination of the civil rights struggle, the absurd triumphs of the antiwar movement, and the profane hopes of a generation that ignores its own lack of power to insist that it will make a revolution and build a new politics concludes, like any systematic professor of political science, that in Vietnam such actions have no relevance.

That is, I think, the saddest thing of all—that these heroic youths and their elders, not only struggling for freedom and peace but also insisting that the well-being of man demands that such struggles be carried on nonviolently, have not won the ardent support of their comrades in the West. It is hard to imagine anything more tragic.

8

They Call It a "Third Solution"

So there is a Third Force in South Vietnam, making its presence and extent known in every way open to it, in the face of brutal, legalized intimidation and suppression. Yet even the people whose actions demonstrate its existence are uneasy with the description. It is not a three-sided war, they insist. The Third Force is a convenient but misleading description of the millions of Vietnamese who would support a "third solution" to this apparently endless conflict. It must not be seen as a new alignment contesting for power against the others, but as a reasonable program that expresses the genuine aspirations of the people for peace.

Inevitably, such a "solution," of course, has important political implications, which is why neither side has grasped at it as a means of bringing the war to a conclusion.

For one thing, it would insist on the complete withdrawal of American military forces, although it would have the new government welcome continued friendly relations and economic aid from the United States and other Western countries as well as from those of the East.

It would resist any attempt to force a South Vietnamese alignment with either side in the contest between the Communist world and the West. Instead it would seek the neutralization, not only of Vietnam itself but also of all of Southeast Asia. (Though its advocates make no demands that North Vietnam become neutralized along with the rest of Indochina, they obviously think that the North Vietnamese would be wise to join them in such a status.)

It would require the Vietnamese Communists, who are in complete control of the National Liberation Front, to share that control in a coalition government constructed by two political groupings rather than by one.

The response of the NLF to such proposals has been equivocal. Communists, like other men, do not gracefully relinquish power they have once acquired. Many of them are deeply and sincerely committed to the belief that only the imposition of a Marxist-Leninist system can solve Vietnam's political and economic problems; they have fought long and vigorously and so are even less disposed to meaningful sharing of power. Consequently, the NLF's inclusion of Buddhists, Catholics, Cao Daiists, and others in its governing committee has been on an individual basis, and its public assurances that all elements in South Vietnam would be welcomed in a coalition government have been carefully phrased not only to exclude supporters of the Thieu-Ky Government but also to refer to such elements in individual, rather than corporate terms.

Nor is this altered by the NLF's claim, similar to those of all revolutionary movements, to be "the authentic voice of the South Vietnamese people." Popular support of a movement is not incompatible with control by an élite bureaucracy but, as Milovan Djilas points out in *The New Class,* such support does not pose anything like the serious threat to its power that a much smaller organized and articulate opposition does. A socialist writer, commenting on the Vietnam war, cautions that "it is necessary to keep clear in our minds the difference between the *mass base* of a party or movement, and its *class basis*—the fact that the mass base of the NLF lies among the peasantry does not mean that the NLF is controlled by the peasantry, or that an NLF victory will establish peasant control of the state and its society. Instead, the NLF is controlled by an incipient bureaucratic ruling class—that is its class basis, and that is the class which would be projected into state power by an NLF victory." [1]

It is this incipient bureaucratic ruling class that recognizes the threat to its exclusive control in the emergence of a significant Third Force, or the backing of a third solution by an articulate, organized group of nationally recognized leaders. In this it resembles similar ruling class groupings of all political positions, including President Thieu and his predecessors, who have also made much of the presence in their governments of individual Buddhists, for example, while carefully excluding any important representatives of the An Quang-centered "militants."

But the NLF is also aware of the realities of the situation, and so, while its representatives reiterate their own pre-eminent claim to represent the people of South Vietnam and carefully emphasize the "divisions" within the Buddhist church—divisions that have been more the propaganda creation of the Thieu government than reality—they have also indicated repeatedly their interest in the emergence of a non-NLF, "interim" government with which peace and long-term arrangements could be negotiated. NLF spokesmen have described the "turmoil" in the cities of South Vietnam as an indication of the popular demand for the replacement of the "Saigon regime," without claiming credit for having initiated it. And references made repeatedly to the desirability of a "peace cabinet" recall that the same suggestion, in the same words, has been made by Vo Van Ai, the Buddhist representative-in-exile, since 1965.

---

[1] Don Bacheller in *The Independent Socialist,* quoted by Martin Oppenheimer in *The Urban Guerrilla* (Chicago: Quadrangle Books, 1969).

Indeed, some Westerners, anxious to end the war and noting the similarity between the proposals of the NLF and the Third Force, and the "willingness" of the National Liberation Front to accept non-NLF "patriotic elements" into a new government, have wondered impatiently why the Buddhists do not simply join the NLF. The answer to that question, in several sections, defines the nature and importance of the forces supporting the Third Solution.

The answer is first a practical one. Neither side, say its proponents, can win a military victory in the war with their present investment of forces. The United States of 1969 is not the France of 1954. Its military power surpasses anything history has ever known, and it is impossible for the NLF and the North Vietnamese to muster sufficient forces to defeat the Americans so long as they are determined to stay. That determination may be relative, deeply affected by the political situation at home, and perhaps at some time in the future susceptible of total erosion, but not for a long time to come, during which the war will continue and Vietnam and the Vietnamese be destroyed. The war is not fought in a vacuum, and even if the United States would like to withdraw, the conception of world political forces in contention held by its bureaucratic élite makes it impossible for it to do so unless some provision is made for easing the appearance of defeat.

On the other hand, neither can the United States and its South Vietnamese, South Korean, and Thai allies win the war. American air power has inflicted great damage on both North and South Vietnam, and, since the Communists are political realists, there could conceivably be a temporary subsiding of the fighting as the other side simply withdraws into the jungles and villages. But even such a development is not in sight, and in any case would be a lull rather than a cessation, with the struggle for "independence from the imperialists" resuming as soon as the "imperialists" had reduced their forces significantly.

From this perspective the Neutralists foresee the continuation of war, whether in set battles or by guerrillas, as far into the future as it has gone on in the past. And, since the ultimate decision must be made in Washington rather than in Saigon or Hanoi, for the Third Force elements openly to join the NLF would be more likely to harden the polarization of both sides than to contribute to an end of the war.

Along with this consideration, paradoxically, is their recognition that either side *could* win the war if it were determined to do so, that the war, however horrifying, has been fought under a type of restraint that is always dangerously strained and that at any time may become untenable. By this reasoning, while the Vietnamese on both sides have been fighting total war, their supporters have not. The United States has poured more bombs on Vietnam than were used against all combatants in the Second World War, but it has refrained from using nuclear weapons, refrained from bombing and mining the port of Haiphong, and refrained from bombing the airfields and railroad terminals and lines just north of the Chinese border so close to Hanoi. On the other hand, the Soviet Union with its immense airpower nearby and China with its overpowering land forces have refrained from using them, as they could, to destroy American power in Vietnam or sweep it into the sea. Each side has operated under restraints imposed by the knowledge that to lift them would almost certainly involve it in nuclear war with a giant opponent.

Such restraints, Vietnamese neutralists reason, are a new element in international war, and undependable. Vietnam, already entangled in the competitions of the Great Powers, stands in imminent danger of becoming the battleground on which they not only test out their new techniques, but also lock in the final death grip of their insane enmity.

"We are torn," declared Vo Van Ai, of the Overseas Vietnamese Buddhist Association, at a conference of the International Peace Bureau, "between choices which have no solution. We can choose to combat aggression, in which case we must ally ourselves with one power bloc for support. We thence fall immediately into the vicious circle of conflict, and are drawn into the orbit of conflict between the two major power blocs. Thus our survival depends on the play of chance in the hands of the power bloc. We will have lost our identity. We are no longer ourselves."

In such circumstances, argue the Third Force adherents, to insist on an elusive and unattainable victory is the ultimate absurdity; only peace can give their people and country the chance to survive. And even if a victory were possible, they add, it would plummet Vietnam inexorably into the grip of one power bloc or the other, dependent "on the play of chance" between them. Since peace is their only hope of survival, neutralism is their only hope not to "lose their identity."

But there are other considerations that reach further and plumb more deeply. These are Vietnamese permeated by a Buddhist tradition of tolerance and compassion, accustomed to accepting and absorbing what seems good in new or alien ideologies, finding fanatic commitment to any political or ideological view completely uncongenial. They know the claims and conflicts that are being fought over them and they are not prepared to accept either set uncritically. They are drawn to and repelled by aspects of both Eastern and Western societal organizations and see important things lacking in both.

They recognize that capitalism as it is practiced in the United States is unadaptable to the Vietnamese situation whatever its relevance at home. The accumulations of capital necessary to establish it do not exist in Vietnam and would be attainable only at the unacceptable price of a new wave of economic imperialism. But more than that, they see capitalism as essentially dehumanizing, focusing on the competition for wealth and possessions rather than on the legitimate needs and nature of human beings. So the statement of the Buddhist Socialist Bloc reads very much like any other socialist manifesto, demanding that the instruments of production be controlled for the benefit of the people as a whole and that neither extreme wealth nor extreme poverty can be tolerated within a decent society.

Yet those constituting the Buddhist-influenced element are not prepared to accept the imposition of socialism as implemented by a Communist party, either. If the egalitarian objectives of economic organization in the Soviet Union and China, for example, are congenial to their sense of economic responsibility, the suppression of the individual for the benefit of the state is not. Nor do they respond to the division of men into classes bent on each other's subjugation. If capitalism is bad economics, the freedom of speech, press, and religion that has accompanied capitalism where it has been most successful is good human relations. No one can be so confident of his grasp on ultimate truth as to have the right to suppress the thoughts and opinions of others, however admirable his intentions.

So the ideologies of communism and capitalism alike seem to the Buddhist-influenced Vietnamese to be unacceptable examples of fanaticism, certain to lead to an inhuman, depersonalized, mechanistic society even if they manage to escape the ultimate horror of nuclear war.

One of the principal causes of the Vietnam War, explained Vo Van Ai, is the "national and political isolationism of international politics, that fails to embrace the essence of the interdependence of mankind which is the basis for peace. . . . Politics has lost its first existential essence, its universality in the mission of establishing social harmony and in solving the problem of human suffering. Today, in the East and in the West, people's faith in political power has become almost worship. We have not yet escaped from pantheism, but have simply replaced the old idols by a number of names drained of meaning, as Peace, Liberty, Democracy, Equality, Reason, Revolution.
. . .

"It is astonishing to hear the warmth and sincerity in the voice of a politician, or to read a party program, full of humanity and good will. But the astonishment becomes tragedy when

compared with reality. The word Revolution has become an ep-
ithet for murder instead of a constructive process to serve
human equality and social justice. We cannot doubt the good
will of the mass of American people, nor that of the Russians.
But why is it that these masses support the intervention of
500,000 American soldiers into South Vietnam, or the invasion
of 500,000 of the Soviet Pact troops into Czechoslovakia? The
good will of the people is not lacking, but it is simply misled by
a handful of powerful men, or by a party. The right of the masses to unbiased information has been violated. They cannot see
the whiteness of the snow because of the colored glasses of state
politics!"

For men who think thus, even national independence is not a
goal sufficient to claim the abandonment of their own convic-
tions to acceptance of the dictates of a party or bloc. But more
than that, they see such independence, even if achieved, as
ephemeral and deceptive. A people does not really achieve its
independence in such ways; it simply transfers its chains from
one bondsman to another. The freedom of the individual is
prerequisite to the good of society. Again, in the words of Vo
Van Ai: "Each individual is a revolutionary center no matter
where or when, whatever his beliefs or customs. The objective
of this revolutionary center, which is the man, is the social justice and equality of mankind. His weapon is refusal, his ammu-
nition respect for life. It is precisely this conscious refusal that
is our way of transcending violence and murder. Only those
who fear and who do not understand are armed with guns to
oppress and murder others."

So the Vietnamese in the Third Force, seeing peace as essential to the survival of their people and nation and despairing of
peace through the military efforts of either side in the war,
offer their Third Solution to both. As a means of ending the
war, it has five simple elements:

1. Replacement of the Thieu-Ky-Khiem regime by an "interim" government representative of the actual popular forces

in South Vietnam and committed to ending the war. Obviously such a government could not be elected. A major part of the struggle in Paris is over the question of who would organize "free" elections, since the organizer could so easily manipulate and control the results. But the "interim" government could come to power without elections, as Duong Van Minh came to power in 1963, the Third Solution people believe, if one thing only happens: that is if the United States withdraws its unqualified support from the Thieu regime.

2. The interim government would immediately order the South Vietnamese army to cease firing, and ask both its allies and adversaries to join in the suspension of hostilities.

3. Simultaneously, the new government would ask the United States for the complete withdrawal of its troops and dismantling of its military bases, and initiate negotiations with the North Vietnamese Government for withdrawal of its troops and on procedures looking toward eventual reunification.

4. Proposals would be made to North Vietnam for the lifting of bans on travel and trade between the two zones to take effect immediately regardless of any ultimate decisions on reunification.

5. Negotiations would begin at once with the National Liberation Front for the holding of genuinely free elections, overseen by whatever form of international supervision was mutually acceptable, to choose a government representing all factions and tendencies in the country.

The proposals have been greeted with skepticism by "practical" Westerners, whether they oppose or back the NLF.

If a cease-fire were declared by such a government, say Washington's supporters, what would prevent the Vietcong and the North Vietnamese from sweeping over the new government and seizing complete control? Or, since the American troops would be there until their withdrawal had been effected, why would not the Vietcong *then* overrun the country? And would there not then be a blood bath? The South Vietnamese army cannot cope with the Vietcong now; how could it hope to do so without American help, or would it even want to?

On the other side, among those whose suspicions of American intentions are without limit, the danger seems to be of a different nature. If such a new and admittedly more representative government were to come to power, even under the designation of "interim," they say, it would simply supply the United States with a new excuse for continuing the war by legitimizing the Saigon government. "Look," they hear Washington saying, "the bad guys are out and the good guys are in. Surely no one now can doubt the sincerity of our efforts to defend freedom!" And even if the new Vietnamese officials sincerely wanted to follow the program they had outlined, say these critics, would not the temptation to reinforce their position by relying on United States power be irresistible?

There are both simple and complicated answers to such questions, and the Vietnamese are often exasperatedly prone to supply the simple ones first.

"Do not believe," wrote the university students to their American counterparts early in 1967, "that the danger of a Communist takeover justifies continuation of the war. We believe we are strong enough to form an independent government. *The decision, however, should be ours, not yours, when it is our lives and our country that are being destroyed!*" [2]

And Thich Nhat Hanh, replying to a questioner who had raised the possibility of a "blood bath," said gently:

"We are not savages; we are a people with an ancient culture, and we are sick in our very bones of war. I do not believe there would be a blood bath, but I wonder when you ask such a question how you would describe what your military forces are doing to my people now."

Then, turning to a questioner who feared that the interim government would be a new ploy for the Americans to continue the war, he said, "I cannot understand you Americans. First

[2] Author's italics.

you insist on fighting a war for us so that we can determine our own destinies; now you insist on telling us how we shall make the peace in order to determine our own destinies. Do you really think that your success in the first has been so great as to warrant your certainty in the second?"

But with the exasperation out of their system, they will explain that serious answers to such questions depend upon a familiarity with the Vietnamese people that few Westerners possess. Compressed, such an understanding would run like this:

The large majority of South Vietnamese are peasants—farmers and workers living in the villages of the Mekong Delta and other parts of the country. Millions of them have been uprooted by the war, forced out of their homes by the terrorization of both sides and the fear of the American bombing, driven out by actual bombing that has destroyed their homes, or removed forcibly to refugee camps in the dreadful campaign euphemistically called the "pacification program." Cities have become vast unsanitary slums as refugees have crowded into them as the only alternative to life in the even more appalling refugee camps. Inevitably many of the displaced peasants will remain displaced even when the war ends, choosing the attractions of the most crowded city over those of the village, or simply despairing of beginning again in a ruined village and on ground that has been chemically poisoned. But whether displaced in the cities or not, they are peasants, with a peasant background and a peasant's view of the world. That view is not ideological; the peasant neither understands nor longs for either communism or free enterprise. He has no fear that communism will take away his property since he has no property; he has no great visions of a people's utopia since his own village democracy seemed a highly satisfactory way of life to him.

Most of the peasants are Buddhists, with about a million each giving allegiance to the Cao Dai and Hoa Hao sects (Hoa Haoism is a variant of Buddhism), but about 10 per cent—

1½ million—are Catholics. About two-thirds of these last *are* ideologized in a strong anti-Communist position. They are the refugees who fled from North Vietnam in 1954 and 1955 in fear of retribution from the Vietminh, against whom many of them had fought beside the French in the long "war of liberation," and only the experience of a tolerant society and the maturing of a post-1954 generation will relieve them of their fears.

For the rest, their first desire is peace, and in this they are at one with most Vietnamese intellectuals and politicians. I have heard Third Force Buddhists and NLF officials echo in almost identical words the mournful sentences of a North Vietnamese ambassador.

"Every Vietnamese wants peace," he said, "because our lives have known almost nothing but war. My father's life was dominated by war, my life has been dominated by it, my son's life now is filled with it. Our children are born and raised in war. Seven-year-olds are taught to lay booby-traps along jungle trails so that men may be killed. What kind of life is that? We all want peace, we must have peace!"

This longing for peace, pervading Vietnamese life in all areas and among all factions, seems to the Third Solution advocates to be their strongest ally. Millions of Vietnamese, despite their longing for independence, would accept almost any form of government if it brought them peace. How much more would they support a government that brought them both peace and independence!

"You see," a Saigon University student explained carefully, "when you Americans ask how many Vietnamese support the Buddhists and how many support the Front, you begin with a misunderstanding. There is not that kind of division. At the top, perhaps, yes. Leaders of both groups understand well what their differences are and where their allegiances lie. But as soon as you get down into the population, the sharp line vanishes. The same people support the Front because of its stand for independence and the Buddhists for their insistence on peace. Combine the two, create a government that demonstrates its independence"—he looked at me apologetically and continued, "You understand that I mean independence from the foreigners, the Americans—and its commitment to peace, and no one could oppose it."

So the picture becomes clearer. The war remains basically a guerrilla campaign despite the presence of many North Vietnamese regulars, and guerrillas, as Mao Tse-tung has said, move among the population as the fish swim in a friendly sea. The peasant, though often unenthusiastic about the Vietcong, who tax him and conscript his sons, still identifies the Vietcong as his own people fighting the white foreigner, and the sea, while not completely friendly, is tolerant enough to hide the fish. But let the sea become unfriendly, and the fish find their task more difficult. And, the Third Force people say, the sea would become definitely hostile if the Vietcong tried to overthrow a Vietnamese government that had achieved an end to the war and was negotiating the removal of the Western imperialists.

"But it's more than that, even," another young Vietnamese faculty member explained. "The VC is full of our friends! You must not think in terms of two irreconcilable hostile forces. Of course the Front is directed by Communists, but most of its members and soldiers are like us, Vietnamese, non-Communist nationalists, longing for peace, Buddhists in their upbringing. I do not believe for a moment that the VC would try to continue the war, or take over militarily, if such a government came to power and declared a cease-fire, but if it did it would disintegrate." He mused a moment, then smiled. "Why should they take the risk of alienating the whole population by continuing the killing when they expect to win the political struggle later on anyway. But they won't, you know, if we can produce a government that will really serve the people. And I think we can. I think we can."

If they were in fact able to do so, the consequences could be of importance to the world beyond even its relief from a war that has tortured the Western conscience more than anything in modern history. The Buddhist thought that permeates the theories of the Third Force speaks directly to the tensions and uncertainties that torment the West and its youth—the dehumanization that seems to accompany a successfully industrialized society, the alienation that comes with satisfaction of material needs in a society that goes no deeper into man's nature, the arraying of groups of men against one another in a senseless and suicidal confrontation. So the Buddhists are not content simply to end the war, but seek to end it in a manner that will contribute to the enrichment of society and perhaps will redirect it.

"This soulless technical civilization is murdering mankind," cried a Buddhist spokesman. "What can we do to save this alienated society?" [3]

The answer lies, they believe, in a more "human" view by men of one another, and by the mobilization of man's spiritual resources in resistance to the perpetuation and deepening of divisions created by ideological disagreements. Men will always disagree, but they must recognize their grasp on truth as partial and relative, always conditioned by the knowledge that to transform a search for truth into a defense of a partial truth against the persons of one's fellows is to destroy even the partial truth one has attained. Men must reverence themselves and one another first as men, subordinating all systems and ideologies to that reality, able to draw from each other's insights enrichment of their common understanding. And never must they close off communication and dialogue.

So Thich Nhat Hanh, in a widely though illegally circulated appeal in Vietnam,[4] made dialogue between Vietnamese Com-

[3] Vo Van Ai, *War Resistance and War Reality,* published by the Overseas Vietnamese Buddhist Association (Paris, 1968).

[4] *Dialogue: The Key to Vietnam Peace,* published by the Overseas Vietnamese Buddhist Association (Paris, 1968).

munists and anti-Communists the first priority in achieving peace. Such a dialogue must come about, he wrote, as Vietnamese look at one another first as Vietnamese rather than ideologues.

"Buddhist thought," he argued, "is capable of engaging in dialogues both with systems of thought whose aim is spiritual salvation and with systems of thought whose aim is social revolution. Buddhists, however, categorically reject one thing: a doctrinal, fanatical, intransigent attitude." If Vietnamese can recall their own commitment to such an attitude, then "Vietnam will be able to write an illuminating page in the history of the world", but "the very first step . . . is to liberate the mind from fanaticism and prejudice. This openmindedness is indispensable for the cultivation of love, compassion and tolerance. It is this aspect of Buddhism which puts its followers right in the middle of conflicting power groups and guides them in their duty as mediators."

It is this same aspect of Buddhism that has led monks and students and a soldier to immolate themselves, and induced ordinary householders to place their precious family altars in the streets of Hue to stop the advance of General Ky's tanks. "They offered this naked spirituality to halt the brutal and inhuman advance of soulless technique," declared Vo Van Ai. They did not produce at the same time tracts or blueprints for the new society. They did not profess even to know how the new society should look. Like the young student Phan Thi Mai, they sought only to bring their own suffering to bear in reminding their fellows that solutions could be found only when they stop killing one another and work at it together.

Whether such blueprints and plans exist in systematic form, whether there have been discussions and agreements among the religious and political leadership of the Third Force, is impossible to demonstrate. The mere revelation that such discussions had taken place would make life impossible for their participants, who would have to disappear from sight, as did the identified members of the abortive Alliance of National, Democratic and Peace Forces announced by the NLF after the launching of the Tet offensive early in 1968.

But it is beyond doubt that such discussions have taken place and that plans have been prepared. The evidence of them can be seen in such statements as the program of the Buddhist Socialist Bloc, publicized by exiled Vietnamese in Paris, and in such acts as Thich Tri Quang's call for a "government of national reconciliation," the organization by Tran Ngoc Lieng, vice-presidential candidate on the aborted ticket of Duong Van Minh, of the Progressive National Force (Luc Luong Quog Gia Tieu Bo) committed to the creation of such a government, and the news released by the Overseas Vietnamese Buddhist Association that unnamed parties had formed a "shadow cabinet" in South Vietnam.[5] That individuals identified with such moves, or even suspected of being identified, promptly deny or minimize the reports when they are questioned, reveals only the continuing mortal danger of expressing any sentiments that the Thieu-Ky-Khiem regime considers unfriendly.

But the difficulties of disclosing anything but the vaguest outlines of a political program or organization are not the only reason for an absence of "hard information." The Vietnamese do not want attention distracted from the essential point, which is ending the war, nor do they want to encourage non-Vietnamese to believe that they have any right to debate or decide the political and economic future of Vietnam.

"The most urgent need is for an immediate cease-fire," the Venerable Thich Tri Quang declared in an interview in November, 1968, "so that the massacre and destruction of people and country might end. The negotiations must go on without attachment to rigid and preconceived formulae, for these only reflect ulterior motives and petty pride. . . . The position of the Buddhists is not within any party, particularly those at war. It is not concerned with rivaling any party, but it must live with,

[5] Michael Morrow, "The Neutralists Speak Out," *Dissent,* September–October 1969.

and work for and with the people. The NLF and others speak of peace, too, but only as a tactic. The strategy of warring parties is victory, not peace. The forces for peace lie in the ardent desire of the people for peace."

So the Buddhists and their allies tread a narrow, difficult path, allying themselves with neither side, seeking no one's defeat for its own sake, but rather showing their ability to mobilize the people behind a genuine program for peace. Their pleas have gone to both sides. To Vietnamese fighting one another they have sent messages asking for a cease-fire and discussions among them as Vietnamese, recognizing the common ties that bind them against the ideological disagreements that divide.

Their most urgent and insistent plea, however, continues to be to the United States. The Americans have the initiative; they are the foreigners who have invaded Vietnam, and until they leave it is inconceivable that Vietnamese resistance to their presence will cease. They are much the stronger, too, able to take the steps that will lead to peace without fearing the reality of defeat or any suffering for their own people. As for the American insistence on "peace with honor," the Vietnamese respond as did Thich Nhat Hanh in the United States.

"How can the United States withdraw with honor? What is honor? The honor of the American devotion to democracy is widely known, but if that honor cannot be shown in Vietnam, then honor is not served. Stopping the bombing and shooting of Vietnamese will not harm honor." And they remind the Americans of France's experience in ending the Algerian war by its own withdrawal, "thereby recovering the honor it had lost in fighting it."

How can the United States withdraw? Millions of Americans have come to share the Vietnamese poet's view: It is in the continuation of the war that dishonor lies; honor is not in the form of the withdrawal, or in conditions attached to it, but in the withdrawal itself.

"They ask me how to withdraw," said a speaker. "The answer is simple: in ships." A highly vocal segment of the anti-war movement echoes the statement. Withdraw, unilaterally, unconditionally, immediately. Let the Vietnamese settle their affairs themselves; we have already interfered too much. "There is nothing to negotiate," said another speaker, "except the timetable of withdrawal."

But of course it is not really that simple, and even negotiation on the "timetable of withdrawal" would necessitate a formidable agenda. Is the timetable to be agreed upon by all four parties in the Paris talks, including the Thieu-Ky government? To ask the question is to answer it. Saigon will approve only token withdrawal, since the Thieu-Ky regime cannot survive if withdrawal is complete. So far, the United States has deferred to Saigon, and if some judicious arm-twisting has been applied to President Thieu, still the White House has not protested his assertion that it will be "years and years" before all American troops can be brought home.

Or will withdrawal occur in spite of Saigon, as a result of agreements between the United States on the one hand and Hanoi and the NLF on the other? In that case, one of two things could be expected to happen in South Vietnam. One would be a desperate attempt by the Saigon Government to retain control of the army and continue the war. That would mean battles fought through and around American troops, who are stationed all over the country, frequently in the same camps and bases as the South Vietnamese, over the months that would be required to move out half a million men and their impedimenta. It would be manifestly impossible, even with maximum cooperation from the NLF, for United States forces to avoid involvement in such actions, even perhaps to the point of finding themselves fighting their erstwhile allies!

More likely, the announcement of an American withdrawal would precipitate the immediate collapse of the Saigon Government and the hasty departure of its top officials for more hospitable climes. Then what would happen? The United States has built up an intricate set of relationships in South Vietnam over the last fifteen years, civilian as well as military and paramilitary. Not only guns and munitions are supplied, but also thousands of tons of rice and other foods for millions of people whose own rice paddies have been poisoned or blasted out of production.

The Saigon Government is riddled with corruption, and much of the material sent to sustain the Vietnamese people finds its way into channels designed to enrich the administrators. Not all of it, probably not even most. Some distribution is accomplished, however inadequately, through Saigon's civil service, and the conclusion is unavoidable that this operation would disintegrate along with the Government itself. Would the United States then set up its own interim government to avert total chaos until it had managed to get all of its people out? There are many precedents for temporary military governments being established by victorious armies to function in occupied territories during the slow process of building new indigenous structures to replace the deposed ones, but none by a military government set up by an army that was acknowledging its "mistake" by leaving.

Or would the "timetable negotiations" make arrangements for NLF cadres to move into the Saigon government offices as the Thieu Government moved out? It may be that the NLF could mobilize the necessary talent, and such an arrangement would at least furnish history with another novelty. After having fought the NLF to save South Vietnam from its rule, the United States would now, with no more consultation than before, impose the same organization on the people!

But these are idle speculations because it is inconceivable that any government, let alone the present American one, would venture anything of the sort. "Withdrawal" is a great slogan—short and crisp and explicit enough to fit on signs and bumper strips—but, when qualified only by such words as "unconditional," "immediate," and "unilateral," it is still only a slogan, the assertion of an objective, not a program for achieving it. For such a program, only the Third Solution provides the answer.

That answer hinges on the replacement of the Thieu-Ky Government as the first move in the equation of withdrawal, not the last. A new government, representative of the people, committed to ending the war and then arranging for honest, countrywide elections for a coalition government, would have as one of its earliest tasks the supervision of United States military withdrawal, while assuming simultaneously the responsibility for running the machinery of civilian government, distributing food and supplies, and carrying on the multitude of other tasks that go with the intricate business of ending a war.

It will not be easy to open the way for such a government without hopelessly prejudicing it in the process. To "arrange" it through a convenient coup engineered by the CIA in its inimitable way would be to give it the kiss of death. Any suspicion that a new Third Force government was in fact a creature of Washington, the result of a "deal," would sentence that government to the same hatred and distrust now directed at the Thieu-Ky-Khiem regime. Fundamentally, the United States is called upon to do one thing: *make clear to the Saigon Government and to the people of South Vietnam its unwillingness any longer to prevent the replacement of that Government with one genuinely representative of the popular will.*

How that message is to be communicated and the replacement accomplished are matters that must perforce be left, respectively, to the State Department's experts in communication and to the Vietnamese themselves. Whether the word is sent through diplomatic channels, confidentially, or made public in a speech at an obscure Midwest college is unimportant so long as its meaning is clear. There are a number of handles to be grasped if the will exists to grasp them. President Nixon could express his shock at learning that Saigon was holding prisoner thousands of non-NLF religious and political dissenters and demand that they be freed, or he could take note of the organization of the Progressive National Force last June and express sympathy with its demands for an immediate cease-fire and a "reconciliatory government . . . composed of nationalists acceptable to all sides," or he could say bluntly that United States aid would terminate and troop withdrawals accelerate unless immediate and credible provisions were made for countrywide elections for a new government. (It is barely conceivable, though not likely, that Mr. Nixon is now attempting such communication through hints that he will withdraw as many as 200,000 troops by the end of 1970. The "Vietnamization" of the war, with the South Vietnamese army taking over all combat operations from the Americans, is so transparent a fiction that something else must lie behind these moves. The probability is that the real explanation is a characteristic political attempt to quiet domestic criticism while stalling for time, but it *could* be something more. Similarly, the welcome release on November 1, 1969, of some 300 political prisoners, headed by Thich Thien Minh, cannot be seen as any fundamental shift in Saigon's policy. But it does demonstrate that both Saigon and Washington are sensitive to this exceedingly vulnerable spot in their pretensions to be the defenders of freedom. It is not likely that many people will be so dazzled by the release of 300 that they will forget the scores of thousands who are still in prison —with more arrested weekly. But the degree to which this direction is being opened up to discussion is further suggested by the resolution—S.R. 268—introduced by Senators Thomas F. Eagleton of Missouri and Harold E. Hughes of Iowa, and co-sponsored by several other Senators. The resolution would have the Senate urge that the Government of South Vietnam be required to take four actions "within the next sixty days" or suffer the termination of all American military, political, and economic assistance. Those actions are:

1. Grant liberty and amnesty to all of those held in custody as political prisoners;
2. Lift the censorship of all communications media, foreign and

domestic, including especially those newspapers which have been closed down;

3. Permit political parties the freedom to organize and operate without governmental controls; and

4. Present a plan for a provisional government, broadly representative of the main political, ethnic, and religious groups of South Vietnam, whose principal function will be to maintain government effectively during the transition from war to peace.)

There is no assurance that such a procedure would "work." The fabric of Vietnamese life has been shredded, and it may be that the battered and persecuted nationalists could not, when the chips are down, summon enough political and personal cohesion to create and sustain a government of the sort they seek against the skillful organization the NLF would bring to the contest. In that case the war might go on, though at a decelerating tempo and between Vietnamese, or it might be that South Vietnam would come quickly under a Communist form of government, albeit a highly nationalistic form of communism. Either would be an improvement over the present endless bloodletting, for both the Vietnamese and us.

But the Third Force spokesmen do not think the outlook is so gloomy. Let the United States declare unequivocally its intention to withdraw all its military forces; let it call for a cease-fire or even announce its intention of declaring one unilaterally; and let it make known that it no longer insists on imposing on the South Vietnamese a government they detest.

"Then," said a young university student, "we will soon have the government we want and be on the way to peace."

9

Why Are We in Vietnam?

When I speak around the country about Vietnam, there is usually a question period following the initial presentation. Questions are asked on substantive matters—What happened to the student who was beaten? What is the future for the School of Youth for Social Service? Is there any chance of my working as a volunteer to help the Vietnamese? But no matter how the others go, there is always one haunting theme:

Why are we in Vietnam? If what you say is true, why did we go there and why do we stay? Are you saying that the people we elect to govern us from Washington don't know these things, and if they do, why are we there?

Why does the press not report the facts as you've given them to us? Why do the papers not print the materials you say they have had? Why do the reporters not find out what you say you have found out?

Why are American boys being sent to die or to be maimed for life? Are you trying to say that someone wants it that way? Why? Why? Why?

For the political "radicals" in the audience, the answer is easy. Yes, somebody wants it that way, not out of personal bloodthirstiness or sadism, but because that's how they get or keep their power and wealth. Yes, the people you elect to government know all about it. Vietnam is no accident, but a reflection of basic United States policy, which is imperialistic and exploitative—witness Cuba and the Dominican Republic. And yes, the press knows all about these things, but the press is the lackey of the imperialistic Establishment, obediently emphasizing what the Establishment wants emphasized and suppressing what it wants suppressed, and sharing in the profits for its obedience. And yes, they are not only willing to see more than 40,000 American boys killed in Vietnam, but are quite matter-of-factly preparing other military ventures in defense of their interests in which thousands more Americans will die.

But that answer does not satisfy the others, the majority, in the audiences. Perhaps there is an uneasy recognition that there is an uncomfortable amount of truth underlying the harsh indictment, but their knowledge of America is different from the radicals' knowledge, and their judgment is at once more self-justifying and more compassionate. America is not all that bad. They know it and they say it.

The radicals' answer does not satisfy me, either, though there is truth in every one of their assertions. But a nation is not a monolithic plot, and neither is its governing élite, though the latter may come closer. Nor is a nation's political and economic system the consequence of a handful of decisions in the smoke-filled back rooms of the politicians or the elegant board rooms of large corporations. Systems and attitudes evolve. Each cause is an effect, the Zen Buddhist says, and each effect a cause. The decisions are not made by impersonal computers but by human beings, and human beings are complex combinations of impulses and emotions, and it is not irrelevant that the chairman of the corporate board or the Secretary of Defense is also a husband and father and a man who suffers heartburn after eating and whose eyes fill with tears at the sight of suffering children. Only because all men are bound more closely together by their common attributes than they are separated by their selfishness is there any hope for the survival of the race.

I am not much for the conspiratorial view of history, though the *de facto* conspiracy of common interests does exist and often greatly affects the course of history. But men are much alike, and even if our experience is that men whose natures have somehow been twisted into an overweaning lust for power are those who almost invariably achieve power—a largely unacknowledged factor in the "failure" of Eugene McCarthy —still the way in which they wield the power rests heavily on the way in which their fellow citizens see and support the policies they make and follow. And the men of power themselves also are never the monoliths they sometimes seem, but are the same combination of good and evil, selfishness and altruism, calculation and impulse, as the rest of us.

There is a decency in Americans, a concern for others, that manifests itself in many ways, including the agonizing *Why?* that greets the recital of their country's misdeeds. But it is a decency that has been often corrupted by the country's history, by ignorance, and by the plethora of material possessions that has become a way of life for many of us.

Americans are right in believing that there are some very good things about their society that are worth preserving. The Bill of Rights was a monumental advance in the organization of human society, and the court system that protects and extends the rights included in it, even though slow and far from perfect, was a majestic achievement. But to understand the importance of such achievements requires a grasp of history and an ability to conceptualize and communicate that still is far from universal, and essayists and pollsters have indicated the unlikelihood that the same Bill of Rights could win a majority vote if submitted to plebiscite today.

The remarkable band of men who created the structure of the United States were dealing with a relatively small population, of whom many had had recent experiences with tyranny, and they managed a spectacular synthesis within a relatively short time. Their motives were not unmixed, of course. Some of the Republic's earliest heroes took advantage of their positions to enrich themselves, and they were woefully, blindly inconsistent in not relating their noblest concepts to slavery and the country's black population, but some of them were passionate about the sovereignty of the people, and they established safeguards that still hold and that are enormously precious. But by 1969 the only Americans conscious of direct experience with tyranny were the black and the poor, for whom tyranny was inflicted by their own country; for the rest the vision of equality had been dimmed by the peculiar circumstances of the country that had led to a level of physical comfort and the accumulation of things unmatched in previous history.

The currents have been mixed and clouded. Millions of Americans have seen themselves and their country as specially blessed, not just with the lucky opportunities that came to the settlers of an unexploited continent, but also with a special kind of moral fiber and industriousness that enabled them to take advantage of these opportunities and even, somehow, to have created them. I have met many Americans who, confronted with the poverty of their immediate neighbors in ghetto or slum, or with their world neighbors in the underdeveloped countries of Asia, Africa, and Latin America, still bask in their own achievements even in the process of commiserating with the victims of poverty. Somehow or other those others could have done as well if they had worked as hard or been as intelligent about it as they. The advantages of the inheritance of a continent unimaginably rich in natural resources whose previous owners had lived in harmony with nature instead of bent on its ravishment, the chance of skin color and all the impediments that go with it, the unearned opportunities for education and training, or their undeserved denial, somehow all disappear in the self-satisfaction that comes from having "made it."

Thus many of us have fallen prey to a form of self-righteousness. The poverty of others becomes an affirmation of the superiority of our system and, by extension, of ourselves, who devised it and made it work. And since "their" poverty is their own fault and we are quite willing to extend a limited amount of charity to them, we are perfectly justified in defending our giant grasp on the world's goods—60 per cent of the world's wealth owned by 6 per cent of the world's people. As Lyndon Johnson put it with the spare and unmistakable succinctness of which he was capable: "Don't forget there are only 200 million of us in a world of three billion. They want what we've got and we're not going to give it to them." [1]

Only in the historically minute period of the last five years have most Americans been aware of any serious challenge to this self-image, and it has been a traumatic experience. Historically and psychologically it is nothing novel for the values of a society to be challenged by its most affluent and educated citizens. What has made it so devastating is that there are so many of these affluent and educated, that they are our own children in many cases, and that we are at the mercy of a machinery of communication that brings it all into our living rooms every night. So there has come not only an awareness that there are problems, but a realization that the problems are many and mammoth, and that their dimensions bring into question some of the most cherished values the society has held.

A generation still conscious of the stringent circumstances of a society gripped by depression has discovered that the acquisition of goods and economic security is not an unmitigated blessing. Suburban families with two cars, two television sets, and a boat on a nearby lake have also a psychiatrist on their payroll and a horrifying generation gap dividing parents from the children on whom they have lavished their best efforts and much of their money.

A nation that has spent more money buying military weapons than the rest of the world earns discovers that it has not bought strength but insecurity, that it is more fearful now,

[1] Speech to troops at Camp Stanley, Korea. Quoted in *Ramparts*, November 20, 1966.

ringed with missiles and their nuclear warheads and stockpiled with ingenious poisons and disease germs, than it ever was before. And that, with all its strength, it cannot win a war against a small, industrially primitive country with one-tenth its population.

At the same time, Americans are slowly hearing the worried tones of the ecologists telling them that the very prosperity that they enjoy and the means of getting it have ravished our environment and threaten our survival. Cars and planes and trucks and ships and factories have poured pollutants into the air and water in quantities that are nearing the saturation point. Natural resources of metals, fossil fuels, and other basics of the industrialized world, accumulated over millennia and necessary to unnumbered future generations, are being exhausted at an impossible rate, while the very best expressions of our altruism in the wiping out of many forms of disease around the world, unaccompanied by provisions for birth control and food rationing, have resulted in a mushrooming population that already presses hard against available food supplies.

And with all this comes the slow realization that the United States, so long the beacon of liberty and the heady example for revolutionaries everywhere, is the focus of a worldwide hatred and contempt that paralyzes the imagination. Alienation within, hatred without—no generation of people in the history of man has had to face so profound a convulsion of values and beliefs as has this one in this country.

None of this is irrelevant to Vietnam, or to the troubled *Why?* that it elicits from troubled audiences. Indeed, Vietnam is the flaring technicolored incarnation of our problems in microcosm, the most dramatic possible demonstration of the typical misunderstanding of what those problems are and of the inability of old attitudes and techniques to deal with them.

Here in Vietnam is a war whose primary motive force is a nation fighting off the last vestiges of nineteenth-century colonialism, with the villainous colonialists represented by the historically anticolonialist United States, so bemused by its half-century obsession with the horrors of communism as to be unaware of what it is doing! The radicals are right when they say that Vietnam will be only the first of many such wars unless the United States comes quickly to a form of political maturity it has not yet displayed. Old-style colonialism has been supplanted by new-style economic imperialism, but the *dramatis personnae* are much the same in the heartland of the empire and the colony itself, and the resistance to it will be just as determined and fanatic as it has been in Vietnam. Already the United States has intervened with its military power or its manipulating, bribing, assassinating CIA in Cuba, Guatemala, Bolivia, and the Dominican Republic in behalf of the Latin-American oligarchies who are the obliging tools of its corporate empire. In every case the villain has been called aggressive communism; as in Vietnam, the tactic can only become a self-fulfilling prophecy. When both the Communists and the United States maintain that it is the Communists who stand behind every nationalist revolt, it is hard for even the most skeptical non-Communist nationalist to maintain his skepticism.

The necessary changes in view and response are not likely to come from the top down, except on the verbal level. We have made much in Vietnam of the need to "win the hearts and minds of the people," but it has not perceptibly altered a policy totally oriented to the military suppression of nationalist aspirations, whether through war against the NLF or support and financing of an antifreedom government in Saigon. So, too, there may be many pious expressions in Washington of righteous appreciation of the difficulties and aspirations of the third world that will be no more than camouflage for the continuation of a policy in support of the vested interests of the wealthy. Only when popular understanding of issues compels it will there be major changes in the attitudes of the nation.

But Vietnam is also the cockpit of struggle between two ideological competitors—communism on the one hand and capitalism-free, enterprise-welfare statism on the other—and that struggle also dominates the world scene and is likely to continue to do so. The two competitors, nominally poles apart in their conceptions of the organization of society, in fact share a commitment to the right to use violence to impose their wills on other people and continue the ravishment of nature for the productivity of the present.

In these the similarities of the two struggling giants are of far greater significance than their differences. The continued use of violence of a military nature in the age of nuclear weapons will bring about the annihilation of capitalist, communist, and nationalist alike, along with the hundreds of millions of human beings who identify consciously with none of them. Violence is synonymous with reaction in our day; only nonviolence can be considered a radical departure from the suicidal old ways, and even then only if it is in the context of a new universalism and not simply a substitute of one tactic of conflict for another.

Meanwhile, the continued rape of the planet in the name of production, resulting in an atmosphere polluted equally by capitalist and socialist factory chimneys and jet planes, is the very basis of the competition between the two systems. Both, in this suddenly altered world, are threats to human survival, enemies of the race.

In Vietnam, obscured by the smoke of battle between colonialist and anticolonialist, Communist and anti-Communist, there is a mode of thought and action that might—just might—rescue us from this rut of conventional thinking and point us in the direction of safety and survival. It is what characterizes the most eloquent spokesmen of the Third Force, and it is more important even than their proposals for ending the war. It is a system of thought still permeated by the teachings of Buddhism, in Vietnam and some other Asian countries, not yet seduced by the blandishments of Western culture and wealth. It has nothing much to do with popular Western myths about Buddhism—begging, meditating monks teaching reincarnation—but it has a great deal to do with the Buddhist view of life as a continuum and of all beings as part of one indefinable whole, and with the Buddhist commitment to tolerance and compassion toward all men.

"Beware!" writes the Vietnamese poet.

> Turn around to face your real enemies—
> Ambition, violence, hatred, greed.
> Men cannot be our enemies—even men called the Vietcong!
> If we kill men, what brothers will we have left?
> With whom then shall we live? [2]

Man's history has been a record of the struggle of two conflicting views of himself and his fellows. One has seen life as competitive, each man for himself. The other has seen men as units in a family, deeply estranged from one another but capable of realizing their potential only as they recognize their relationship and turn to modes of life designed for mutual help and cooperation.

The first, which leads inexorably to violence and war, has dominated the events of human history; the second has shaped man's religions, his poetry, and his art, and occasionally has broken through into the world of events. One such breakthrough was the Gandhian movement in India, when the astute lawyer-turned-mahatma mobilized the "soul force" in his people to win freedom from the British raj without violence. Another occurred in the United States in the nineteen-fifties when Martin Luther King mobilized the soul force in *his* people to win significant advances in civil rights and, more important, to give black Americans themselves a new and necessary sense of their dignity and worth. The third of our century, and potentially the most significant, is what Nhat Hanh has described as "the nonviolent struggle for peace in Vietnam." [3]

[2] Thich Nhat Hanh, from *Condemnation* (New York: Unicorn Press, 1967).

[3] That is the title of his essay published by the Overseas Vietnamese Buddhist Association, available in the United States from the Fellowship of Reconciliation, Nyack, New York.

It is potentially the most significant because of the circumstances in which it has taken shape. The nonviolent struggle in India was a product of Gandhi's genius of leadership. It spoke to a strain in Indian history and character that was congenial to nonviolence, but it achieved its support from a people united against the ruling colonialists and who had no other means of struggling for independence. The civil rights movement in the United States was also a rising of the weak against the strong, though in a quite different context, and if there was a strong strain of nonviolence in Negro life, so was there an articulate segment which described that strain as a manifestation of subservience to "the man."

In Vietnam the concept of Satyagraha is not isolated from the ethos of the people. It is not a tactic so much as the tactical expression of a view of life. Its practitioners do not lack for a violent alternative; all the weapons they need are available for the asking if they simply enlist in the NLF forces also struggling for independence. That they have not so enlisted represents their understanding that violence represents the grip of fanaticism and intolerance on men and that Satyagraha, as Gandhi said, is not only "a better and more expeditious way of righting wrongs" than other forms of politics, but that it seeks to cure men of the "righteous and fanatic moralism" that is the principal source of irrational violence.[4]

"True help," the Supreme Patriarch of the Unified Buddhist Church declared as his country staggered with suffering, "does not consist in using help to bypass those who receive help and compel them to do our bidding. Liberation does not mean using rifles to kill those who do not share the same ideology. Liberation in modern times cannot tolerate violence, even for the sake of emancipating human beings and nations. Because, as long as violence is used, it will be challenged by violence . . ."[5]

[4] Erik Erikson, *Gandhi's Truth* (New York: W. W. Norton, 1969).
[5] "Peace for Vietnam," a communication by the Venerable Thich Tinh Khiet, to the Unified Buddhist Church, Saigon, February, 1969.

What would a society run by such people look like? An economist in Britain, E. F. Schumacher, taken with the notion of a "Buddhist economics," outlined the ways in which it would differ from the classic economics of the West, and how the differences would be relevant to the massive problems of our times.

It would look to a simpler life, unquestionably, since "simplicity and nonviolence are obviously closely related." Since the earth's physical resources are far too limited to permit of a universal rate of consumption on the level reached by Western societies, "people satisfying their needs by means of a modest use of resources are obviously less likely to be at each other's throats than people dependent on a high rate of use."

At the same time, Buddhism is a "middle way," not an exercise in asceticism, so it would move to the use of modern technology effectively applied for men's good rather than to an unrealistic suppression of technology. Work, in the same way, would be seen neither as an impersonal commodity to be directed and exploited by managers nor as an unmitigated evil to be avoided at all costs. Work, conducted in conditions of freedom and dignity, fulfills man's needs as truly as do eating and sleeping, and contributes to the formation of character. "Since the Buddhist sees the essence of civilization not in a multiplication of wants but in the purification of human character," Schumacher writes, it is apparent that an economics shaped by Buddhist thought would be very different from that of Western materialism. Technology's objective would be the elimination of the unrewarding and uncreative toil of life, in order to free men to apply themselves to the artistic and creative work of their own choice.

A Buddhist economics would make a distinction between renewable and nonrenewable materials in a way that modern economics, evaluating everything in terms of a money price, does not do. "The Buddhist economist would insist that a population basing its economic life on nonrenewable fuels (coal and oil) is living parasitically, on capital instead of income. Such a way of life could have no permanence, and could therefore be justified only as a purely temporary expedient." And since the "nonrenewable" resources, including fossil fuels, are unevenly distributed throughout the world, a continued dependence on them for a standard of living leads inevitably to violent competition for their possession.[6]

It will be hard for Americans, products of a society that has made the constant multiplication of human wants to be the irrational motive power of its whole economy, to see such a movement toward simplicity and sharing as anything but unreal and utopian. Yet the finger writing on the wall becomes daily more visible, and the irrationality of our own society less tolerable, and perhaps we should remove ourselves from the path of a nation that just might produce some experiments in political and economic organization that would save us all.

In Vietnam the Third Force represents the potential for such experiments, even beyond its immediate potential for ending the war. Its appeal is more universal than we think, and more helpful. It is the appeal for a human life, in which men seek each other out for their mutual enrichment, and for a rejection of the violence that rejects them. Thousands of miles from Saigon, in late November, 1968, some 65,000 Czechoslovak students stayed in their dormitories for seventy-two hours in a nonviolent "strike" protesting the Soviet invasion of their country. Outside the Comenius Theological Faculty in Prague, the strike posters included this proclamation:

> *Nonviolent resistance against injustice and despotism is the only way of carrying forward the truth.*
> *The use of violence is madness.*
> *Returning evil for evil leads to hatred and war which employs any and every means of vanquishing the adversary.*
> *The issue is not the conquest-of-the-adversary "victory."*

[6] E. F. Schumacher, "Buddhist Economics," published in *Resurgence,* London, January–February, 1968. Reprinted by *Manas,* August 13, 1969.

The issue is the victory of solid truth binding the black as the white, the good as the wicked, the conservative as the liberal, the student as the Secretary of the Central Committee of the Communist Party of Czechoslovakia.[7]

In Prague the students who think that way are suppressed by Soviet troops. In Saigon they are suppressed by American hirelings. It is time we got off their backs.

[7] Milton Mayer, "The Art of the Impossible," A Center Occasional Paper, published by the Center for the Study of Democratic Institutions, April, 1969.

APPENDICES

i

"In the Name of God, Stop It!"

A full-page advertisement in *The New York Times* of Sunday, April 4, 1965, under the auspices of the Clergymen's Emergency Committee on Vietnam, created by the Fellowship of Reconciliation. Initiators were Methodist Bishop John Wesley Lord; Dr. Dana McLean Greeley, president of the Unitarian-Universalist Association; Dr. Edwin T. Dahlberg, former president of the National Council of Churches and the American Baptist Convention; Dr. Isidor B. Hoffman, chaplain to Jewish students at Columbia University; Dr. Henry J. Cadbury, Biblical scholar and former chairman of the American Friends Service Committee, and the Rev. Peter Riga, moderator of the Catholic Council on Civil Liberties. More than 3,000 other clergymen of all faiths endorsed the statement, which led to the trip to Vietnam of twelve religious leaders, including Drs. Dahlberg and Greeley, a few months later.

2700 Ministers, Priests and Rabbis Say:
MR. PRESIDENT:

In the Name of God, STOP IT!

We are aware of the awesome responsibilities you carry; we can imagine the difficulties of making important decisions in the face of conflicting advice from many sources; nor do we doubt your devotion to this nation or to the great goal of peace among all nations. Yet in offering our concerns over American involvement in Vietnam we must be as blunt as honesty requires us to be.

Mr. President, every one of us is deeply, personally dismayed by the role the United States is playing in Vietnam.

It is not a light thing for an American to say that he is dismayed by his country's actions. We do not say it lightly, but soberly and in deep distress. Our government's actions in Vietnam have been and continue to be unworthy either of the high standards of our common religious faith, or of the lofty aspirations on which this country was founded.

Now the United States has begun the process of extending the war beyond the borders of South Vietnam, with all the attendant dangers of precipitating a far greater conflict, perhaps even on a global and nuclear scale.

Mr. President, we plead with you to reverse this course. Let us admit our mistakes and work for an immediate cease-fire. Let us call a conference of all the nations involved, including China, not alone to conclude peace but to launch at once a major and cooperative effort to heal and rebuild that wounded land.

Let us declare our intention to withdraw our troops, calling on other states to do the same, thereby allowing the Vietnamese the right of self-determination. We cannot dictate their course, and we may well regret it, but the risk is to be preferred over the certainty that the moral bankruptcy of our present policy is setting the stage for the ultimate victory of totalitarian forces, and even of thermonuclear war.

The prophets and teachers of our Judeo-Christian faith admonished the people of their day, and of all times, to go beyond the old restraints by which injuries might be exactly recompensed, and instead to deal with their enemies with love and good deeds. Yet in Vietnam this nation, so-proudly self-described as "under God," is not content even with "eye for an eye" retaliation, but returns evil for evil on a multiplying scale.

No nation has ever saved either its life or its soul by such methods, and ours will not be an exception. As men and women who have committed their lives to the attempt to explain and interpret the will of God, we have no alternative but to assert on every occasion and in every way open to us our conviction that these methods are not God's methods, but will bring the judgment of God upon our nation.

Mr. President, we plead with you with the utmost urgency to turn our nation's course, before it is too late, from cruelty to compassion, from destruction to healing, from retaliation to reconcilation, from war to peace.

ii

"They Are Our Brothers Whom We Kill!"

The statement that inaugurated the International Committee of Conscience. Invited by key members of the Clergymen's Emergency Committee to join them in signing it, more than 10,000 religious leaders of all faiths, from forty countries including Communist ones, put their names to this appeal to both sides to end the war. It appeared first as a two-page advertisement in *The New York Times* January 23, 1966, and was subsequently reprinted in many publications and languages.

They Are Our Brothers Whom We Kill!

No generation has had shown to it more clearly than ours the interdependence of all men. No matter what the reasons we advance for the killing we do—in Vietnam or elsewhere—they are our brothers whom we kill. More indeed than our brothers—they are ourselves and our children, for as surely as we do not find other ways than war for solving our human problems, we destroy the future for ourselves and for them.

We who sign this statement are impelled to speak by the tragedy of Vietnam, and by the failure of governments to end that terrible conflict. Yet we think not only of Vietnam, but of all our apprehensive world, torn by contending ideologies and ambitions, of which Vietnam is the present symbol. We, who in various ways have assumed the terrible responsibility of articulating the human conscience, must speak or, literally, we should expect the very stones to cry out.

We know the claims of both sides in the Vietnamese conflict. Each professes its own moral rectitude. The United States and its allies assert their determination to stop what they describe as "ruthless Communist aggression" in order to defend freedom, both for Vietnam and for the world. North Vietnam, the National Liberation Front of South Vietnam, and the People's Republic of China vigorously proclaim their intention to throw back the "ruthlessly aggressive American imperialists" in defense of the right of the Vietnamese to govern themselves, and on behalf of all those nations that are seeking "national liberation." Each side rejects with scorn the claims of the other, and ridicules the possibility that its antagonist may be sincere.

We do not question the sincerity of either side. On the contrary, the passionate conviction that each has of its own absolute rightness profoundly alarms us. Their determination seems to have no terminal point; to prove its case, each seems willing to risk the ultimate nuclear conflict and jeopardize the future of the human race.

Helpless villagers in Vietnam, unable either to escape or defend themselves, recoil from the bombing of one side and from the terror of the other. War has become a way of life for them, dominating their rice paddies and market places, conscripting their young men, making widows of their women and orphans of their children, holding a whole population hostage to horror. In such circumstances, the claims of both sides become a mockery of the noble words they use. Freedom and justice are for men; they are not achieved by the tormenting of men.

We address ourselves to the rulers of nations,
and to those associated with them:
Lyndon B. Johnson—Ho Chi Minh—Nguyen Cao Ky
Mao Tse-Tung

Continuation of the war will not prove which side is right and which wrong. It will only increasingly force both sides to commit such atrocities as will mock all their claims. It will draw both sides farther and farther into a maelstrom of destruction in which mankind as a whole may finally be engulfed.

You—each of you—has the opportunity at least to try to reverse this dreadful course, and each of you has the responsibility. We plead with you to accept it—now—today—in the interest of all humanity.

We address ourselves to our fellow
human beings everywhere.

Each of our nations has its hopes and aspirations, its own history and grievances and resentments. We live in widely differing social systems and ideologies which seem to have in common only one thing: a willingness to resort to war in their own interests.

But war cannot serve the interests of men any longer, if it ever could. In this age, no matter for what ends war is fought, it can only destroy all our hopes and all our accomplishments. We must find new, non-military ways of dealing with the conflicts and misunderstandings that inevitably arise among us, and to secure justice for all men.

We recognize and respect the necessary functions of government. We are not disloyal; we honor the accomplishments and particular values of our respective societies. But governments have as their proper responsibility the safety and well-being of their citizens, and in our world that well-being cannot be achieved through the military confrontation of competing states.

It is your responsibility and ours to make this known, unmistakably and in every way open to us. To this end, we who sign this statement have committed ourselves as a beginning. We represent many religious faiths in many countries, but we are of a common mind in our plea to all the contending parties.

To the People and Government
of the United States of America:

The horrors that your planes and massive firepower are inflicting on the people of Vietnam are beyond any moral or political justification. The destruction of whole villages and the murder of masses of non-combatants which are the consequences of your policies cannot be excused on any grounds whatever. We believe that there is wrong on both sides, but that, as the only one of the world's major powers directly involved, you bear the heaviest responsibility for the initiation of peace moves. We call on you:

—to stop the air attacks in both North and South Vietnam at once, unilaterally, not simply as a political move in the direction of negotiations, but because those attacks are an affront to human decency and unworthy of a great people;

—to express a clear intention to withdraw all U.S. military

forces from Vietnam, consistent with the 1954 Geneva Agreements, to take effect immediately on conclusion of satisfactory arrangements to assure the Vietnamese people a free choice of government;

—to state unequivocally your readiness to negotiate an end of the war on the basis of the 1954 Agreements, with the National Liberation Front as one of the principals in the negotiations.

To the People and Government of North Vietnam,
and to the National Liberation Front of South Vietnam:

The opposition to your cause is not motivated solely by what you call the "aggressive imperialism" of the United States. Honest, brave Vietnamese patriots who fought beside you in the Viet Minh against the French are among those who fight against you now. They distrust your intentions; they cherish certain rights and freedoms which they suspect you of wanting to destroy; they are shocked and repelled by some of the methods you use. We believe that a heavy responsibility for ending the war honorably rests with the United States, but that there is also a very heavy responsibility on you to create the conditions of peace. We call on you:

—to abandon the methods of torture, assassination, the indiscriminate bombing of civilians and other forms of terror. They are an affront to the whole concept of human decency, and hopelessly degrade your cause. No consideration whatever of either justice or vengeance can excuse such tactics;

—to issue a clear statement that any Vietnamese government in which you may have a part will honor the right of its citizens to practice their religions in absolute freedom, and that there will be no reprisal against those who have fought against you;

—to express your unqualified willingness to meet with representatives of the United States and the present South Vietnamese government to negotiate peace and the future of your country, based on the 1954 Agreements.

To the People and Government of
the People's Republic of China:

Your influence in Southeast Asia is enormous, your words and actions are weighted throughout the world as portents of the future. We call on you:

—to refrain from statements and actions that harden already bitter attitudes on both sides, and so perpetuate the war;

—to make clear your willingness to see the countries of Southeast Asia develop their institutions of government and society free from outside intervention by force, and free from the military presence of any foreign powers.

It is hard to imagine a world so torn by suspicion and hatred as is ours turning away from war and toward the resolution of conflict and the building of justice by non-violent means, yet we humans have no other choice, and in our great religious heritage we have the guidelines we need to make this difficult decision. We call on all those, of whatever faith and nationality, who share our concern, to join us in our efforts to build a truly human society on earth.

An Appeal to
American Students

Signed by fifty-nine student leaders and eleven professors from South Vietnam's five universities, this appeal for help took the place of the intention of twenty of the students to take their own lives to protest the continuation of the war. After the complete failure of American students or press to respond, it was published as part of an advertisement in *The New York Times* on April 9, 1967. A few weeks later Phan Thi Mai, a 20-year old student who had signed the statement, burned herself to death on the steps of a Cholon pagoda.

Dear Fellow Students,

We are students and professors from all the universities of South Vietnam (Saigon, Hue, Dalat, Can Tho and Van Hanh), who write to thank you for your action in trying to stop this terrible war in our country. We cannot act officially, as you did, because the universities here are not permitted by the Government to express themselves freely. We have made petitions and appeals, but we cannot let our names be made public, because we would be arrested and imprisoned. That is the kind of society we live in here today.

Nevertheless, we write to thank you for your actions and to plead with you to continue. We ask you to consider these facts:

1. In South Vietnam cities the American power has become so great in support of the Ky government that no one can speak against the war without risking his life or his liberty.

2. If it were not so, millions would speak out. The people of South Vietnam desperately want the war to end, but they are losing hope. They are not Communists, but if the war does not soon end, they will join the National Liberation Front because they see no other way out.

3. Americans should not believe that they are protecting the South Vietnamese against communism. Most of us believe that the United States only wants to control our country in order to prepare for war with China.

4. The present government of South Vietnam is not our government and is not representing our people. It was imposed on us by the United States, and is controlled by military men who fought for the French against the Vietnamese before 1954. If we were free to vote freely, that government would not last one day. We want a government of our own, not controlled by either side, so that we may be able to settle the problems of Vietnam by ourselves on the basis of national brotherhood: to negotiate peace with the National Liberation Front and North Vietnam, and negotiate the withdrawal of American troops with the United States.

5. Do not believe that the danger of a Communist takeover justifies continuation of the war. We believe we are strong enough to form an independent government. The decision, however, should be ours, not yours, when it is our lives and our country that are being destroyed.

6. We endorse the proposals outlined in the book written by our friend THICH NHAT HANH, *Vietnam: Lotus In A Sea of Fire,* and ask your help in realizing them.

Finally, we send you the best wishes of ours and also of the Vietnamese people.

Done in Saigon, the 20th of February, 1967

Signed by:

Cao Ngoc phuong

Pham hiu Tai

sinh vien chinh tri
Vien Dai Hoc Dalat

giang vien
Dai Hoc Khoa Hor
Vien Dai Hoc Saigon
Vien Dai Hoc Hue

iv

The Poems of Phan Thi Mai

Early in the morning of May 16, 1967, a number of young Vietnamese met at the steps of the Tu Nghiem Pagoda in Cholon, the Chinese section of Saigon. They had all received notes from one of their friends, Phan Thi Mai, a 20-year old student, asking them to meet her there. They found her in the lotus position before statues of the Virgin Mary and the (Mother) Bodhisattva Kwan Yin. Before they could interfere, she had poured a basin of gasoline over herself and ignited it. She remained in the same position until death, when her body slowly toppled over. An estimated total of fifty thousand people took part in her funeral procession, which thereby became a peace march. Phan Thi Mai left behind her these and other expressions of her longing for peace.

Letter of the Heart

My fellowmen, listen to me
Because I love my people
Because I love my country
I want to be a light
even a dim one
in this dark night
in order to prove
the presence of 'man'

I wish to use my body as a torch
to dissipate the darkness
to waken Love among men
and to bring Peace to Viet Nam

she hung this poem in front of her during
the ceremony of sacrifice.

The Last Words of One Who Loves Vietnam

O Vietnam, Vietnam
Please listen
to the last words
of one
who loves Vietnam!

I am on the side
of my forefathers
of Revolution
of the young generation
of all those who suffer:
orphans, widows,
the injured,
the exiled.

I am for the fatherland:
I cry because of the shedding of blood
of both innocents and wicked.

O Vietnam, Vietnam
why this hatred among men?
why this killing of one another?
who will be the defeated?
who will be the winner?

O please remove all labels!
we all are vietnamese
we all are vietnamese

let us take each others' hand
to protect the fatherland.

O Vietnam, Vietnam!

the one who burns herself for Peace.
Phan Thi Mai, May 1967

To My Fellow Countrymen

I do not know how to address my countrymen,

I do not know how to make the suffering of my people known—my people have been victims of ambition and hatred—for more than 20 years!

I do not know how to help my countrymen remember that they are of the same origin, that they will share the same future, so that they may accept each other and stop the killing.

I do not know how to help enemies to become friends regardless of race, religion, political affiliation, so that love and wisdom may come to them, so that they will stop all massacre, all fanaticism and injustice.

I do not know how!

In order for my love to all and my aspiration for Peace will not be misunderstood or deliberately distorted,

I AM BURNING MYSELF

asserting that my sacrifice is for *Peace in Vietnam* and for *Love and Justice*.

I am doing what Thich Quang Duc and N. Morrison [1] have done.

I pray that the flame that is consuming my body will burn away all ambition and hatred which have been pushing many of us into the Hell of the Soul and creating so much sufferings among human beings.

I pray that the human race will be able to inherit Buddha's Compassion, Jesus' Love and the legacy of man's humaneness.

Homage to the Compassionate Buddha, and
to the Spirit of the Nation.
Phan Thi Mai

[1] Norman R. Morrison, a 32-year-old American Quaker, burned himself to death at an entrance to the Pentagon on November 2, 1965.

A Letter Addressed to the Governments
of the North and of the South—May 1967

Gentlemen,

Being a Vietnamese citizen, I share the responsibility towards the history of the nation and towards the people of our country.

I believe I do have the right to express my ideas and aspirations concerning my own country. But you have not allowed me to say anything, even in this 'free' part of the fatherland. This is why I have to die in order that my desperate voice be heard, my voice and that of the peasants who have no power and no means to make known their unjust sufferings!

Please let my last words to be heard everywhere. Let the people speak their mind. Listen to them in order to act for them as you have often declared. Be courageous to listen to the voice of the people even if what this voice has to say is not fitted to your ideas.

We poor peasants, we don't need ideologies, we don't need labels, we only want to live peacefully and with dignity. But in the present situation, under your rule, we are living under opposite conditions.

You have been taking modern foreign weapons or asking hundreds of thousands of foreigners to come to kill our people in the name of your empty words. One side is motivated by ambition, the other side by hatred. You are shouting from your comfortable palaces without being aware of our sufferings.

Are you aware of the fact that much injustices and corruptions have been created? That our society has been miserably degenerated because of your reliance on foreign aid?

Please be lucid to find a way out for Vietnam.

Please negotiate peace.

Please solve the problem by ourselves.

Please remove all labels in order to cooperate with each other.

Millions of Vietnamese are waiting for Justice and Compassion from your part. History waits for good actions of yours.

                              Respectfully,
                              the one who burns herself for peace,
                              Phan Thi Mai

A Letter to the U. S. Government
Through President Johnson

May 1967

I am only an ordinary Vietnamese woman, without any talent or ability. But I feel painful everytime I look at the situation of my country.

I want to say that the empty words you have been using, 'to defend Freedom and Happiness for Vietnam', have lost all their meaning and become ridiculous.

How many tons of dollars and bombs have been dropped on our people to destroy both their souls and bodies?

How many patriotic Vietnamese have been suppressed and liquidated by your policy?

How many courageous, humanitarian and enlightened Americans who dared to point out to you your mistakes, have been condemned and imprisoned?

All this is neither freedom nor happiness.

Do you realize that most of us Vietnamese feel in the bottom of our heart this hatred towards those Americans who have brought the sufferings of the war to our country?

The more you escalate the war, the more you intensify your efforts here, the greater defeat you will get. Because of your mistakes, you are now without a right cause. Please re-read the Vietnamese history.

I feel painful everytime I think of the sufferings of my people, and I also feel sorry for the fate of American soldiers and their family. They have too been pushed into this absurd and ugly war! People have been using beautiful words to intoxicate them!

What kind of honor will the U.S. get from a 'victory' over a tiny country like Vietnam and perhaps more than 20 years from now?

What kind of dishonor will the U.S. have to encounter if she realizes that being a big power she only wants to stop something she has done wrong?

In the hope to save the lives of millions of Vietnamese, I am appealing to the Americans and to the powerful U.S:

1/ to stop the bombing over North and South Vietnam.

2/ to gradually withdraw their troops, and let the Vietnamese to decide what regime they are going to adapt.

3/ to let the U.N. sponsor free elections in Vietnam. The Vietnamese will be wise enough to make their own choice in order to get freedom and happiness.

4/ to help the Vietnamese rebuild their country which has been destroyed by your bombs. Vietnam consents to be a small brother of the powerful U.S.

The history of Vietnam of the U.S. and of the world will record your civilized and humanist acts.

Respectfully,

the one who burns herself to oppose War

Phan Thi Mai

V

Appeal of the Professors

Sixty-five Saigon University professors released the following statement on January 16, 1968. They were called in to the Ministry of Education, and those who refused to sign a retraction were arrested.

Considering the critical situation that may be decisive for the future of the country, we, a number of university teachers, feel we have the responsibility to make public the following statement:

1)—The present conflict is seriously endangering the very existence of the Vietnamese people from both material and moral standpoints. Therefore every Vietnamese has the duty to contribute to the finding of a suitable way out for his fatherland. As educators we are all the more convinced of this obligation because there is nothing more harmful to education than violence, destruction, killing, deprivation and corruption bred by war.

2)—In view of the horror of an ever-expanding war as well as the nascent hope for an ever-elusive peace we cannot but appeal to all Vietnamese who have the responsibilities of this land not to forfeit this precious opportunity, because opportunity is quite rare in history, to sit together, to recognize one another as Vietnamese in order to find a formula for peace based on the supreme interest of the nation.

3)—The complex differences between the official positions require subtle solutions that can only be reached after long deliberations and drawn-out negotiations.

In order to create a suitable atmosphere for such an open-hearted discussion between the belligerent parties and above all to save thousands of people from death and suffering while a peaceful settlement is being sought, we APPEAL TO ALL THE BELLIGERENT PARTIES TO EXTEND INDEFINITELY THE TET CEASE FIRE AND TO NEGOTIATE IMMEDIATELY A PEACEFUL SETTLEMENT.

Saigon, Jan. 16, 1968

vi

Plea from a Draft Center

The draft is often used by the South Vietnamese Government to punish students involved in peace protests, since it is regarded as less likely to arouse public opinion than would imprisoning them. Drafted students can expect to be sent to the areas of heaviest combat immediately. This plea, dated November 21, 1967, came from seventeen of South Vietnam's student leaders whose protests against the September, 1967, elections had been met by their arrest and drafting.

AN APPEAL TO THE STUDENTS OF AMERICA
AND THE WEST
from the
INTERUNIVERSITY STUDENT COMMITTEE
STRUGGLING FOR DEMOCRACY
of
South Vietnam

We appeal to you from the Lam Son draft center, in Nha Trang, where we have been fasting since our arrest more than a week ago. We are seventeen student leaders of South Vietnam's universities, who were arrested and ordered to be drafted into the South Vietnamese army because of our activities in demonstrating against the undemocratic and unrepresentative elections of September and October.

We know how much some of you have struggled to ease the sufferings of our country, and we thank you for your efforts. Yet the disaster continues and can only be ended when we of South Vietnam are free to choose a government that will genuinely represent our aspirations. To deny us the right to such a government, as the present Saigon government has done with the help of the United States, is to deny democracy.

We appeal to you for your support in our efforts, for your intervention on our behalf, and for your continued solidarity with our efforts for the well-being of our tormented country.

(signed) HO HUU NHUT
Chairman, Student Council,
Saigon University
For the Committee.

vii

Buddhist Socialist Policy Statement

The Buddhist Socialist Bloc is a coalition consisting of Vietnamese Buddhist groups, non-Buddhist religious groups, and secular groups—which are willing to accept the guidance of the Buddhist Church in the seeking of a means for the preservation and reconstruction of the fatherland. The Buddhist Socialist Bloc is a reflection of engaged Buddhism, a historically precedented expression of Buddhism which does not restrict itself to the sacred aspects of religious activity but which encompasses and guides the daily actions of earthly living. The position which the Buddhist Socialist Bloc takes on matters of major contemporary importance in Vietnam is outlined on the following pages.

Policy for the Ending of the War and for Reunification

The Buddhist Socialist Bloc began its struggle against the policies of war and of foreign dependency, policies instituted by dictatorial and militarist circles in 1964. The aim of the Bloc is the establishment of an interim civilian government which will enjoy the support of the non-communist, non-NLF political groups, and of the religious groups, with a view toward preparing for the election of a government strong enough to negotiate: (1) with the Front for the ending of the hostilities; (2) with the government in Washington for the withdrawal of foreign troops; and (3) with Hanoi for the withdrawal of the North Vietnamese troops. The withdrawal of the U.S. and North Vietnamese troops would be effected under the supervision and control of the International Control Commission, in the true spirit of the 1954 Geneva agreements.

Our policy, and we believe that in essence it would be the policy of any honestly elected government, will be: (1) to ask the U.S. to stop all bombing and military operations; (2) to order the South Vietnamese army to observe a cease fire and to adopt a defensive position adequate for protecting the people; and (3) to call on the NLF to stop the fighting and to arrange for peace. The basic negotiations should be carried out between the civilian government and the leadership of the Front, that is to say, between Vietnamese only. The objective of these negotiations will be the re-establishment of peace and the formation of a coalition government, a truly neutralist government for a truly neutralist South Vietnam.

Every effort will be made to put an end to all intervention and political influence by the two blocs in the internal affairs of the country. Although the Buddhist Socialist Bloc aims ultimately at seeing a unified and neutralist Vietnam, the neutralist South must first build up its own strength and only when it feels strong enough will it reunify politically with the North. During the interval, the government will establish economic and cultural relations with the North.

Policy of Unity

The Buddhist Socialist Bloc works initially for unified action on the part of all religious communities in Vietnam. With the Cao Dai and Hoa Hao sects the Bloc will strengthen the existing relationships and fraternal ties. The Bloc places particular stress on unity of action and brotherhood with the Catholic organizations. It supports the policy of the progressive Catholics who propose to integrate Catholicism into the heart of the nation and who are prepared to share the responsibility of saving and rebuilding the country in cooperation with other segments of the population.

The Buddhist Socialist Bloc invites all religious communities in Vietnam to link their progressive efforts in the common task of reconstructing the national economy and culture through an exploration of their social and spiritual potentialities. The Bloc believes that the dynamic and enlightened efforts by the religious communities, which alone speak to the spiritual needs of the Vietnamese people, offer the best guarantee for the neutrality and independence of the country.

All compatriots, whether Buddhist or non-Buddhist, who have been imprisoned for their activities for peace and democracy, will be immediately released. The Buddhist Socialist Bloc recognizes freedom of action for all political beliefs and parties but will not accept bloody conflict among peoples of the same nation. The Bloc is prepared to cooperate with the National Liberation Front in accordance with the principle of putting the survival and the independence of the country above all ideological conflicts. The Bloc does not consider the regime of North Vietnam as an enemy but will work with it, as with all factions in the South to build a sound basis for reunification under a truly neutralist regime. Immediate postal exchange between families and individuals in the two zones, North and South, will be instituted.

Regarding the ethnic minorities, the Bloc supports the respect of their autonomy, at the same time seeking all ways and means to assist them. All legitimate rights of the foreign residents in Vietnam will be guaranteed.

Economic Policy

The Buddhist Socialist Bloc feels that a proper reconstruction of Vietnamese society on a basis of nationalism and social justice must begin with an economic revolution in South Vietnam. Corruption and special privilege in whatever form must be vigorously uprooted. The traditional, feudal relationships, especially the excessive power of the large landlords, must be broken, and a socio-economic system installed which can win the willing cooperation of the people, without whose such support no free society can hope to progress. The necessary condition for such support from the people is that the national economy operate in a fashion which visibly improves the lot of the masses instead of disproportionately enriching that of the privileged classes.

To achieve such a system the Buddhist Socialist Bloc favors a planned economy with government control of basic industries and government responsibility for the over-all functioning of the economy. Small and medium size business will be open to private enterprise. A limited amount of foreign participation in government and private industry may be permitted on an individual case basis and with provision for adequate safeguards. Efforts will also be made to encourage cooperative forms of ownership and new forms of worker participation in industry control.

A truly independent Vietnam will raise its national income primarily through mobilizing the efforts and sacrifices of its own people, not through the generosity of foreigners. The Vietnamese people are accustomed to hard work and the Buddhist Socialist Bloc believes that if the fruits of the peoples' efforts are efficiently and equitably allocated, the need for foreign assistance will be modest once the destruction caused by the war is repaired. Meanwhile, foreign aid will be welcomed from all sources so long as it is not used to undermine our national sovereignty. The magnitude of this aid must not be so large as to dominate our national budget, as has been the case in the past, for such heavy dependence upon foreigners is incompatible with Vietnamese independence. As a matter of policy the Buddhist Socialist Bloc proposes that Vietnam's dependence on foreign assistance be terminated within ten years, and will bend its efforts toward achievement of that objective. The Buddhist Socialist Bloc favors regional economic integration, especially with North Vietnam, Cambodia, and Laos, so as to expand the market area of each of the Indo-China states. In recognition of the distribution of natural resources within our country, special effort will be made to develop the agricultural potential in South Vietnam so as to complement the industrial potential in the North. This does not preclude some industrial development of the South so as to permit the Southern economy to enjoy an autonomous existence pending reunification.

Community development programs will be encouraged, not on the political pattern which has proved so ineffective in the past, but by mobilizing the voluntary spirit of Vietnamese youth along lines currently being pioneered by the Buddhist Youth Movement. To assure the success of all of these programs a particular effort will be made to overcome the alienation of the Vietnamese intellectuals. This alienation has been a response to the corruption, nepotism, and sycophantism toward foreigners which have provided the paths to success since 1954. By appealing to the national pride and by demonstrating a genuine concern for the welfare of the nation and of all classes of its inhabitants, the Buddhist Socialist Bloc hopes to involve the Vietnamese intellectuals in the reconstruction of the country and to attract home hundreds of our most promising young people who have demonstrated their disdain for the present and previous Vietnamese governments by their refusal to return.

A cornerstone of the Buddhist Socialist Bloc's economic revolution will be the implementation of an effective land reform based on the spirit of national responsibility for all sufferings and social injustice. There will be land for all farmers. The land distribution already instituted by the Resistance to the poor peasants will be legalized. A program of voluntary land donations will be encouraged. The Buddhist Socialist Bloc believes in humanitarian as well as in juridical means to prevent and abolish ownership of excessive possessions by a minority of our citizenry.

Special programs of technical assistance will be extended to the peasants with a view to raising agricultural productivity. Government-sponsored rural credit programs will be developed and enlarged, and production and marketing cooperatives will be organized with a view to helping the rural people to eliminate the poverty which infests our countryside. Expanded education and health services will also be brought to the Vietnamese masses, as well as measures for their social security.

Foreign Policy

The Bloc proposes to establish diplomatic relations with all countries which recognize and respect the independence and neutrality of Vietnam, without antagonism toward either the socialist or the capitalist camp. At the same time, the Bloc will not permit either camp to influence Vietnamese policy or to use Vietnam as a means for antagonizing the other camp. The Bloc will refuse Vietnam's participation in any military alliance whatsoever. It will not accept the presence on the territory of Vietnam of armed forces of any foreign country.

The Bloc proposes to cooperate closely with the uncommitted Afro-Asian bloc to re-establish diplomatic relations with Laos and Cambodia, and to establish economic and political alliances with these neighbors. Economic and cultural relations will be established with North Vietnam and steps will be taken to create favorable conditions for agreement between the two zones in preparation for the unification and neutralization of the whole of Vietnam.

Cultural Policy

The Bloc will strive to develop and consolidate the national culture. It will abolish the cult of materialistic fulfillment and irresponsibility. It welcomes foreign technical ideas and is hospitable to all national cultures, but vigorously opposes cultural enslavement and cultural bastardization. The Bloc proposes to reorganize the educational system to accord with the needs of the national development program. It will re-examine the problems of studying abroad. It will welcome home and effectively utilize in the service of the nation Vietnamese students who have finished their studies abroad. It will enlarge the existing Universities in the country and will introduce Vietnamese as the language of instruction throughout the educational system.

Military Policy

The Bloc proposes that the armed forces return to their non-political role, and will take all necessary measures to prevent the resurgence of militarism.

viii

Bishop Armstrong's Statement

Following is the statement made by Bishop James Armstrong of the Methodist Church to the Kennedy Subcommittee on Refugees of the Senate Judiciary Committee on June 25, 1969:

I have two points to make before the more specific and detailed presentation of my colleague(s):

1. The Thieu-Ky government does not represent the majority of the people of South Vietnam.
2. The American military machine is systematically and unremittingly destroying a people and a land in southeast Asia.

I. *The Thieu-Ky government does not represent the majority of the people of South Vietnam.*

According to the U.S. Embassy in Saigon there are about 45,000 prisoners in the official prisons and detention centers of South Vietnam. There are thousands more held in military custody, in refugee camps, and in detention centers manned by secret police. More than 70 per cent of those being held are "political prisoners."

The majority of the "political prisoners" are classified as Communists or NLF agents. In a sense, because of the nature of the war, they are "prisoners of war." However, there are thousands more who are not VC agents, but whose only crimes consist of opposing the Saigon government or of advocating peace.

The U.S. Study Team on Religious and Political Freedom visited the Con Son Island prison, Chi Hoa and Thu Duc prisons, and the National Police Headquarters in Saigon. We talked with hundreds of "political prisoners." Many of them represented the so-called Third Force or "third solution." They were nationalists: persons who are not pro-Communist, but who are opposed to the present government in Saigon, a government they consider to be a military dictatorship.

We saw Truong Dinh Dzu, now sentenced to five years at forced labor, in the Chi Hoa prison. He was runner-up in the 1967 presidential election. He was imprisoned because he advocated negotiations with the NLF, and later advocated a coalition government.

We saw Thich Thien Minh, one of the most influential Buddhist monks in Vietnam. He was being held in military custody under tight security. Several months ago he argued that loyal Vietnamese could neither tolerate the "terrorism" of Communism nor the "corrupt militarism" of President Thieu. He was summoned to the office of the Minister of the Interior and warned to stop preaching "peace sermons." On February 23, he was arrested and sentenced to ten and five years in prison (the sentences to run concurrently). The sentence has been reduced to three years.

We were denied access to Nguyen Lau, owner and publisher of *The Saigon Daily News,* now thought to be held in the National Police Headquarters. He was arrested on April 16. His newspaper had been closed down at least once a year since 1963. Recently he had criticized the treatment of prisoners in his editorial columns and had likened press censorship to that under Diem. (More than 25 newspapers and several magazines have been suppressed during the past twelve months.)

At Thu Duc we talked with two girls who had been officers in the Student Union at Saigon University. Though these girls were classified as "Communist" at Thu Duc, their sole offense, according to their dossiers, was that they had "leftist tendencies." They had attended a peace meeting at their school and some VC pamphlets were found in a Student Union desk.

We asked to see thirteen other prisoners by name, but were denied access to them.

Without question there are thousands of prisoners in South Vietnam who have been denied all procedural protection during the time of their detention and interrogation, who have been erroneously classified as "Communist," who have been physically mistreated (see *Congressional Record* for June 17, 1969), and who represent a broad middle-ground of nationalism and progressive political sentiment.

More than 80 per cent of the South Vietnamese people are Buddhists. Buddhists are by nature and doctrine non-violent. They have been regularly and systematically persecuted by a succession of Saigon governments since the time of Diem. We saw 120 Buddhist monks in Chi Hoa prison alone. President Thieu, a Catholic, told us that though Catholics supported both the war and his policies, the Buddhists gave him "trouble."

The National Buddhist Shrine, headed by Thich Tam Chau, has the blessing of the Thieu-Ky regime. However, the An Quang Pagoda in Saigon, the seat of the Unified Buddhist Congregation, is more representative of Vietnamese Buddhism. It represents both the Mahayana and Therevada wings of the faith and has consistently been anti-government and anti-war. Thich Tri Quang, the leader of the so-called "militant Buddhists," is identified with the An Quang Pagoda.

The Thieu-Ky government does *not* have the support of the nation's Buddhists, the old-line nationalists who fought in the resistance movement against the French, the student leaders, most of the labor leaders, the so-called intellectuals and a broad cross-section of the citizenry who refuse to believe that the only alternatives to Communism are corruption, militarism and police state terrorism.

No government can long pretend to be free and democratic when it uses the words "Communism," "neutralism," and "coalition" interchangeably; when it silences its opposition, denying its critics any semblance of "due process"; when it imprisons or forces into exile multiplied thousands of persons who could lend balance and strength to a truly representative government; and when it arrogantly denies its people the right to discuss the obvious options open to them.

President Thieu told us, as he told his first Saigon press conference following Midway, that talk about a coalition government will not be tolerated. This from the man who says, when speaking with the American president, that there should be self-determination for his people.

II. *The American military presence is systematically and unremittingly destroying a land and a people in southeast Asia.*

In all fairness, let it be said that we were more impressed by General Abrams than by any other American official with whom we met. He seemed profoundly moved by the devastation of the war, was deeply sensitive to the needs of the Vietnamese people and appeared to welcome the kind of inquiry our Study Team was conducting. After all, freedom is indivisible. When it is denied a people it makes a lie of any war fought in its name.

We talked with Peter Arnett and other correspondents in the

field who argue that, given our present manpower and military hardware south of the 17th parallel, we could not pursue our stated military goals with greater intensity and maximal effectiveness.

It almost goes without saying, now, that we have dropped almost twice the bomb tonnage on Vietnam that the Allies dropped on the enemy during World War II.

Operation Phoenix, the pacification program, "search and destroy," "hunt and kill"—call it what you will—has been heatedly debated in the Lower House of Saigon's Congress within the past two weeks. Even those committed to the present government in South Vietnam are not willing to stand by silently while their nation is turned into a smoldering ash heap.

Defoliation, napalm, indiscriminate bombing and intensified search and destroy operations are laying waste the countryside, tearing peasants from their lands and splintering their families, and glutting the cities with millions of nameless refugees.

The American soldier, a valued friend of the Vietnamese people during World War II, has become a hated presence since the Vietnamese war was "Americanized" in 1964 and 1965, and for two reasons:

One, the American presence is turning the Vietnamese people (Buddhist and Catholic, but all Confucian) *away from their ancient and treasured heritage.* I asked Thich Tri Quang to compare French colonial rule with the American presence today. He said the American presence is far more destructive because the French, at least, appreciated and protected the traditions of the past. And, he said, the French were relatively poor. The Americans, with their money and their western value system, are turning the head and destroying the soul of Vietnam.

It isn't just the subversion of culture, however, *it is the destruction of life that is gaining the United States the enmity of the Vietnamese people.*

I walked through the children's surgical unit in a Saigon hospital. By my side was a distinguished physician, a member of the medical faculty of Saigon University and a former Minister of Education of the South Vietnamese government. He explained the sights I was seeing. Each year between 5,000 and 6,000 children are brought into that one unit of that one Saigon hospital. They are brought in from a range of 30 or 40 kilometers out. Eighty per cent of them are war victims. Twenty-five per cent of that 80 per cent suffer from burns. The remainder have shell fragments, bomb fragments and other kinds of military hardware in their little bodies. The doctors, by now sophisticated in determining the nature of aggressive weaponry, insist that only a handful of the children brought in over the past year had been wounded by VC weapons. Almost all of them were victims of our search and destroy tactics. I saw the amputees: youngsters without hands, arms, legs. I saw those disfigured for life with horrible burns. My nostrils caught the stench of open wounds. I heard the moans and cries. I wish those who speak so glibly on this Hill of defending "freedom" and stopping Communism 10,000 miles away could hear and see these pitiful "trophies" of our distant efforts.

One day a group of deputies from the Lower House gave a lunch for us. Duong Minh Kinh, one of their number, spoke of the resources being poured into North Vietnam by Russia and China. He spoke of the men and money the United States is pumping into South Vietnam. And then he said, "We are begging from all of the people in the world in order to destroy ourselves. That is the greatest tragedy of all."

In Paris we saw a gentle little Buddhist scholar in exile, a monk named Thich Nhat Hanh. He has written a poignant book about the war called, *Vietnam: Lotus in a Sea of Fire*. In it he describes the overwhelming destructive capacity of the American war machine and says: "More than anything else, Vietnam needs to be saved from [America's] salvation."

ix

Peace for Vietnam

The following is a communication from the Supreme Patriarch of the Unified Vietnam Buddhist Congregation:

In the sad recollection of the past Mau Than New Year and under the daily worries brought about by this protracted war that is destroying our motherland, I am sending to all the Venerables and Reverends of the Sangha and to the people of the country, at home and abroad my dear and best wishes for a Happy New Year and earnestly appeal to all of you to join me in praying for an early peace in Vietnam and in the world.

The Vietnam war is a common source of anxiety and headache to all mankind. Every kind of destruction and killing has become a daily occurrence throughout our dear motherland. The human being here is being forced to adopt an attitude of self-defense for the sake of self-preservation. Since the Vietnam war happens to be the outcome of the confrontation and clashes between international ideologies, the longer this protracted war is dragging on, the more useless and wasteful would be the shedding of blood both of the Vietnamese people and their enemies. And those who suffer the utmost in terms of human lives and material as well as spiritual values, are the Vietnamese people. Really, we are the victims who have been sacrificed and are being sacrificed and humiliated by this unjust war.

Bombs and bullets at the battlefield cannot uphold any just cause, nor words alone defend reason at the conference table.

And a peace conference will never yield results as long as the lives of the people, the rights of the Vietnamese and of the under-developed countries cannot be truly safeguarded. Peace has true meaning only when it can guarantee the right of self-determination for the nation and the rights for basic democratic freedom for the people in the community of the world.

In presenting the above-mentioned view, we do not aim at fostering hatred but only at exhorting ourselves and all peace-loving people to unite our efforts and be very clear-sighted in our endeavor to seek peace for Vietnam and for the world. True and lasting peace cannot be found in intricate devices to enslave people and small nations. True and lasting peace can be found only in respect for human dignity and human lives: with the human being as our final objective and with respect for the interests of all peoples living in this world.

So the mission and duties of the honest Vietnamese are clearly defined: first, to earnestly demand all fighting parties in Vietnam to stop at once all killing and acts of terrorism, especially when there is a peace conference going on. Secondly, not to have any faith in a peace which is false and pre-arranged, but to earnestly endeavor for ourselves to seek to establish a true Vietnam peace, where human beings should have the right of self-determination and the people should be securely protected.

We appeal to spiritual leaders, writers, politicians and all peace-loving people to be with us in our common endeavor to implement the two above-mentioned decisions, confident of their response and worthy contribution.

May all sister religions, writers, political and revolutionary parties, may all Vietnamese people let down barriers of ideology, personal views, opinions and self-interest so as to see in their true perspective the real facts that are confronting and threatening us and to change our destinies for the better.

Vietnamese Buddhism is always being threatened and misunderstood. Its leaders and the Buddhists are forever living in a state of insecurity and even the Church organization is being challenged and undermined. But the situation in Vietnam shows every day that the aspirations of Vietnamese Buddhism are correct, both in the light of mankind's aspirations and in the interests of our people. Because of that, we earnestly appeal to all Venerables and Reverends of the Sangha and to all the Buddhists to continually contribute and actively be ready to contribute more and more to the security and peace for our people.

We have sacrificed to serve our religion. We shall unitedly exert ourselves to better serve our people in the light of the Dharma.

We do not consider the powers that create suffering to Buddhism and to our people as enemies. But we should do our utmost to stop their unenlightened schemes and activities that make us and them suffer. The words "aid, help" as well as the word "liberation" should be correctly re-examined. True help does not consist in using help to bypass those who receive help and compel them to do our bidding. Liberation does not mean using rifles to kill those who do not share the same ideology. Liberation in modern times cannot tolerate violence, even for the sake of emancipating human beings and nations. Because, as long as violence is used, it will be challenged by violence. True liberation means liberation of the mind from unenlightened scheming and activities. So we could not share in any kind of fictitious help or any kind of bogus and violent liberation. From beginning to end, we support a nonviolent campaign aiming at happiness for the individual self, strength for peoples and progress for the world. Liberation by nonviolent methods is true liberation: to liberate oneself and the unenlightened forces from all cravings that are the root cause of suffering to oneself and to mankind.

In the past, we have more than once demonstrated the efficacy of the nonviolent method in our campaign against despotism. Now and in the future, we shall not depart from this method in our campaign for peace for our country. If sacrifice is needed we are ready to sacrifice ourselves to enlighten our opponents but not to crush them.

Our Buddhist Church is not afraid to be misunderstood. But I call on our Buddhists to be clear-sighted, not to allow ourselves to be influenced by any kind of parties or forces, in the name of peace or of war. The honest Buddhist, and all Vietnamese who truly care for their country, should resolve not to side with any parties who are now the tools of some unenlightened international forces. Only we, the Vietnamese people who are between the devil and the deep blue sea, whose right to live even is thwarted and who are the victims of destruction, only we have the right to decide what would be better for the destiny of our nation, a nation whose system of government should be selected only by ourselves.

We should assert ourselves as a dynamic entity which truly reflects the aspirations for peace of our people, so as to speak out from the heart and soul of a human being and the latent forces of our nation. We have no right to hand over the destiny of our people to those who are sham-people, bogus people and anti-people.

We should march forward, resolute, fearless but always nonviolent. We should make it known that the Unified Vietnam Buddhist Congregation has no ambition to take over the government for our own religion. The Buddhist Church works only for the true interests of the nation and hopes to see that the system of our government should be a humanist government which respects and promotes human dignity. This government should put the national interests and the interests of the people above self-interest and party interests. It should be a government elected freely, without pressure or fraud.

After having suffered the utmost, the people of Vietnam should have the right to live in an atmosphere of freedom, independence and justice, without any wide gap between standards of living, and without a class struggle. All that is done for the Vietnamese people should be dictated by the authentic needs of the Vietnamese people. We do not accept any foreign ideology, any anti-humanitarian government, any system which promotes materialistic preponderance over spiritual values as over true Vietnamese traditions.

Do not use a mechanic's eye to look into the needs of the Vietnamese people and label us as rightist, leftist or neutral. All these attitudes are those of a mechanized society and not ours. The Vietnamese people up to now has had only one purpose: that is to resolutely uplift human dignity and the independence of the nation, so that this nation can march forward along with other nations to build up a world where peace, compassion and justice prevail.

Vietnam will not refuse any aid from friendly nations who sincerely want to help a friend in need. We will struggle only against those who want to enslave human beings, the Vietnamese people and the world, through an ideology, a system of thought and under the false pretext of giving aid with a view to taking away the right to live as human beings from this nation or from other small nations.

Those who have died in this unjust war, those who are being dragged into the battlefield, those who are under training to use firearms, and our future generations, all are compelling us to think over, to act in time and to stop this war at once.

If they have any conscience and love for the country and for the people, both governments of North and South Vietnam should not prolong this killing any more. The other powers should not import to this country any more firearms to compel the Vietnamese people and human beings to kill each other. The international political and economic issues can be settled by other means than war. You should be ready to compromise so as to solve the problem in mutual understanding and mutual interest.

Wisdom, respect for human dignity, respect for the interests and right of the people, social justice would lead this world out of its present lack of sense of direction and dedication, so as to build up for mankind a world of peace, progress, material security and happiness. I put all my faith in the positive contribution for peace in Vietnam by all Buddhists at home and abroad, by all sister-religions, by all Vietnamese people and peace-loving people in the world.

May all be united to bring back a true and lasting peace for Vietnam and for the world.

In this spirit, I beg to request the Buddhist Clergy and laity to observe a week of fasting and prayer from the first day of the New Year to pray for National Unity and an early peace, for a speedy return of Eternal Di-Lac Spring to our beloved country.

May peace be with us, this year.

Saigon, Ky-Dau Spring,
Buddha era 2513 Christ era 1969

His Holiness The Supreme Patriarch of the Unified Vietnam Buddhist Congregation.

Mahathera: Thich Tinh Khiet

X

A Letter from the White House

Washington
March 19, 1969

Dear Mr. Hassler:

Dr. Kissinger has asked me to thank you for your letter of March 6, 1969, a copy of which was also addressed to President Nixon.

As you know, this Administration has been engaged in a fullscale review of American policy toward Vietnam. The general objective of this review has been to determine what policies could best be implemented in order to achieve a quick and just settlement of the war.

In a real sense, the Administration's interest in continuing to seek a just solution to the war is based on a desire to see a political situation established in South Vietnam in which the "third force" elements which you support can continue to exist. It is the view of this Administration that this situation can best be obtained by continued support of the present constitutional government.

I regret that the pressure of business on both the President and Dr. Kissinger makes it impossible to personally discuss your views at the present time.

Sincerely yours,

/s/ Richard L. Sneider
Senior Staff Member
National Security Council

xi

Letter from the
Department of State

Washington, D.C.
May 9, 1969

Honorable Charles E. Goodell
United States Senate
Washington, D.C.

Dear Senator Goodell:

I am responding to your recent communication enclosing a letter
to you from Mr. David McReynolds of the War Resisters League,
who states that he is in receipt of a letter from Vo Van Ai of the
Overseas Vietnamese Buddhist Association.

Allegations such as the one quoted in Mr. McReynolds' letter that
there are "tens of thousands of Buddhists under arrest and held in
prison" in South Viet-Nam are not borne out by the evidence available to us. There are, of course, a varying number of known or suspected members of the Viet Cong who are not prisoners of war and
who are imprisoned in South Viet-Nam. But, so far as we can determine, the number of persons in prison—apart from common
criminals and known or suspected Communists—is not only small
but is also decreasing. By June 1968 the Government of Viet-Nam
had released all of the militant Buddhist leaders and other "political
oppositionists" who were placed in "protective custody" after the
1968 Tet offensive. In December the Government released the last

three figures of any importance involved in the 1966 Buddhist uprising in Hue and Da Nang. Presently, the Government of Viet-
Nam is reviewing the cases of other, less well-known "civil defendants" and is releasing those against whom there is insufficient
evidence and remanding others for early trial.

With specific regard to the arrest and imprisonment of the Venerable Thich Thien Minh, the facts available to us are as follows:
Thich Thien Minh was arrested on February 23 in the course of a
police raid on the Quang Duc Buddhist Youth Center in Saigon, of
which he was the director. The raid reportedly was prompted by
the prior arrest of a confessed member of the Viet Cong, who had
been staying at the Center and who led the authorities to a weapon
and explosives he had concealed in his room there. Communist propaganda documents were reportedly found elsewhere on the prem-
ises. Arrested along with Thich Thien Minh were some twenty
young men who were accused of being members of the Viet Cong,
draft-dodgers, or deserters from the South Vietnamese armed
forces. The Center itself was closed.

As a consequence, Thich Thien Minh was tried on March 15 by
a military mobile field court on charges of hiding "rebels" (Viet
Cong) and concealing weapons and illegal documents. He was convicted of these charges and sentenced to ten years' imprisonment
at hard labor. Eight other persons arrested with him were tried at
the same time and also convicted and sentenced; among them was
the Viet Cong member mentioned earlier, who was sentenced to
20 years at hard labor.

Thich Thien Minh was tried again on March 17 by a different
military court on the lesser charge of sheltering deserters and draft-
dodgers. He was also convicted of this offense and was sentenced
to five years' solitary confinement, to be served concurrently with
the earlier sentence. Three other persons arrested with him were
tried on this occasion and were also convicted and sentenced; all
three reportedly testified that they were in fact deserters.

On March 18, the office of President Nguyen Van Thieu made
public a special order concerning the execution of Thich Thien
Minh's sentences. The order directed the Prime Minister to insure
that Thich Thien Minh is held in a place and manner different from
other criminals; that he be permitted to observe religious obliga-
tions and to perform religious ceremonies required of him as member of the Buddhist clergy; and that he be guaranteed any special
privileges and care that his health may require. We are reliably informed that these conditions are in fact being observed.

The action of the Government of Viet-Nam in bringing Thich Thien Minh to trial is in the first instance an internal matter between a sovereign government and one of its own citizens. However, as Secretary of State Rogers said at his news conference on April 7, "We are obviously concerned about civil liberties in South Viet-Nam," and he noted that we have discussed the matter with the Government of Viet-Nam.

I trust that this information will prove useful to you, and I hope that you will not hesitate to call on me if I can be of further assistance.

Sincerely yours,

William B. Macomber, Jr.
Assistant Secretary for
Congressional Relations

Enclosure:
Correspondence returned.

xii

Letter from Eleven Students

Eleven Students of the Saigon University Student Union and the Faculty-Student Representative Committee from the Prison of the Central Police, in Saigon.

To:
    The Rector of Saigon University
    The Deans of the Faculties of Saigon University
    The Professors of Saigon University

Our dear Teachers:

We eleven students who are being held in the prison of the Central Police, we your students have something to present with respect to you, our teachers.

Our dear Teachers:

For many years we have studied and worked closely with you in order to absorb the high and beautiful ideas, the love for your country and people with which you have led us. As a result we are aware of the responsibility of students in the present situation of the country; we have tried to develop our potentials to the highest degree; and we have not hesitated to contribute all that we have learned and all the energy of our youth to serving the interests of the students and the country. We have been well received by people in all walks of life. This indicates that we can use with precision what we have learned from you.

However, under the eye of the Saigon Government we are always considered to be offenders and are often oppressed, arrested, to the extent that the government does not hesitate to put its hands directly into many of our activities: in student elections, in student press, etc.

Our dear Teachers:

This fact offends seriously the reputation of the University community, interfering in University autonomy, which you and we consider to be the last stronghold left to protect.

Dear Teachers:

When this letter from the heart reaches your hands we will be on our way to "ai tri." [1] And there also other students will follow us. The government works in this way with the intention of pushing the students out of the national community. In this way the government can push patriotic students to the wall and turn their attitudes against the national interest. The last words that we, patriotic students, are trying to send to you is to present to you our respect and our love, and at the same time we hope with all our hearts that you will speak out for the honor of the university and for the interest of the students against all the injustices put upon the students.

In this situation, in which we are wrenched away from all liberty, we hope with all our hearts that there are no obstacles that can separate the close and deep relations between professors and students. We believe that the sentiment between teachers and students will remain close forever.

Yours respectfully,
Central National Police Station
May 21, 1969

Cosigned:
    Tran van Chi
        Vice-President for Internal Affairs
        Executive Committee, Saigon Student Union
    Huynh Quan Thu
        Secretary General, Executive Comm.
        Saigon Student Union
    Do Huu Canh
        Acting President, Executive Comm.
        Faculty of Law, Saigon University
    Phan Hao Quang
        President, Executive Committee
        Faculty of Science, Saigon Univ.

[1] "ai tri" means to keep one's mind quiet, with the connotation of being put into a grave. It refers to the prisons where people are held without trial.

Trinh Dinh Ba
Vice President for Planning,
Executive Committee, Faculty of Law
Lam Ba Phat
Vice President for Internal Affairs
Permanent Committee Representative
Faculty of Letters
Truong Van Khoe
Vice President for Internal Affairs
Executive Committee, Faculty of Pedagogy
Dao Thi Nguyet Thanh
Secretary General, Committee of Youth,
High-school and University Students
for Relief of War Victims
Ha Thu Thuan
Editor of the Student Paper *Khai Pha*
Tran Hoang San
Graduate student, faculty of Law
Graduate student, Fac. of Administration
Nguyen Dang Lien
Student of Law

xiii

An Appeal to the People

Tokyo,
May 30, 1969.

Mr. Al Hassler,
Fellowship of Reconciliation,
Box 271, Nyack,
N.Y. 10960,
U.S.A.

Dear Mr. Hassler,

On behalf of the Vietnamese people whom I represent, I have just issued in Tokyo an appeal to the People of the United States of America and Japan. I have pleasure in sending you a copy of my statement as a substantial proposal for the Vietnam Peace Solution.

I am deeply grateful for the work you are doing in bringing peace to our people, and I hope that this statement may be of some use to you in promoting better understanding of the feelings of the Vietnamese people.

I would appreciate having your comments and views on this problem. Kindly address your mail to me in Tokyo:

P.O. Box 5159, TOKYO INT. 100-31 *JAPAN*

With my best regards,

Sincerely yours,

Pham The Truc,
Member, House of Representatives,
Republic of Vietnam,
Province of Binh Thuan.

An Appeal to the People
of the United States of America and Japan

May 30, 1969.
Pham The Truc,
Member, House of Representatives,
Republic of Vietnam,
Province of Binh Thuan.

Thousands of people every day are being killed and the land devastated in the cruel war in Vietnam. Why can't peace be established in Vietnam—a peace for which not only the people of Vietnam but also all peace-loving peoples of the world are longing?

The following is my view on this question.

The regime of Nguyen Van Thieu and Nguyen Cao Ky which is the offspring of a military clique is still, in its basic nature, a military dictatorship. It has only been able to maintain its status by the continuation of this war. In order to buy the favor of supporters, this regime encourages them to exploit the poor and acquiesce in their activities of corruption. The corruption in Vietnam is no less inhuman for the people of Vietnam than the war itself and the fundamental rights of the Vietnamese people are being trampled upon.

Furthermore, the present Saigon regime never hesitates to enact whatever repressive measure it can lay hands on in trying to banish, detain, and oppress religious leaders, politicians, intellectuals and students. The recent arrests of the Rev. Thich Thien Minh as well as a number of students are good examples of this oppression.

The government tries to control the Diet to keep the people quiet and their voices unheard. The government is, for example, giving special favor to pro-governmental Congressmen while threatening those who try to alert the people of the cor-

ruption existing in society. Furthermore, the regime is even op-
pressing the judicial sectors of their own government.

Thus, the principles of democracy in Vietnam are being
trampled upon and the morale of the people is facing a fatal
crisis.

In other words, the present government is a regime which
lacks the support of the majority of the people, exclusively relying on a few people who gain profits out of war procurements
and exploit the poor.

It is the United States government which supports this unpopular government of Vietnam, and by advocating the "Vietnamization of the war" it intensifies the military actions. Thus, the
United States government is making the solution of the war all
the more difficult and adding to the atrocities of an already
bloody war.

Through these serious errors, leaders of the United States
government have proved again that there is not the slightest improvement in their basic understanding of Vietnam and Asia.

As a citizen of Vietnam and also as a member of the Congress, I present the following requests of the United States government:

1) The United States government should immediately stop
   supporting the military regime of Nguyen Van Thieu
   and Nguyen Cao Ky.

   (All the treaties which have been concluded between
   the United States government and the military regime of
   Vietnam have no value to the Vietnamese people whatsoever.)

2) The United States government should withdraw all military forces from Vietnam.

   (There is no ground for President Nixon's view expressed in his eight-point proposals of May 14, namely,
   that the United States military forces cannot be with-
   drawn without the risk of mass slaughter.)

3) The United States government should be sincere in the

Paris Peace Talks. By being "sincere" I mean that *Peace*
for the Vietnamese people, and not the "face" of the
United States government, should be the priority. Political
settlement, and not military settlement, should be the priority.

A believer in God, I pay my respects to the people of the
United States who love peace, freedom and equality. I pray
from my heart that God and the American people's pious faith
in God will reflect the noble traditions of the United States and
will show leaders of the United States the right policy toward
peace in Vietnam.

XIV

Findings on
Trip to Vietnam,
U. S. Study Team,
May 25 – June 10, 1969

Introduction

Background:

The U.S. Study Team was sent to South Vietnam by an ad hoc committee organized in late 1968 by a group of well-known churchmen concerned about the war and the repression of those religious and political forces in South Vietnam who urge an end to hostilities. This committee has wide national interreligious representation. The officers named were: Chairman, Barton Hunter, Executive Secretary of the Department of Church in Society of the Christian Church; Secretary, Gerhard Elston of the National Council of Churches; Executive Director, Allan Brick, Associate Secretary for National Program of the Fellowship of Reconciliation, who also served as a member of the team.

The sponsoring committee defined the team's goals as follows: "First, they will seek to identify the variety of religious forces in South Vietnam and the range of political expression existing there. They will seek to investigate the situation of religious groups and the extent of the imprisonment of leaders of nonaligned groups who represent potentially important political sentiment. The team will be interested, for example, in visiting both Mr. Dzu and Thich Thien Minh. Second, the team will seek to investigate the situation of all prisoners in South Vietnam. Recognizing the difficulties of doing this in a wartime situation, the team will nonetheless attempt to obtain realistic information."

Team Members:

Members of the team were: Bishop James Armstrong of the United Methodist Church, Dakotas Area; Mrs. John C. Bennett, Protestant churchwoman; Allan Brick, Associate Secretary for National Program, Fellowship of Reconciliation; Hon. John Conyers, Jr., M.C. of Detroit, Michigan; Robert F. Drinan, S.J., Dean of the Boston College Law School; John de J. Pemberton, Executive Director of the American Civil Liberties Union; Rabbi Seymour Siegel, Professor of Theology at the Jewish Theological Seminary; and Rear Admiral Arnold E. True, United States Navy (retired).

Summary:

A report issued by the team following the Vietnam trip documents police and military suppression of religious and political expression in South Vietnam under the Thieu-Ky Government. The chief findings of the team are:

1. Many thousands of persons being arrested in South Vietnam are denied all procedural protection. Arrests are made by a variety of local and national officials—by District police, special security forces, military forces and intelligence units —each exercising "relatively unfettered discretion."

2. The Thieu-Ky Government's widespread and increasing

use of the extra-constitutional Military Field Tribunal has been responsible for the sentencing and imprisonment of additional thousands of persons, denying them the fundamental elements of a fair hearing and often failure to serve prior notice of the charges against them. Many of these prisoners remain without trial in the hands of the arresting authorities while the remainder have been removed to prisons by administrative action without charges or trials.

3. The Study Team agrees with those who say that repression, though not as obvious and violent as under the Diem Government, continues to be pervasive and brutal. While some persons visited appear to reflect modern notions of penal administration and certain prison officials seemed sensitive to the needs of inmates, the sheer weight of witnesses' statements concerning physical abuse seemed overwhelmingly conclusive. It became clear that whatever amelioration appeared in the formal correctional institutions, torture and brutality are widespread in the arresting and interrogation process.

4. Without question the Thieu-Ky Government uses the words "communism", "neutralism" and "coalition" to silence dissent and weaken political and religious opposition. Student peace movements, Buddhist pleas for nonviolence and a "third solution," and the freedom of the press have been systematically suppressed by an insecure government that relies more on police state tactics and American support than upon true representation and popular support. As one Vietnamese attorney phrased it: "One cannot fight for freedom without insuring freedom at home."

I. Limitations on Religious and Political Freedom in South Vietnam

The eight-member U.S. Study Team met with President Thieu, Minister of Interior Tran Thien Khiem and members of his staff, Ambassador Ellsworth Bunker and members of his staff, national religious leaders, lawmakers, intellectuals, attorneys, students, a variety of persons of different political persuasions and talked with scores of political prisoners. It visited prisons at Thu Duc, Chi Hoa, and on Con Son Island, as well as the National Police Headquarters. The Government of South Vietnam was helpful in providing data, in permitting team members to visit prisons, and in making accessible certain prisoners.

Three things are readily apparent in South Vietnam: (1) A state of war exists and any meaningful study of freedom must be done against that background; (2) South Vietnam is poor and is unable to provide from its own resources institutional facilities and forms of care which are taken for granted in the Western world; and, (3) whereas the United States of America has lived under the guarantee of its present Constitution for nearly two hundred years, South Vietnam does not have a tradition of political liberty and its Constitution is only two years old. Notwithstanding this, in a message cabled directly to President Nixon from Saigon, the Study Team said:

Speaking for peace or in any other way opposing the government [in South Vietnam] easily brings the charge of Communist sympathy and subsequent arrest. . . . There must be no illusion that this climate of religious and political suppression is compatible with either a representative or a stable government.

Many persons interviewed argued that President Thieu's government is less repressive than the ten years of brutal intimidation under Ngo Dinh Diem. Others, while agreeing that repression is not as obvious and violent, argued that it is equally pervasive though more subtle today. (Some of the following documentation will indicate that there is still unsubtle, violent intimidation.)

Three celebrated cases of political arrest have claimed international attention in recent months. They are the cases of Thich Thien Minh, one of the most influential Buddhist monks in

South Vietnam; Truong Dinh Dzu, runner-up in the Presidential Election of 1967; and Nguyen Lau, wealthy publisher of *The Saigon Daily News.*

Thich Thien Minh was arrested on February 23, 1969, at the Buddhist Youth Center and charged with "harboring rebels, concealing weapons and illegal documents . . . harboring deserters and supporting draft dodgers." After appearing before a military field tribunal, he was sentenced to serve terms of ten and five years at hard labor, the sentences to run concurrently. Last month, his sentence was reduced to three years.

It is assumed by many that Thich Thien Minh was arrested not because of the specific crimes with which he was charged but for his public criticism of the Thieu-Ky Government and his strong advocacy of peace.

In February, he was summoned to the Ministry of the Interior and warned to tone down his sermons which were said to be disrespectful to the government of President Thieu. He had earlier said that the people of South Vietnam could accept neither the "terrorist regime" of North Vietnam nor the "corrupt government" in Saigon. Replying to Thien Minh, President Thieu said, "My government can die because of those pacifists, but before we die, they will have to die first."

The Study Team visited both Thich Thien Minh and Quang Duc Buddhist Youth Center. The Youth Center, closed at the time of Thich Thien Minh's arrest (20 other Buddhists were arrested at the same time), was handed back by the Government and re-opened during the team's stay in Saigon. Team members saw Thich Thien Minh's room, as well as the many hallways, rooms and stairways that separated him from the tiny room and wooden closet with the false back that were said to be the hiding place of the V.C. agent and a cache of small arms. Seeing the distances and buildings involved, it is not difficult to believe the monk's assertion that he had no personal knowledge of a V.C. agent's presence in that hidden room.

The team talked with Thich Thien Minh, who has been held

in military custody. They interviewed him in a small house, a part of a larger complex of carefully guarded government officials pointedly left the room that the discussion might be private. However, it had been determined during the conversations that there was a government agent only four feet from the Venerable, behind a thin wall. Thus, the interview was necessarily inhibited. Thich Thien Minh had been moved four times since his arrest and was kept under the strictest security. Though badly injured in 1966 by a hand grenade, said to have been thrown by a V.C., he said his health was good. He added, "My only offense is that I believe in peace."

On May 1, 1968, Truong Dinh Dzu was arrested "on charges of urging the formation of a coalition government as a step toward peace." In August, he was sentenced to five years of forced labor. Although the N.L.F. is now participating in the Paris peace talks and a coalition government is being widely discussed by responsible government officials in the United States, Mr. Dzu has not yet been released.

In a national election that denied certain candidates the right to run[1] because they were peace advocates, and that heavily favored the Thieu-Ky regime because of its domination of the military and political structures of South Vietnam and because of the well-known support of the American 'presence' in Vietnam, Mr. Dzu ran second, polling 18 per cent of the vote. He wisely did not announce his "white dove" platform until after his candidacy had been approved. (It is interesting to note that in the election, the Thieu-Ky ticket gained only 35 per cent of the vote. In May, 1968, Vice-President Ky told an Italian journalist, "Our last elections were a loss of time and money, a mockery.") Dzu has never been accused of being pro-Communist and is, as President Thieu openly acknowledged, a "politi-

---

[1] General "Big" Minh was kept in exile in Bangkok, and Au Truong Thanh, the other leading contender, was refused candidate status because of his alleged "neutralism." The Study Team talked with Au Truong Thanh in exile in Paris.

cal prisoner." The fact that, running as a peace candidate and advocating direct talks with the N.L.F., he ran second only to the President, accounts more than anything else for his imprisonment. Mr. Dzu was moved from Con Son Prison Island to Chi Hoa Prison in Saigon during the last week in May, 1969. U.S. Study Team members saw him in his cell in Chi Hoa. Suffering from a heart condition, he looked well and various kinds of medicines were in evidence. He said he wanted to serve his country as a nationalist. On June 5, President Thieu told the team that support for a coalition government cannot be tolerated.

On April 16, 1969, Nguyen Lau, publisher and owner of *The Saigon Daily News,* was arrested for "having maintained private contacts with a Vietcong political agent." The agent, a boyhood friend of Lau, returned to Saigon in 1964 from North Vietnam. He talked with Lau many times during the past five years and had, at one time, asked him to supply information for the V.C. According to both Lau and Tran Ngoc Hiem, the agent, Lau had refused to supply the information.

In discussing Lau's case with a member of the team, one of Saigon's most highly regarded foreign correspondents explained its background. In Vietnam, a culture influenced immeasurably by Confucianism, family ties and friendship are revered. Mr. Lau, in a press conference held by government officials at National Police Headquarters, made no attempt to deny his associations with Hiem. He said that Communism was poisoning the minds of many, but that Vietnam would surely survive Communism. He added, "Even today, sitting before you, I keep wondering if as a publisher and as a Vietnamese intellectual, I should denounce a friend whom I have known since boyhood."

Mr. Lau was educated at Oxford and the Sorbonne. As a member of an old and important family of wealth he has no respect for war profiteers and little sympathy for curruption in the government. As a respected journalist and an avowed anti-Communist, he considered it part of his responsibility to be open to every facet of Vietnamese life. He once said, "If people are free to walk the streets, they are free to talk to me."

He insisted upon his right to criticize. On March 24, 1969, *The New York Times* quoted him as saying, "Diem said bluntly that he was not going to tolerate freedom of the press. There were no illusions then. We are living a lie now. People say they are giving you freedom and someone without experience in journalism may be innocent enough to believe that this is paradise. Now you may be carried away by your illusions and land in trouble." Less than a month later Nguyen Lau was arrested.

Members of the Study Team visited the National Police Headquarters. There, Lt. Col. Nguyen Mau, Chief of Special Branch, told them about the Government's case against the publisher. The only "evidence" he produced was the photostat of a press card, allegedly issued by Mr. Lau to one Tan That Dong, the alleged V.C. alias of Tran Ngoc Hiem. Such "evidence", however, raises serious questions. Two days following Lau's arrest, police brought a "so-called Vietcong" to the Lau home. In Mrs. Lau's absence, they proceeded to take pictures of him in various positions around the house. When her two sons (aged 10 and 14) protested, they were handcuffed while the picture-taking continued. When told of the incident, Mrs. Lau courageously went to the authorities. A senior police official did admit that police had visited the house with a V.C. agent and camera to gather "evidence."

Members of the Study Team were not permitted to see Mr. Lau, still being held without sentence. Nor were they permitted to see thirteen other prisioners they had made specific requests to visit.

These three cases have not been isolated because they are more important than others, but because they are more well known. They are symptomatic of a climate of intellectual, religious and political repression that has led to the imprisonment, exile or silencing of thousands of loyal Vietnamese nationalists, persons who are not pro-Communist, but who are critical of the

Thieu-Ky Government and who insist upon the right to think for themselves.

The government's sensitivity at this point is revealed in its attitudes toward dissenters, so-called "militant Buddhists," students and intellectuals, political opponents and the press.

The religious picture in South Vietnam is confused. About one-tenth of the nation's population is Roman Catholic. Yet, from the time of Diem and the Nhu's on, Catholicism has played a dominant role in Vietnamese political life. (Actually, this goes back to the 18th-century French missionary-priest, Pigneau de Behaine, and the continuing influence of French Catholicism during colonial days.) President Thieu reminded the Study Team that, though he had trouble with Buddhists, Catholics had supported his administration. The former editor of a Catholic magazine, a friend and confidante of Archbishop Nguyen Van Binh, agrees that fewer than 10% of the Catholics in South Vietnam are critical of the war and of Thieu's government. It must be remembered that about 1,000,000 of South Vietnam's Catholics were born in what is now North Vietnam and came south following 1954. They are, for the most part, vigorous anti-Communists.

However, there are Catholics who want a closer tie with Buddhists and who are seeking what some call a "third solution." They are trying to find answers between Communism and corrupt militarism. Father Hoang Quynh, an active leader of the All-Religion Citizen's Front, has worked with Buddhists in trying to prevent further friction between the Buddhist and Catholic communities. He has said, "Catholic faithful must learn to live a responsible political life." There are other Catholics who seem close to the Pope's views on meaningful negotiations and peace. They have won the confidence of Buddhist leaders.

When, in January, 1968, all of the bishops of South Vietnam released a four-page statement supporting Pope Paul's message on Vietnam and calling for a bombing halt in North Vietnam, it seemed that there had been a breakthrough. However, and without exception, those with whom Study Team members spoke indicated that the hierarchy in South Vietnam had confined themselves to what the Pope had said with no desire or inclination to supplement or further interpret the Vatican's plea concerning peace. There continues to be sharp feeling between Buddhists and Catholics. As one Buddhist complained, "When Catholics talk about peace, the Thieu Government hears it one way. When we use the word, it is supposed to mean something else." Many Buddhists feel, and justifiably so, that they have been discriminated against by a succession of governments in Saigon.

There are two major Buddhist factions in South Vietnam; the "moderate" government-authorized faction of Thich Tam Chau, and the "activist" [2] faction of Thich Tri Quang and the An Quang Pagoda. However, the Unified Buddhist Church of the An Quang Pagoda is made up of both Mahayana (northern) and Therevada (southern) Buddhists. Early in 1967, the Government sought to fragment the Buddhists, withdrawing the charter of the Unified Church and recognizing the "moderate" wing of Thich Tam Chau. However, the An Quang Pagoda continues to be a major factor in the religious and political life of the country. On the Buddha's 2513th birthday, celebrated May 30, at the An Quang Pagoda, former Chief of State Phan Khac Suu, Tran Ngoc Chau, General Secretary of the House of Representatives, other deputies and senators, Father Quynh, as well as Cao Dai and Hoa Hao leaders were present, indicating a broad base of popular support among disparate groups. During the ceremonies, white doves of peace were released as a crowd of more than 3,000 people looked on, and Thich Tinh Khiet, Supreme Patriarch of the Unified Buddhist Congrega-

[2] The term "militant" is usually applied to the An Quang Pagoda faction. However, Buddhists are committed to nonviolence. In French, "militant" means an "active supporter or worker in a political group."

tion, said, "Every hostile tendency of the world has jostled its way into the Vietnam war in order to exploit it and seek for victory, whereas all the Vietnamese people—either on this side or on the other side of the 17th Parallel—are mere victims of this atrocious war. Our nation is thus forced to accept ready-made decisions without having any right to make our own choice." President Thieu and pro-government supporters may insist that such peace talk is "political". If so, it is an obvious expression of that freedom essential to an emerging democracy. And it is no more political than a caravan of government-owned cars driving Thich Tam Chau to the Saigon Airport on June 5, to meet the Nepalese delegation to a World Buddhist Conference on Social Welfare; no more political than the imprisonment of hundreds of Buddhist monks.

Often the Buddhists who protest Government policy are students. Following the government-controlled elections of 1967, Buddhist students joined by some of their professors were promptly singled out by the Government for retaliatory acts. A professor of law said, "Van Hanh University (Buddhist) was the chief target for attack. . . . If students go to meetings, the police follow them and they can be arrested any time. Many times, they are drafted before the legal age or before their deferments as students expire."

As a result of a peace meeting held in September, 1968, in Saigon University, the Student Union was closed by police. Students, professors, deputies from the Lower House and some Buddhist monks had participated in the meeting. Thirty persons, mostly students, were arrested. More arrests followed.

At about the same time, a student in the Medical School was murdered. He had been kidnapped by the N.L.F. and later rescued by American troops. He was accused of having "leftist tendencies." He was found dead with his hands tied behind his back, having been pushed from a third-floor window. The police called it "probable suicide" and made no investigation.

Student resistance continued. On Christmas Eve, responding to the Pope's plea for peace, 2,000 students, many of them Catholic, held a peace procession. In the aftermath, hundreds were arrested.

In spite of set-back and discouragement, spirit of the student peace movement remains unbroken. A Buddhist student stepped out of a sullen mass of prisoners at Camp No. 7 on Con Son Island and addressed members of the team. The government translator said, "He is here because he refuses to be drafted. He says he doesn't want to serve the United States. As a Vietnamese citizen he will go into the Army only when we have independence." A student, recently released from Con Son, reacting to the devastation visited on his country by modern instruments of war, said much the same thing: "I will not serve a country that has done so much to my own."

Students, intellectuals and Buddhist monks do not comprise the only opponents who threaten President Thieu's government.

There is a growing mood of independence in the Lower House. It is only found in a few deputies, but they are voicing increasing opposition to the policies and practices of the Thieu-Ky Government. There have been criticisms of Operation Phoenix in the National Assembly. Two members of the Lower House raised serious questions about prison policies early in May. The president's tax program has been challenged. Constitutional questions challenging the prerogatives of the executive branch are frequently raised.

President Thieu proudly points to the "new alliance" of political parties in South Vietnam as an indication of the breadth of his support. This alliance includes the Greater Union Force, the political arm of militant Roman Catholic refugees, the Social Humanist Party, a rebirth of Ngo Dinh Nhu's Can Lao party, the Dai Viet, an erstwhile grouping of anti-French nationalists, a faction of the Hoa Hao sect based in the Delta and the Viet Kuomintang, a pro-government bloc formed after the Tet offensive in 1968. All of these parties together, combined with the Thieu-Ky vote, failed to capture half of the popular vote in the 1967 elections.[3]

While there is genuine political opposition, most of it has been driven underground. Members of the Study Team met with leaders of five old-line political parties no longer permitted to function as recognized entities. These men had all been active in the resistance movement against the French and were ardent nationalists. Their parties have been outlawed, their requests to publish a newspaper have gone unanswered and their voices have been muted. These men, and they reflect a vast middle-position in South Vietnam, struggled against the French and consider the Americans their new colonial masters. Over the past twenty-five years, they have known imprisonment and sacrifice. (A retired general present had been in prison eleven times.) They argue that unity and independence cannot be achieved under present circumstances. One of them said, "We know the American Government is anti-Communist and they help us fight Communism. But when they look at Viet Communists, they think of them as western Communists. That is a bad mistake." It is the conviction of the Study Team that there will be no truly representative government in South Vietnam until voices such as these can be legitimatized and participate in the democratic processes of the republic.

One further evidence of political oppression is the Government's attitude toward the press. Although it seems reasonably tolerant of foreign correspondents, and they are permitted to function without too many instances of censorship, the Government's relationship to the Vietnamese press is far more direct and inhibiting. Twelve months ago, censorship was officially eliminated in South Vietnam. Since then, at least twenty-five newspapers and two magazines have been suspended. Mr. Lau's

[3] The United States sent election "observers" to Vietnam to report on election procedures. As one cynical Vietnamese put it: "We are planning to send twenty-two Vietnamese observers who don't speak English to the United States . . . for four days to see if your elections are fair."

Daily News has been suspended for thirty days for hinting that
Thich Thien Minh's trial might have been unfair. *Ting Sang*
was closed when it suggested that Prime Minister Huong (one
of the more highly regarded members of the Thieu Government
and a former political prisoner himself) once yielded to pressure in a cabinet appointment.[4] Nguyen Thanh Tai a UPI combat photographer, was arrested in May, 1968, for taking pictures "detrimental" to South Vietnam.

One of the most credible and influential anti-government nationalist leaders with whom we talked prepared a three-page
position paper for the team. The English translation was his
own. In part, he said:

> The range of political expression as legally exists here is narrow
> indeed . . .
>
> Let us imagine for a moment that those people are given a
> chance. What would they do?
>
> They would firstly negotiate with the Government of the United
> States an agreement on the Allied Forces Establishment in Viet
> Nam which would provide for progressive withdrawals when the
> situation warrants it. Of course, they would bear in mind the secu-
> rity and the honor of the Allied troops who came here to protect
> ourselves and prevent a Communist domination.
>
> They would secondly invite the Vietnamese people to actively
> participate in national affairs and take their share of responsibility.
> Democratic freedom would be enforced without restrictions, how
> adventurous this might first look. Live forces such as students, intel-
> lectuals, religious leaders and workers' unions would be given an au-
> thorized say. Unjust treatment would be redeemed. One cannot
> fight for freedom without ensuring freedom at home . . .

Many, not all, of the nationalist leaders with whom the Study
Team talked believed that a continuing American presence in
South Vietnam is an unfortunate necessity until the political sit-
uation can be stabilized and made more representative. One
student leader who had been imprisoned twice by the Thieu
Government for his activities on behalf of peace argued that no

---

[4] *The New York Times,* March 24, 1969.

truly representative democracy can come into being as long as U.S. troops are present and U.S. policy is being enforced. He said, "By now, we should have learned the irony of having any Vietnamese Government that is embraced by U.S. power. The Americans must depart leaving us to decide our own future." He spoke those words with anguish, obviously knowing the problems that Vietnamese nationalism and many of its long-suffering advocates would face in dealing with the N.L.F. in the wake of an American withdrawal. Yet, he bitterly insisted that after many years of American military presence and American good intentions, there was no other way.

At the luncheon given the team by members of the Lower House, Deputy Duong Minh Kinh talked about the vast expenditures poured into North Vietnam by the Soviet Union and China, and into South Vietnam by America. He said, "We are beggars from all of the people in the world in order to destroy ourselves. That is the greatest tragedy of all."

II. Detention, Interrogation, Imprisonment and Treatment of Prisoners

The large majority of those imprisoned in South Vietnam are held because they oppose the Government; they are "political prisoners". Undoubtedly, a great many of these are, as the Government classifies them, "Viet Cong". Legally speaking, they are properly prisoners of war—although they are kept in a separate category from military prisoners. Others are "civilians related to Communist activities;" i.e., V.C. agents, and are accurately classified as such. Still others, many of them detained without hearing or trial, should be classified differently. Some of these have been picked up in "search and destroy" sweeps and are innocent of anything save being present in an area of military operations. Others are clearly political prisoners. They are nationalists and not Communists, but are seen by the Gov-

ernment as inimical to its continuing control. In the official statistics very few "detainees" and "political prisoners" are so
classified. The Government places the vast majority of prisoners in either the "Communist" or the "criminal" category.

The classification of prisoners in 41 Correctional Centers as
given by Col. Nguyen Psu Sanh, Director of Correctional Institutions, is:

16.98%	Criminals
64.25%	Communists
4.16%	Civilians related to Communist activities
11.91%	Military
.21%	Political activities harmful to national interest
2.49%	War prisoners temporarily in correctional centers

Colonel Sanh said that there are 35,000 prisoners in these
Correctional Centers. The senior American adviser to Col.
Sanh, Mr. Don Bordenkercher, estimated that, in addition,
there are 10,000 held in interrogation centers. He reported that
the number had gone up gradually since the Tet offensive of
1968 when the jump was precipitate. Ambassador Colby, General Abrams' Deputy for Pacification, said that the number of
prisoners had gone up and will continue to go up as the pacification program (Civil Operations and Revolutionary Development Support) develops.

The national police in Saigon and in the provinces are the official organ for making arrests. In addition, there appear to be
many other arrest and detention agencies.[1] It is clear that those
arrested are taken to a variety of detention centers for interrogation and that many are held in these centers for periods of
time up to two years. According to the U.S. Mission, American
advisers are involved only with cases of Viet Cong or suspected
Viet Cong sympathizers and with persons apprehended during
military operations; e.g., "Operation Phoenix", the 18-month-
old program which pools information from half a dozen U.S.

[1] See Section III, B.

and South Vietnamese intelligence and security agencies with the purpose of identifying and capturing Viet Cong political agents.

Doubtless the total number of political prisoners in South Vietnam—including those held as prisoners of war by intelligence agencies and in military prisons, as well as those in the correctional institutions and those held by various other arresting agencies—far exceeds the official statistics and estimates. Due to the wide range of arresting and detention agencies, and the inadequacy of statistical methods, no accurate count of prisoners can be made.

In addition to the provincial Correctional Centers, there are four large prisons for essentially civilian prisoners. These are Chi Hoa in Saigon, Phu Nu in Thu Duc (for female prisoners), Tan Hiep near Bien Hoa, and Con Son on an island off the southeastern coast. Team members were enabled by the Ministry of the Interior to visit Chi Hoa, Thu Duc, and Con Son Island Prison. They were also shown through the interrogation center at National Police Headquarters.

The following statistics, provided by prison officials, further illustrate the Government's desire to de-emphasize the so-called "political prisoner" category. Warden Pham Van Lien of Chi Hoa prison reported to team members on June 3, 1969, this prisoner classification:

45	%	Criminals
40	%	Communists
4	%	Civilians condemned by military court
10	%	Military
.6%		Political—non-Communist

Prison Governor Minh, of Thu Duc prison, classified the 1,126 prisoners held by him on June 3, 1969, as:

265	Criminal offenders
843	Communists
15	Civilians condemned by military courts

3   Military prisoners
0   Political prisoners
0   Prisoners of war

The Warden of Con Son Island prison reported that there were 7,021 men and boys in Con Son, of whom:

984   were soldiers who committed political offenses (helped or sympathized with the V.C.),
2,700   were civilians who had worked directly with the V.C.,
769   were soldiers who committed criminal offenses,
252   were civilians who committed criminal offenses, and
2,316   were detainees, never tried or sentenced.

(Note that only the Warden of Con Son Island Prison separately identified unsentenced detainees in his statistics. The rest of the breakdowns presumably distribute the detainees among the classifications according to file, or dossier, information.)

There are no figures available on the religious affiliation of prisoners. Warden Lien reported that there were about 120 Buddhist monks in Chi Hoa prison on June 3 when team members visited.

Thu Duc (*Women's Prison*)

Members of the Study Team spent several hours at the Women's Prison, where the staff, headed by Prison Governor Minh, explained the prison's operation and enabled members to see what they requested. The administration of the prison seemed commendable in many respects. The dispensary was reasonably clean. There were two large rooms filled with power sewing machines where the inmates made military uniforms. There were sewing classes, classes in English and other educational opportunities provided.

The cells and large prison rooms were overcrowded. This was especially hard on nursing mothers and those with small children. Fifty women, some with babies, lived in a crude building 40 x 30 feet. Sanitation was primitive and inadequate. There was evidence that some prisoners had not received needed medical attention.

Team members were especially concerned about the large number of prisoners who had not been sentenced after many months of detention, the looseness and inaccuracy of prisoner classification, the inhumanity of some sentences (one slight old woman who, according to her dossier had passed V.C. letters, had served ten years of a fifteen-year sentence), and the extreme youthfulness of many of the inmates. Governor Minh told the team that there were fifty children from birth to 13 years of age in prison (the very youngest, of course, belonged to the women prisoners), and forty young offenders from 13 to 17 years.

To judge from both interviews and official explanations, the circumstances of many classified as "Communist" did not justify this classification. Two students who were called "Communist" were found by the team members to be unsentenced detainees. Their dossiers said that they were being held because they had exhibited "leftist tendencies" and had written for a Saigon University paper which was later suspended. In another building 20 per cent of the women said they had not been tried or sentenced. It seemed obvious that prisoners who had been accused of "leftist tendencies" or who had not yet been tried could not justly be categorized as "Communist." Yet they were and were forced to live with persons who were considered "hard core Communists."

Chi Hoa

Chi Hoa is often referred to as the "showcase prison." Since 1963 American funds have been available for the improvement of facilities, and American advisers have helped set up rehabilitation programs. The team was given an attractive brochure with pictures of prisoners in classes, at worship, and enjoying recreational activities. The brochure states that "the present Vietnamese system of corrections is . . . based on the principles of humanity, charity and equality."

The Warden said that there were about 5,500 men and boys now in prison of whom 40 per cent were "Communist" and only .6 per cent were "non-Communist political" prisoners. Each prisoner wore a colored badge indicating his classification. The Warden estimated that 40 per cent of the inmates had not yet been tried or sentenced. He said someone from the Ministry checked the lists every month and an effort was made to have those prisoners who had been in longer than six months brought to trial and sentenced.

The team members were taken on a tour of the prison. Wherever they went, they found the halls and cells clean. They were shown the vocational classes in which about 300 prisoners were enrolled and met daily over a six-month period.

Team members saw the Catholic Chapel, a Buddhist shrine and a Buddhist pagoda. In the pagoda, they talked with several monks who are in prison for resisting the draft. These monks were the only prisoners in any of the institutions who did not stand at rigid attention. Sometimes prisoners shouted ear-splitting anti-Communist slogans when team members stopped to see them.

The Warden estimated that there were 200 children from 10 to 14 years of age and 200 from 14 to 18 in the prison not yet sentenced. All children, he said, were in a separate section and given education. Team members asked to see the children's section and were shown two cells. In a room, about 40 x 25 feet, there were 47 children *under 8 years of age*. One child, 4 years old, said he was in prison because he had been caught stealing a necklace. The children were squatting in one end of the room eating when the team members entered. They live in a bare room, with sanitary facilities at one end. No materials for play or study were in evidence. The food was rice with vegetables and fish. It looked adequate. The children seemed to be well physically. When the team entered, the children left their bowls of food and assembled in lines without any order from the adult in the room or from the Warden. All, even the 4-year-old, stood at attention and did not move or speak; only their eyes followed the visitor's moves. In the next cell, similar in size, there were 67 children slightly older but under 10 years. The situation was the same in all respects.

The team members saw three cells in the men's section, the same size as the cells for children. There were about 50 men in each of the rooms viewed. Some of the men were preparing over tiny burners various kinds of food which had been brought by friends or relatives. None of the men in these three cells had been sentenced.

Upon asking to see the disciplinary cells, the team members were shown a room with iron rings for shackling prisoners, which, we were told, were seldom used. The iron looked rusty. Team members did not get to see any of the 100 prisoners who the Warden said were in solitary.

The prison is in the form of a hexagon, four stories high facing inside. The wedge-shaped area in front of each of the six sections contains water tanks for bathing and washing clothes and an open space. The Warden said that after 5 P.M. the inmates are allowed here for sports and bathing. Since there is an average of about 1,000 inmates in each section, it is obvious that only a very small proportion of the inmates could play soccer, volley ball, bathe or wash clothes at one time.

Con Son Island Prison

Con Son Island Prison, an escape-proof prison about 50 miles off the southeast coast, is said by officials to contain 7,021 prisoners, most of them "political." In many of the barracks, the majority of the prisoners were "political" prisoners who had been "tried" before a Military Field Court, usually without legal representation. They wore red tags which identified them as either V.C. or V.C. sympathizers. Those with yellow badges (detainees) presented another kind of problem. A show of hands, taken in a number of barracks, revealed that many detainees had been imprisoned as long as a year and a half with little hope of being released unless, conceivably, a place was required for new prisoners. It was explained that frequently the means or records necessary to determine whether charges should be brought were unavailable. There was a failure to observe even a minimum amount of due process in the overwhelming majority of cases. The same circumstances were recited over and over by the prisoners; they were either being held on charges of sympathizing with or aiding the enemy, or they had been rounded up after a military action in their village and were held. Others were students who had indicated their support for peace.

The tour had been carefully arranged by prison officials. The only time the team members deviated from the prepared pattern, successfully demanding to see Camp No. 4 instead of the camp that the prison authorities had scheduled, they saw something of significance. There were large dark dormitory cells (three out of about ten such cells were inspected) in which there were from 70 to 90 prisoners each, all of whom (as determined by a show of hands) were condemned to life in prison. None had had lawyers or any trial other than a judgment by a military tribunal.

The prison authorities denied the existence of "tiger cages", reputed small barred cells in which prisoners being disciplined were chained to the floor in a prone position. Although recently released prisoners referred to this practice from actual experience, the team members were unable to elicit any more from the prison officials than that the "tiger cages" were no longer in existence. (At first any knowledge of such things was denied). One prisoner, however, speaking surreptitiously to the team members said, in answer to a question, "Yes, the "tiger cages" are here, behind Camp No. 2 and Camp No. 3. You looked in the wrong place." The team members had looked behind Camp No. 4.

Taking into consideration the conditions under which such a prison had to operate, it seemed that an attempt was being made by the prison officials to conduct as clean and sanitary an operation as they could. There was a 1.3 million dollar expansion under way (funded and supervised by the U.S.A.) which would provide 72 additional barracks.

Pursuing further the question of how prisoners were disciplined, the team members were told that only 10 out of the 7,021 prisoners were under discipline. On request, the visitors were shown two of these ten. They had been in solitary for six months because of their refusal to salute the flag. One said he would never salute it. His legs were deeply marked, the Colonel in charge explained this was the result of a past disease. Questioned directly, the prisoner said it was the result of a long period in leg irons.

Although team members observed no brutality, they felt that to have no disciplinary barracks other than a small number of maximum security cells was highly unusual. The team members noted the fearful reaction of the inmates whenever prison officials appeared, surmising that there must exist a high degree of punitive regimentation.

A disturbing aspect of the prison situation in Vietnam is physical abuse of prisoners. U.S. officials (there are American advisers at every level of Vietnamese bureaucracy) agree that there is torture, but insist that it does not take place in the correctional centers but in the interrogation and detention centers where the prisoners are taken first. Accounts by ex-prisoners verified the fact that torture in detention and interrogation centers is general procedure.

Frequently, the interrogation center at the National Police Headquarters in Saigon was mentioned as a scene of torture. However, many informants said that the types and extent of torture administered in some of the detention centers in the provinces were far worse than in the National Police Interrogation Center in Saigon.

Although team members were allowed to visit the National Police Headquarters in Saigon, it was an arranged visit. There was no evidence of the forms of torture here described. Colonel Mau said that modern interrogation techniques ruled out the need for physical violence. Team members saw the interrogation rooms but no prisoners were being questioned. The team's evidence for the tortures described come from interviews with ex-prisoners testifying to what they had endured and seen, together with the statements of doctors and others who had treated the victims. While the testimony of prison officials and the appearances of the National Police Headquarters cannot be lightly dismissed, the sheer weight of witnesses' statements seemed overwhelming and conclusive to team members.

All prisoners are oppressed by conditions of overcrowding. Sometimes, however, many prisoners are stuffed into small cells which do not allow for lying down or, sometimes, even for sitting; and this, when it is steaming hot, when excrement accumulates, and when the prisoners are seldom released for exercise, is torture indeed.

Beating is the most common form of abuse. Intellectuals appear to receive "favored" treatment and seldom are subjected to torture other than beating. This is done with wooden sticks and clubs. ("Metal" was mentioned by one observer.) The blows are applied to the back and to the bony parts of the legs, to the hands, and, in a particularly painful form, to the elevated soles of the feet when the body is in a prone position. Beating of the genitals also occurs. A number of commentators also described the immersion of prisoners into tanks of water which are then beaten with a stick on the outside. The pain is said to be particularly intense and the resultant injuries are internal.

Another type of water torture in which a soaked cloth is placed over the nose and mouth of a prisoner tied back-down to a bench is said to be very common. The cloth is removed at the last moment before the victim chokes to death, and then is reapplied. In a related form, water is pumped into the nose.

The most common procedure is said to be the elevation of

the victim on a rope bound to his hands which are crossed behind his back. One witness described a "bicycle torture" used in this center. For about a week the prisoner is forced to maintain a squat position with an iron bar locking his wrists to his ankles; "afterwards he cannot walk or even straighten up," it was said.

An intellectual who was arrested in 1966 and spent the first six months of his two-and one-half year term in an interrogation center described what he called the "typical case" of a woman law student in a nearby cell. She had been in the interrogation center for six months when he arrived and stayed for the next six months during his own imprisonment there. Throughout this year, she was tortured mostly by beating. When she was finally called before a tribunal to hear the charges, she had to be carried by two fellow prisoners. The tribunal, apparently because of her status, heard her case carefully and determined that it was a case of misidentification. Someone in Zone D had reported a V.C. returnee or spy who looked like her.

The same informant said, as a number of others did, that sexual torture was common. Though apparently it was not used on this woman student, it was used on many women. Frequently coke and beer bottles were prodded into the vagina. Also, there were a number of accounts of electrical wires applied to the genitals of males and females, as well as to other sensitive parts of the body. Another informant told of the torture by electricity of an eight-year-old girl for the purpose of finding her father: "She said her father was dead and they just kept torturing her . . . They tortured her mother too." This was said to have occurred in the National Police Interrogation Center (Saigon) during 1968. Several ex-prisoners testified that it is not unusual to torture family members, including children, before the eyes of the prisoner. "Then," explained a woman teacher who had been imprisoned twice, "the prisoner will tell anything."

A respected physician told team members that recently po-

lice brought a dead girl from an interrogation center to a city
hospital and asked the Doctor there to certify to death from
natural causes. On examination of the cadaver, the Doctor
found signs of beating and sexual violation. He refused to so
certify. Pressure was brought on the head of the hospital to
issue the certificate. Such incidents are not unusual.

III. Legal Standards and Procedures

The heart of the problem of assessing the conditions of political imprisonment in South Vietnam lies in the matters of
standards and procedures. The key questions are: who is subject to arrest and imprisonment; and, how in each case is this
determination made? If either the standards for determining
who is subject to arrest, or the procedures for making the determination is loose, then enormous potential for official capri-
ciousness exists and the freedoms of those subject to such cap-
rice are ephemeral.

The Study Team found both the standards and the procedures to be loose by any measure, even by the most generous
measure of allowance for the exigencies of civil and guerrilla
warfare. The evidence is more than adequate to sustain the conviction of the Study Team that this looseness is used deliberately to suppress political dissent and to oppress some religious
groups. In particular, loyal nationalists who are in basic disa-
greement with the Government fear with good reason retaliation for expressing their views.

Naturally, the particular kind of war being waged in South
Vietnam bears upon the judgments of the team. Government
of Vietnam officials quite properly see an analogy between the
civilians arrested for guerrilla war activities—sabotage, es-
pionage and the organization and support of National Liberation Front military cadres—and soldiers taken as prisoners
in more conventional war. The validity of the analogy should

be granted. We cannot class as suppression of political freedoms the imprisonment of those actively engaged in conducting war against the government. Moreover, the need for procedures to permit speedy imprisonment without exposing the government to the risk of further warlike activity on the part of the arrested persons must be conceded.

It is humbling for Americans to be reminded that their own history is replete with invasions of individual rights made in the name of wartime emergency: the suspension of the writ of habeas corpus during the Civil War, for instance, and the evacuation of persons of Japanese ancestry from the West Coast during World War II. An American cannot presume to sit with clean hands in judgment upon the Government of South Vietnam. But both the principles of justice to which their constitutions commit the United States and the Republic of Vietnam, and the pragmatic concern for winning popular support for democratic principles compels this Team to confine the restrictions on freedom made in the name of wartime exigency to those actually necessitated by war.

Loose and inadequate standards and procedures do not represent concessions of those wartime exigencies. Minimization of risk of warlike activities against the Government is not achieved by the imprisonment, for instance, of loyal nationalists who advocate forming a coalition government with N.L.F. representatives. Nor does minimization of such risks require imprisonment of powerless people who scurry to avoid exposure to the demands of both N.L.F. and government forces, in so-called "insecure" areas, and are arrested on suspicion with the expectation that brutal interrogation may yield a "confession" which will warrant detention.[1]

In fact, imprisonments of this kind create the unnecessary risk of alienating loyalties; a hazard made doubly severe by the highly political character of a war in Vietnam. The seriousness

---

[1] Credible testimony of instances of arrests fitting both these examples was given the Study Team from many sources. (See Section II.)

of this hazard is underscored by the statement to the team of one young man, a resident of a rural province, that probably a majority of the men his age who reside in "secure" areas (under Government of South Vietnam control) of that province have experienced arrest and detention at least once during their lives. The evidence available to the team suggests that the number of such arrests is steadily and continuously increasing.

The limits of the "war exigencies" justification are well illustrated by Article 29 of the Republic of Vietnam Constitution, which clearly contemplates the existence of exceptional circumstances such as war. It provides:

Any restriction upon the basic rights of the citizens must be prescribed by law and the time and place within which such a restriction is in force must be clearly specified. In any event the essence of all basic freedoms cannot be violated.

A. Standards

Authority for imprisonment of non-conventional criminals is found in the State of War Law, Law No. 10/68, adopted by the National Assembly and promulgated by the President on November 5, 1968. It amends the State of War Decree promulgated prior to the present Constitution, on June 24, 1965, and as amended authorizes, among other things:

—The search of private houses, both by day and night;
—Fixing the place of residence of those elements judged dangerous to national security;
—Prohibition of all demonstrations or gatherings harmful to public security and order;
—Prohibition of the distribution of all printed matter harmful to national security;
—Control and restriction of communications and travel, consonant with security requirements; . . .

In particular, the euphemistic language of the second paragraph quoted requires elaboration. Under it, numbers of persons are "assigned residence" in one or another of the provincial or national prisons by action of a Provincial Security Council for specified but renewable terms, not exceeding two years, because they are "judged" to be "elements . . . dangerous to national security." Such a standard patently abidicates to the judging body the determination of who is to be subject to such imprisonments, with little, if any, legislative guidance or control. In fact, it was determined that students with nothing more than the notation in their files that they exhibited "leftwing tendencies" were being incarcerated in national prisons whose administrator classified them in his census as "Communists"; i.e., in the same category with individuals found to have assumed leadership roles in organizing warlike activity for the N.L.F. Others claimed to the team that they had been detained for no other reason than that local officials responsible for their arrests expected to extort bribes as conditions for their release.

Under the heading of "prohibition of . . . gatherings," the team learned of a Saigon political leader who was sentenced by a Military Field Court to imprisonment for one year because he called a press conference without proper advance clearance from Republic of Vietnam authorities. (In this man's case, a known requirement appeared to have been deliberately violated, but the sentence suggests that the State of War Law is being used for more than minimization of military risks to national security.)

The standards just quoted should be read in conjunction with Article 4 of the Constitution, which provides:

Article 4. (1) The Republic of Vietnam opposes Communism in any form.
(2) Every activity designed to publicize or carry out Communism is prohibited.

The looseness of the prohibition against activity designed to "publicize or carry out" Communism parallels that inherent in the other standards we have discussed. Under it, President Thieu, in an interview he generously afforded the members of the team, justified the detention of Truong Dinh Dzu as a "political prisoner" on the ground that he had allegedly advocated the formation of a coalition government in which the N.L.F. would participate. This would violate Article 4, President Thieu reasoned, since such advocacy is *ipso facto* prohibited by that article. It may be unnecessary to point out, in response to this reasoning, that the Constitution also provides machinery for its own amendment, a process hardly likely to be completed without someone having first advocated a result barred by the language of the provisions being amended.

B. Procedure

1. Arrest, detention and interrogation.

Because of the long periods for which individuals are often held and interrogated prior to any disposition, often for six months or more—the procedures for determining who is to be arrested and for how long he is to be detained and interrogated take on a special importance. Moreover, the frequent and serious physical abuses about which the team heard most often occur during this period. Although they seem to be employed as "aids" to interrogation, they are forms of cruel and barbarous punishment against which the citizen needs every conceivable procedural protection.

In fact, procedural protections are essentially nonexistent at the arrest and interrogation stage. Arrests are made by a wide variety of local and national officials—by district police, special security forces, military forces and intelligence units—each exercising a relatively unfettered discretion. The arrest may occur for no other reason than that the arrestee was found near the scene of a guerrilla raid. Unless the arrested person is of exceptional importance, he will usually be detained by the arresting unit or by the district or security police in the district or province where arrested, and subjected to whatever interrogation methods authorities in that unit choose to apply.

Such detention for interrogation frequently continues for

many months and it is at this stage that the bestial brutality the team encountered occurs.

Despite the constitutional provision that:

> (6) A defendant has the right to a defense lawyer for counsel in every phase of interrogation, including the preliminary investigation.

the team was unequivocally assured by Colonel Mau, Chief of the Special Branch of the National Police Forces, that no one within his knowledge ever saw a lawyer at this stage— certainly never when detained at the Interrogation Center of the National Directorate of Police in Saigon. All of the team's information tended to confirm that this generalization applied to other places of interrogation, both in Saigon and in the provinces.

Not only is the arrestee denied a right to counsel at this stage, he is frequently denied all contact with outsiders, including members of his family. Often families are not notified of the arrest, and they may go for days or months in ignorance of any fact save that their loved-one has disappeared. In one instance, occasional visits were stopped after several weeks on the ground that they interfered with the interrogation. Isolation itself may be used as an interrogation "aid" or technique.

2. "Assigned Residence" by Provincial Security Councils.

An unknown proportion of the persons held in the correctional system—the four national and thirty-seven provincial prisons of the system—are assigned there by action of Provincial Security Councils rather than by the judgment and sentence of any court. An official of one province reported that 50 per cent of the 1,400 occupants of the local provincial prison were assigned there by the action of the Provincial Security Council.

When Prime Minister Huong took office in May, 1968, the team was told he made a major effort to improve the functioning of these bodies, enlarging them to include an elected official (in the provinces where elections have been held) and causing them to pare their backlogs of undisposed business. As a result, it may be assumed that dispositions in some provinces show a greater sensitivity to local opinion and that the periods of preliminary detentions—to the extent they exceed the length of interrogation desired—have been reduced.

One of the Prime Minister Huong's first acts was to initiate a remarkable admission of wrongdoing on the part of the Thieu Government in the release and commutation of the sentences of a number of political prisoners whose total has been variously estimated from 2,000 to 6,000.

On another occasion Deputy Prime Minister Khiem commendably acknowledged in response to questions raised in the National Assembly the arbitrary nature of the arrest and interrogation procedures and the official fear of repercussions which could result from the conditions of brutality.

When a team member shared with Minister Khiem a preliminary sketch of team findings; i.e., loose prisoner classification, denial of due process and the arbitrary action of Military Field Courts, he agreed that these were concerns he and his staff had been considering.

But these steps only sweeten a system that is intolerable. No society can pretend to be free that permits "administrative" detentions of the kind handled by Provincial Security Councils. One team member was privileged to visit the members of one such Council as its regular weekly session was being concluded. Members of the Council each possessed a type-written list of the names of the individuals whose cases were being considered; approximately 100 names were on the list for a single afternoon's consideration. He was told that on heavy business days the Council sometimes continued to meet into the evening. An officer brought the relevant files to the meeting and read to the Council the information required for consideration. Without notice to the arrested person, without his presence or that of witnesses to the facts relevant for determination, without confrontation or opportunity for rebuttal, to say nothing of rights of counsel or to appeal, the liberty of each of the 100 persons listed was summarily determined and detentions in prison were ordered for periods—renewable by like procedure—of up to two years. No wartime conditions, nor any other justification, can be offered to reconcile such a procedure with the democracy which is claimed to be the object of the Constitution of the Republic of Vietnam. Undoubtedly, the system succeeds in detaining some people for whom a real connection with the activities of the N.L.F. has been shown, although the team was told that all serious wartime offenses are referred to a Military Field Court for disposition. But no other purpose than convenience to the interests of local or national officials which are adverse to those of the detainees—whether to suppress political opposition or otherwise—can really be served by this mechanism.

3. Military Field Tribunals

The Study Team has reached the conclusion that the Thieu-Ky Government has, through the extensive and increasing use of the extra-constitutional Military Field Courts, imprisoned thousands of persons without the most fundamental elements of a fair hearing and, in a shocking number of instances, without even apprising the imprisoned persons of the charges against them. This extraordinary development has had such a devastating effect on the people of South Vietnam and such a chilling impact on all political activities that it seems important to chronicle in some detail the process by which the present Saigon Government, in the name of a wartime emergency, can deny persons arrested for political "offenses" all of the guarantees which Vietnamese constitutional and statutory law gives to persons accused of crime.

The Constitution of the Republic of Vietnam, promulgated on April 1, 1967, confers in Article 7 a series of guarantees upon those accused of crime which are among the most generous and progressive of any democracy in the world. Because these rights have been denied to probably 65 to 75 per cent of all of the persons committed to prisons in South Vietnam, it is important to set them forth in some detail. Article 7 reads as follows:

(1)   The State respects and protects the security of each individual and the right of every citizen to plead his case before a court of law.

(2)   No one can be arrested or detained without a legal order issued by an agency with judicial powers conferred upon it by law, except in case of flagrant violation of the law.

(3)   The accused and his next of kin must be informed of the accusation against him within the time limit prescribed by law. Detentions must be controlled by an agency of the judiciary.

(4)   No citizen can be tortured, threatened or forced to confess. A confession obtained by torture, threat or coercion will not be considered as valid evidence.

(5)   A defendant is entitled to a speedy and public trial.

(6)   A defendant has the right to a defense lawyer for counsel in every phase of the interrogation, including the preliminary investigation.

(7)   Any person accused of a minor offense who does not have a record of more than three months' imprisonment for an intentional crime may be released pending trial, provided that he or she is employed and has a fixed residence. Women pregnant more than three months accused of minor offenses who are employed and have fixed residence can be released pending trial.

(8)   Accused persons will be considered innocent until sentence recognizing their guilt is handed down.

In the event of doubt, the court will rule in favor of the accused.

(9)   If unjustly detained, a person has the right to demand compensation for damages from the State after he has been pronounced innocent, in accordance with the provisions of law.

All of these carefully spelled-out guarantees were nullified for political offenders by Law No. 10/68 of November 5, 1968, which we have earlier described. This law amends and revitalizes a pre-constitutional decree issued June 24, 1965. By its legitimation of the Military Field Courts, this law, in effect, amended the Constitution although none of the Articles of the Constitution related to amending the document (Nos. 103–107) were complied with.

The November 5, 1968 law, in addition to authorizing the invasions of individual rights previously recited, authorizes local proclamations of martial law and in its Article 2 declares that:

All violations of the law related to national security fall within the Military Field Courts which will try them in accordance with emergency procedures.

The creation of these "Military Field Courts" is nowhere authorized in Article 76 through Article 87 of the Constitution, which provide in detail for the structure of Vietnam's judiciary. Nor is the "Military Field Court" related to military tribunals which exist in the armed forces of South Vietnam for the prosecution of offenses committed by military personnel. *The "Military Field Courts" are not really courts at all.*

The Study Team is convinced that the number of arrests and imprisonments continues to grow larger under the law of November 5, 1968. Moreover, it is clear that the 1968 law, unlike the 1965 decree, abrogates and amends the 1967 Constitution of South Vietnam in an illegal way. Indeed, the 1968 law eviscerates that Constitution and suggests that the President and the National Assembly disregarded the Constitution in several respects and, relying on "a state of war," undertook to legitimize the Military Field Courts which imprison persons in proceedings having few if any of the features of a real trial. No matter how favorably they are viewed, these courts serve as the instrument by which the Thieu Government imprisons and thereby silences its critics.

The inadequacies of the Military Field Courts are many. Among their more glaring defects are the following:

(1) These courts violate Article 77 of the Constitution which stipulates that every court should be composed of "an element that judges and an element that prosecutes, both of which are

professionally qualified." In the Military Field Court, the judge is a military official not necessarily trained in law.

(2) The offenses triable by the Military Field Courts are non-appealable. The denial of these basic rights violates the Vietnam Constitution as well as the practices which have become customary in most of the judicial processes in the civilized world.

(3) The Military Field Courts also violate Article 9 of the Universal Declaration of Human Rights which states that, "No one shall be subjected to arbitrary arrest or detention." This statement is now incorporated in the draft Covenant on Civil and Political Rights and is broadened to read as follows:

Everyone has the right to liberty and security of person. No one shall be subjected to arbitrary arrest and detention. No one shall be deprived of his liberty except on such grounds and in accordance with such procedures as are established by law.

These provisions are being violated in South Vietnam. Their violation is thus a violation of the Constitution of South Vietnam which states in Article 5 that "the Republic of Vietnam will comply with provisions of international law which are not contrary to its national sovereignty and the principle of equality between nations."

IV. Team Members

JAMES ARMSTRONG, Bishop of the United Methodist Church, Dakotas Area. Bishop Armstrong received his A.B. from Florida Southern College, a B.D. from Emory University, and D.D. from Florida Southern and DePauw University. Elected to the episcopacy in 1968, James Armstrong is the youngest United Methodist Bishop in the United States. He taught for eight years at the Christian Theological Seminary (Disciples of Christ) in Indianapolis, served for ten years as minister of the Broadway United Methodist Church in Indianapolis. Known for his interest in public affairs, he was a board member of the Community Service Council, the Urban League and the Indianapolis Progress Committee, and was singled out as "one of the leaders who builds cities" by Time-Life in its book *The Heartland.* He himself is the author of the book *The Journey That Men Make,* published by Abingdon Press.

MRS. JOHN C. BENNETT (Anne McGrew Bennett). Mrs. Bennett received a B.Sc. in Education from the University of Nebraska and a Master of Religious Education from Auburn Theological Seminary. She taught for several years in country schools in Nebraska, was married in 1931 to John C. Bennett, now president of the Union Theological Seminary in New York City. Mrs. Bennett has been active in denominational and interdenominational affairs for many years. She is a member of the U.S. Inter-Religious Committee on Peace, a former board member of the Council for Christian Social Action of the United Church of Christ, and served from 1960 to 1964 on the General Board of the National Council of Churches.

ALLAN BRICK, Associate Secretary for National Program, Fellowship of Reconciliation. Dr. Brick received an A.B. from Haverford College, an M.A. and a Ph.D. in English from Yale University. A former professor of English at Dartmouth and Goucher Colleges, Dr. Brick served as Peace Education Director for the American Friends Service Committee, Middle Atlantic Region, from 1966 to 1968. He has published articles on English and American literature, as well as articles on student and protest movements and is co-author of *The Draft,* a report by the American Friends Service Committee, published by Hill and Wang, New York.

JOHN CONYERS, JR., Representative in Congress of the First Congressional District, Detroit, Michigan. Congressman Conyers received his B.A. and his law degree from Wayne State University. Currently serving his third term both as a

Representative and a member of the Judiciary Committee, he has been an active supporter of civil rights legislation in Congress. In this capacity he has made trips to Selma, Charleston, Mississippi and other places to investigate cases of civil rights violations. Prior to election to Congress, Mr. Conyers was a labor and civil rights lawyer, also serving as Director of Education for Local 900 of the United Auto Workers, an executive board member of the Detroit NAACP and an advisory council member of the Michigan Civil Liberties Union. During the Korean conflict, he served as a Second Lieutenant in the Corps of Engineers.

ROBERT F. DRINAN, S.J., Dean, Boston College Law School, and Professor of Family Law and Church-State Relations. Father Drinan received his A.B. and M.A. from Boston College, his LL.B. and LL.M. from Georgetown University Law Center, an S.T.L. (Licentiate in Sacred Theology) from Gregorian University in Rome. He is author of several books, the latest of which is *Democracy and Disorder,* published in 1969 by the Seabury Press, and is a contributor to many publications, including *Commonweal* and *The Harvard Law Review.* Father Drinan has served widely in legal, civic and education organizations and committees. He is a former vice president of the Massachusetts Bar Association, is currently chairman of the association's Committee on the Administration of Justice and chairman of the Advisory Committee for Massachusetts to the United States Commission on Civil Rights.

JOHN DE J. PEMBERTON, JR., Executive Director of the American Civil Liberties Union. Mr. Pemberton received his B.A. at Swarthmore in 1940, an LL.B. cum laude at Harvard in 1947. As a student at Harvard Law School, Mr. Pemberton served on the board of editors of *The Harvard Law Review;* after graduation, taught commercial and bankruptcy law at Duke University until 1950. From 1950 to 1962, he practiced law in Rochester, Minnesota, as a member of the firm of Pemberton, Michaels, Bishop & Seeger. In Rochester, he served on the Minnesota Advisory Committee to the United States Civil Rights Commission and the Minnesota Fair Employment Practices Commission. An active member of the ACLU since 1950, Mr. Pemberton was appointed its Executive Director in 1962.

SEYMOUR SIEGEL, Professor of Theology in the Jewish Theological Seminary of America and Assistant Dean of its Herman H. Lehman Institute of Ethics. Dr. Siegel graduated from the University of Chicago. In 1951 he was ordained by the Jewish Theological Seminary and in 1958 received the seminary's degree of Doctor of Hebrew Literature. As representative of the World Council of Synagogues, Dr. Siegel has traveled widely to Jewish communities abroad; in 1962, he became the first Visiting Professor from the seminary to serve at the Seminario Rabbinico Latinoamericano in Buenos Aires. He is a member of the editorial boards of *Conservative Judaism and Jewish Heritage,* and editorial consultant to Benziger Brothers Publishing Company. Now completing work on his second book, *Jewish Theology Today,* he has also contributed many articles and reviews to both scholarly and popular journals, among them the *Saturday Review* and *Commentary.*

ARNOLD E. TRUE, Rear Admiral, United States Navy, Retired; Professor Emeritus of Meteorology, San Jose College. Admirial True received a B.S. at the U.S. Naval Academy in 1920, and an M.S. from M.I.T. in 1931, and graduated from the Naval War College in 1939. He served in the United States Asiatic Fleet in the Far East, commanded the USS Hammann and two destroyers in World War II, and was on the staff of the Commander in Chief of the United States Atlantic Fleet between 1944 and 1946. During the Battle of Midway he received injuries which necessitated his retirement. From 1947 to 1967 he was professor of meteorology at San Jose College. Admiral True recently presented testimony to the Senate Armed Services Committee concerning budget requests of the Department of Defense.

THE REVEREND PETER JENKINS, of Congregational Church, Wimbledon, England and Treasurer of Eirene International Christian Service for Peace Organization, met the team in Paris and accompanied it to Saigon.

V. Cable to President Nixon

SAIGON
JUNE 5, 1969

PRESIDENT NIXON
WASHINGTON, D.C., U.S.A.

THE INDEPENDENT STUDY TEAM ON RELIGIOUS AND POLITICAL FREEDOM IN VIETNAM HAS COMPLETED ITS STUDY HERE AND IS PREPARING A DETAILED REPORT. THE TEAM MET WITH SOUTH VIETNAMESE AND UNITED STATES OFFICIALS, VARIOUS BUDDHIST AND ROMAN CATHOLIC LEADERS, REPRESENTATIVES OF OTHER PRINCIPAL SECTS, MEMBERS OF THE NATIONAL ASSEMBLY, ATTORNEYS AND OTHER SPECIALISTS IN JURISPRUDENCE AS WELL AS NUMEROUS PRIVATE INDIVIDUALS, INCLUDING SOME PRISONERS.

THE TEAM INSPECTED PRISONS IN SAIGON, THU DUC AND CON SON. OUR FINAL REPORT WILL BE RELATED TO THE FOLLOWING FIRM IMPRESSIONS:

THE GOVERNMENT OF SOUTH VIETNAM DOES NOT PRESENTLY EXEMPLIFY AT LEAST ONE OF THE GOALS SET FORTH IN YOUR MAY 14TH STATEMENT. (QUOTE) THERE SHOULD BE AN OPPORTUNITY FOR FULL PARTICIPATION IN THE POLITICAL LIFE OF SOUTH VIETNAM FOR ALL POLITICAL ELEMENTS THAT ARE PREPARED TO DO SO WITHOUT THE USE OF FORCE OR INTIMIDATION. (UNQUOTE.)

RELIGIOUS AND POLITICAL SUPPRESSION IS WIDESPREAD. SPEAKING FOR PEACE OR IN ANY OTHER WAY OPPOSING THE GOVERNMENT EASILY BRINGS THE CHARGE OF COMMUNIST SYMPATHY AND SUBSEQUENT ARREST. LONG DETENTION WITHOUT TRIAL IS FREQUENTLY THE RESULT.

THE NUMBER OF POLITICAL PRISONERS CONTINUES TO INCREASE.

THERE MUST BE NO ILLUSION THAT THIS CLIMATE OF POLITICAL AND RELIGIOUS SUPPRESSION IS COMPATIBLE WITH EITHER A REPRESENTATIVE OR STABLE GOVERNMENT.

WE RESPECTFULLY REQUEST THAT YOU CONSIDER THIS IN WEIGH-
ING ANY COMMITMENTS TO THE THIEU GOVERNMENT.

ON BEHALF OF THE STUDY TEAM ON
RELIGIOUS AND POLITICAL FREEDOM
IN VIETNAM,

HON. JOHN CONYERS, JR., M.C.

Signed: *

James Armstrong, Bishop, United
Methodist Church

Anne M. Bennett (Mrs. John C.)

Allan Brick, Director of National
Program, Fellowship of
Reconciliation

John Conyers, Jr., Member of Congress

Robert Drinan, S.J., Dean, Boston
College Law School

Peter W. Jenkins, Pastor, Congregational
Church, Wimbledon, England

John de J. Pemberton, Executive Director,
American Civil Liberties Union

Seymour Siegel, Rabbi, Professor of
Theology, Jewish Theological Seminary

Arnold E. True, Rear Admiral, U.S.N. (Ret.)

June 11, 1969

* Organizational associations listed for purposes of identification only.

INDEX

ALFRED HASSLER is the national executive secretary of the Fellowship of Reconciliation, an interdenominational association dedicated to the goal of achieving a peaceful world community. He is also editor of the editorial page of *Fellowship,* the organization's monthly magazine. Mr. Hassler has made fact-finding trips to Vietnam several times in the last few years, and has written and spoken widely in this country about the Vietnamese war. His efforts were largely responsible for the formation of the U.S. Study Team on Religious and Political Freedom in Vietnam, which made an inspection tour there in the spring of 1969. The team included bishops and a member of the United States Congress. Mr. Hassler is the author of *Diary of a Self-Made Convict,* an account of his experiences following imprisonment as a conscientious objector in World War II.